BLOND'S INTERNATIONAL LAW

SULZBURGER & GRAHAM
Publishing Ltd.

New York

BLOND'S
INTERNATIONAL
LAW

By
Neil C. Blond
Nicole L. Fenton
Amy Johannesen
Edward B. Johnson
Charles Wertman

Edited By
John Marafino

Also Available in this Series:

Blond's Torts
Blond's Evidence
Blond's Property
Blond's Contracts
Blond's Income Tax
Blond's Family Law
Blond's Corporations
Blond's Criminal Law
Blond's Corporate Tax
Blond's Civil Procedure
Blond's International Law
Blond's Criminal Procedure
Blond's Administrative Law
Blond's Constitutional Law
Blond's Multistate Questions

ISBN 0-945-819-12-9

printed in the USA

Abbreviations Used in this Book

D   Defendant

P   Plaintiff

HPSS   Henkin, Pugh, Schachter & Smit, International Law, Cases and Materials

SOL   Sweeney, Oliver & Leech, The International Legal System, Cases and Materials

ICJ   International Court of Justice

PCIJ   Permanent Court of International Justice

S.Ct.   The Supreme Court of the United States

Restatement (Revised)   Restatement of the Foreign Relations Law of the United States (Revised) (1986).

U.N.   The United Nations

*Note   Cases without a specific court listing did not take place in a municipal court or a court of the United Nations.

The case listing (U.S.) signifies all courts in the United States judicial system except for the Supreme Court.

Blond's International Law	Henkin	Sweeny
Chapter 1 Foundations of International Law	1-34	
Chapter 2 Sources & Evidence of International Law	35-136	1-83, 1261-1294
Chapter 3 The Relation of International Law To Municipal Law	137-227	383-445
Chapter 4 States	228-317	851-929
Chapter 5 Organizations, Companies & Individuals in International Law	318-385	515-579, 734-850
Chapter 6 Treaties	386-518	993-1130
Chapter 7 International Responsibility & Remedies	519-564	
Chapter 8 Peaceful Settlement of Disputes	565-658	
Chapter 9 The Use of Force	659-819	1295-1496

How To Use This Book

"You teach yourself the law, we teach you how to think"
- Professor Kingsfield, The Paper Chase

Law school is very different from your previous educational experiences. In the past, course material was presented in a straightforward manner both in lectures and texts. You did well by memorizing and regurgitating. In law school, your fat casebooks are stuffed with material, most of which will be useless when finals arrive. Your professors ask a lot of questions but don't seem to be teaching you either the law or how to think. Sifting through voluminous material seeking out the important concepts is a hard, time-consuming chore. We've done that job for you. This book will help you study effectively. We hope to teach you the law and how to think.

Preparing for class

Most students start their first year by reading and briefing all their cases. They spend too much time copying unimportant details. After finals they realize they wasted time on facts that were useless on the exam.

Case Clips

Case Clips help you focus on what your professor wants you to get out of your cases. Facts, Issues, and Rules are carefully and succinctly stated. Left out are details irrelevant to what you need to learn from the case. In general we skip procedural matters in lower courts, we don't care which party is the appellant, petitioner etc. because the trivia is not relevant to the law. Case Clips should be read before you read the actual case. You will have a good idea what to look for in the case, and appreciate the significance of what you are reading. Inevitably you will not have time to read all your cases before class. Case Clips allow you to prepare for class in about five minutes. You will be able to follow the discussion and listen without fear of being called upon.

This book contains a case clip of every major case covered in your case book. Each case clip is followed by a code identifying the case book(s) in which it appears as a principal case. Since we tried to accommodate all the major casebooks, the case clips may not follow the same sequence as they do in your text. The easiest way to study is to leaf through your text and find the corresponding case in this book by checking the table of cases.

"Should I read all the cases even if they aren't from my casebook?"

Yes, if you feel you have the time. Most major cases from other texts will be covered at least as a note case in your book. The principles of these cases are universal and the fact patterns should help your understanding. The Case Clips are written in a way that should provide a tremendous amount of understanding in a relatively short period of time.

Hanau Charts

When asked how he managed to graduate in the top 10 percent of his class at one of the 10 most prestigious law schools in the land, Paul Hanau introduced his system which included charts now called Hanau Charts.

A very common complaint among first year students is that they "can't put it all together." It is difficult to read 100 pages of material and then understand how it fits in with material read weeks or months earlier. It's hard to spend an entire day reading cases about a defense and then to understand the relationship between the defense and other defenses when you have read cases for three or four other classes in between. Hanau Charts will help you put the whole course together. They are designed to help you memorize fundamentals. They reinforce your learning by showing you the material from another perspective.

Outlines

More than one-hundred lawyers and law students were interviewed as part of the development of this series. Most complained that their casebooks did not teach them the law and were far too voluminous to be useful before an exam. They also told us that the commercial outlines they purchased were excellent when used as hornbooks to explain the law, but were too wordy and redundant to be effective during the weeks before finals. Few students can read four 500-page outlines during the last month of classes. It is virtually impossible to memorize that much material and even harder to decide what is and is not important. Almost every student interviewed said he or she studied from homemade outlines. We've written the outline you should use to study.

"But writing my own outline will be a learning experience."

True, but unfortunately many students spend so much time outlining they don't leave time to learn and memorize. Many students told us they spent six weeks outlining, and only one day studying before each final!

Mnemonics

Most law students spend too much time reading, and not enough time memorizing. Mnemonics are included to help you organize your essays and spot issues. They tell what is important and which areas deserve your time.

Table of Contents

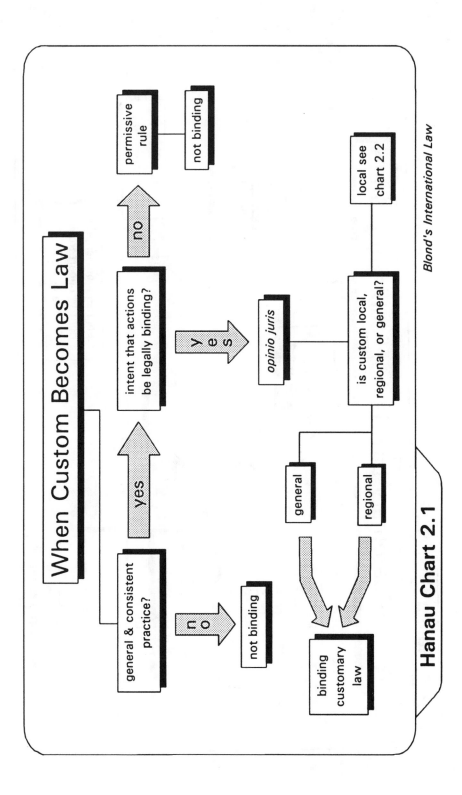

When Custom Becomes Law

general & consistent practice?

- **n o** → **not binding**

- **yes** →

intent that actions be legally binding?

- **no** → **permissive rule** → **not binding**

- **y e s** → **opinio juris**

is custom local, regional, or general?

- **general** →
- **regional** →
  → **binding customary law**
- **local see chart 2.2**

Hanau Chart 2.1

Hanau Chart 2.2

When Customary Law is Applicable to a State

```
                    general custom          regional
                    see chart 2.3
```

```
local
from chart 2.1
```

regional

has state adhered
to custom?

yes → state is bound
by customary law

no → state has a prescriptive
right to depart from
the custom

local from chart 2.1

has the custom existed for
a substantial period?

yes →

has custom been subject to the
approval of an affected state?

no →

has the custom been formally
opposed by an affected nation?

no →

binding customary law

no → not binding

yes → not binding

yes → not binding

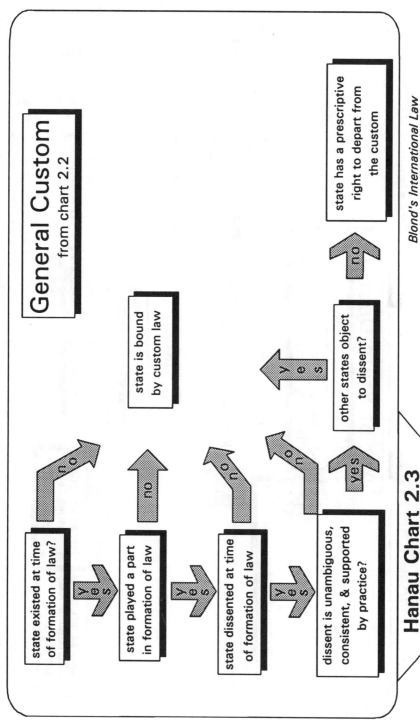

General Custom
from chart 2.2

state existed at time of formation of law? — **no** → state is bound by custom law

state existed at time of formation of law? — **yes** ↓

state played a part in formation of law — **no** → state is bound by custom law

state played a part in formation of law — **yes** ↓

state dissented at time of formation of law — **no** → state is bound by custom law

state dissented at time of formation of law — **yes** ↓

dissent is unambiguous, consistent, & supported by practice? — **no** → state is bound by custom law

dissent is unambiguous, consistent, & supported by practice? — **yes** ↓

other states object to dissent? — **yes** → state is bound by custom law

other states object to dissent? — **no** → state has a prescriptive right to depart from the custom

Blond's International Law

Hanau Chart 2.3

Hanau Chart 5.1

Act of State Doctrine

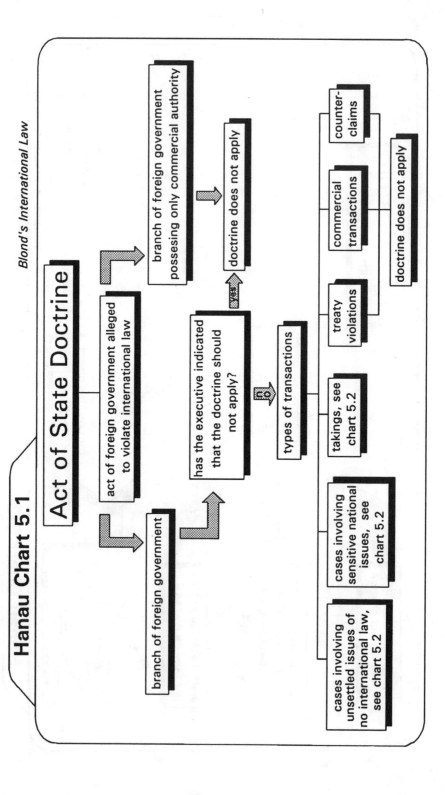

act of foreign government alleged to violate international law

branch of foreign government possesing only commercial authority

→ doctrine does not apply

branch of foreign government

has the executive indicated that the doctrine should not apply?

yes ⇒ doctrine does not apply

no ⇒ types of transactions

cases involving unsettled issues of no international law, see chart 5.2

cases involving sensitive national issues, see chart 5.2

takings, see chart 5.2

treaty violations

commercial transactions

counter-claims

doctrine does not apply

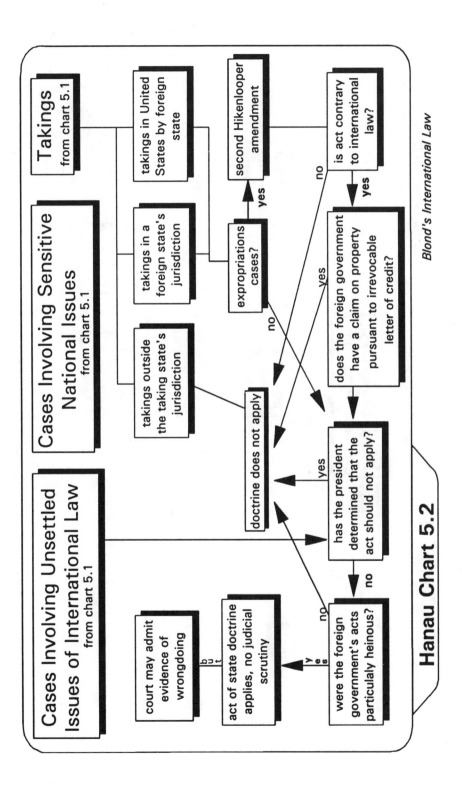

Takings from chart 5.1

takings in United States by foreign state

Cases Involving Sensitive National Issues from chart 5.1

takings in a foreign state's jurisdiction

takings outside the taking state's jurisdiction

Cases Involving Unsettled Issues of International Law from chart 5.1

second Hikenlooper amendment

expropriations cases?

yes

no

is act contrary to international law?

no

yes

does the foreign government have a claim on property pursuant to irrevocable letter of credit?

yes

doctrine does not apply

has the president determined that the act should not apply?

yes

no

were the foreign government's acts particularly heinous?

yes

no

court may admit evidence of wrongdoing

but

act of state doctrine applies, no judicial scrutiny

Blond's International Law

Hanau Chart 5.2

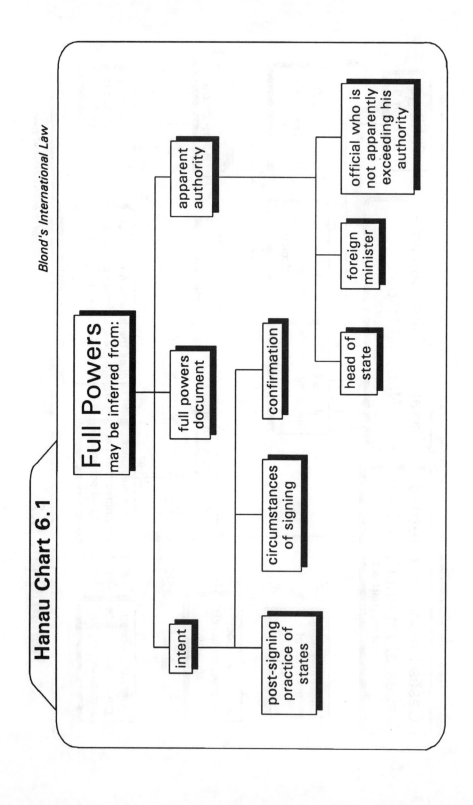

Hanau Chart 6.1

Full Powers
may be inferred from:

- intent
  - post-signing practice of states
  - circumstances of signing
- full powers document
  - confirmation
- apparent authority
  - head of state
  - foreign minister
  - official who is not apparently exceeding his authority

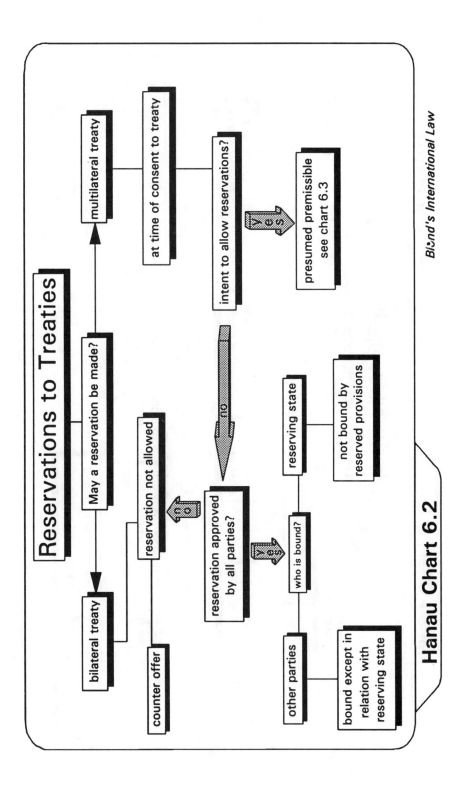

Reservations to Treaties

May a reservation be made?

multilateral treaty

bilateral treaty

at time of consent to treaty

intent to allow reservations?

Yes → presumed premissible see chart 6.3

no ↓

reservation not allowed

counter offer

reservation approved by all parties?

No →

Yes → who is bound?

reserving state — not bound by reserved provisions

other parties — bound except in relation with reserving state

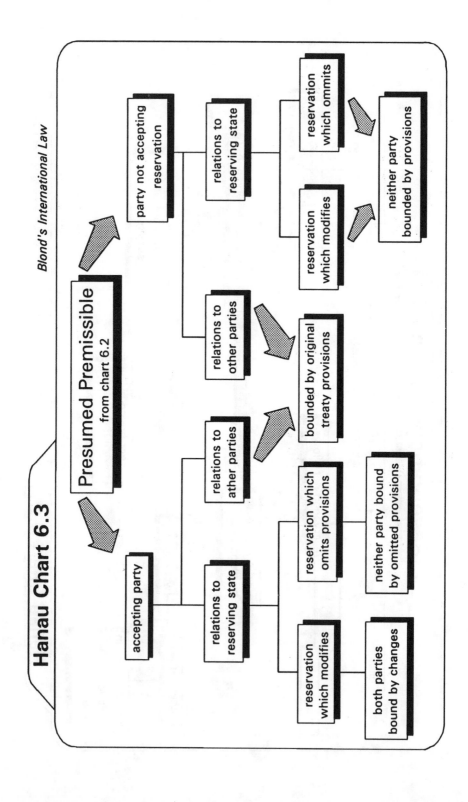

Hanau Chart 6.3

Blond's International Law

Presumed Premissible
from chart 6.2

accepting party

relations to
reserving state

reservation
which modifies

both parties
bound by changes

reservation which
omits provisions

neither party bound
by omitted provisions

relations to
ather parties

bounded by original
treaty provisions

relations to
other parties

bounded by original
treaty provisions

**party not accepting
reservation**

relations to
reserving state

reservation
which modifies

reservation
which ommits

neither party
bounded by provisions

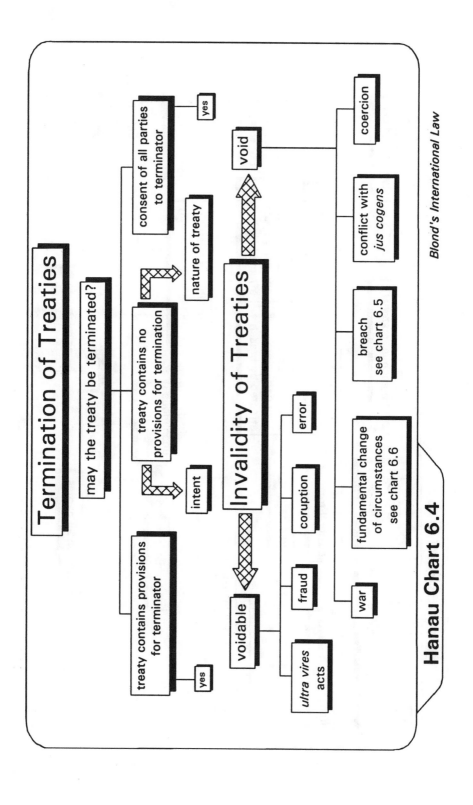

Termination of Treaties

may the treaty be terminated?

treaty contains provisions for terminator — yes

treaty contains no provisions for termination

consent of all parties to terminator — yes

nature of treaty

intent

Invalidity of Treaties

voidable
- ultra vires acts
- fraud
- war
- corruption
- fundamental change of circumstances see chart 6.6
- error

void
- breach see chart 6.5
- conflict with *jus cogens*
- coercion

Hanau Chart 6.4

Blond's International Law

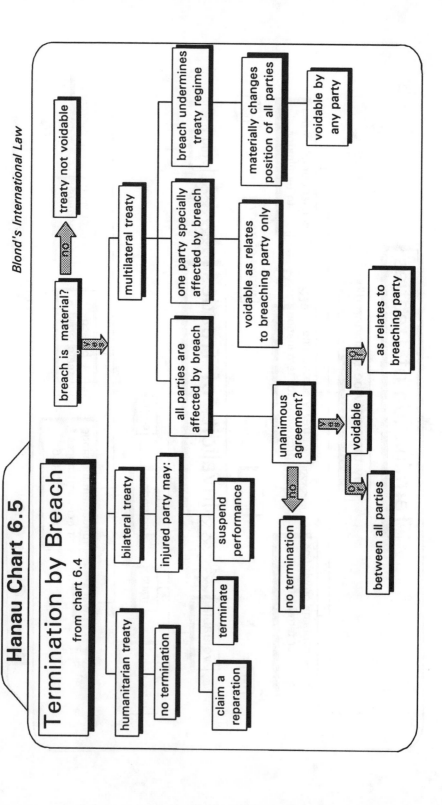

Blond's International Law

Hanau Chart 6.5

Termination by Breach

from chart 6.4

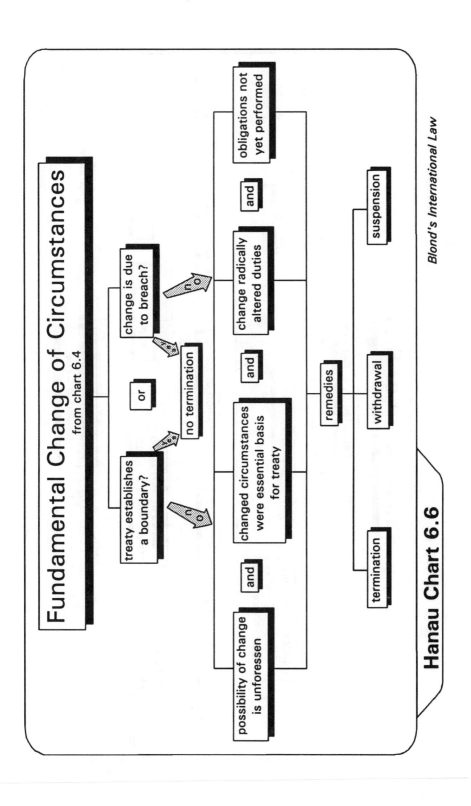

Fundamental Change of Circumstances
from chart 6.4

Blond's International Law

Hanau Chart 6.6

Hanau Chart 6.7

Succession of States

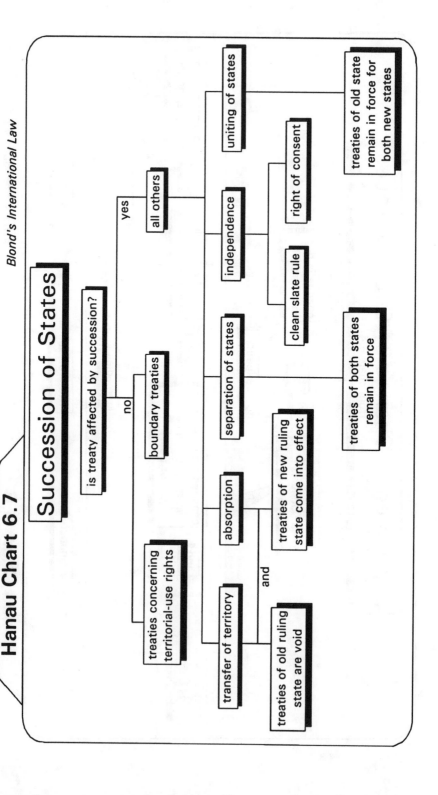

is treaty affected by succession?

no

treaties concerning territorial-use rights

boundary treaties

transfer of territory

treaties of old ruling state are void

and

absorption

treaties of new ruling state come into effect

yes

all others

separation of states

treaties of both states remain in force

independence

clean slate rule

right of consent

uniting of states

treaties of old state remain in force for both new states

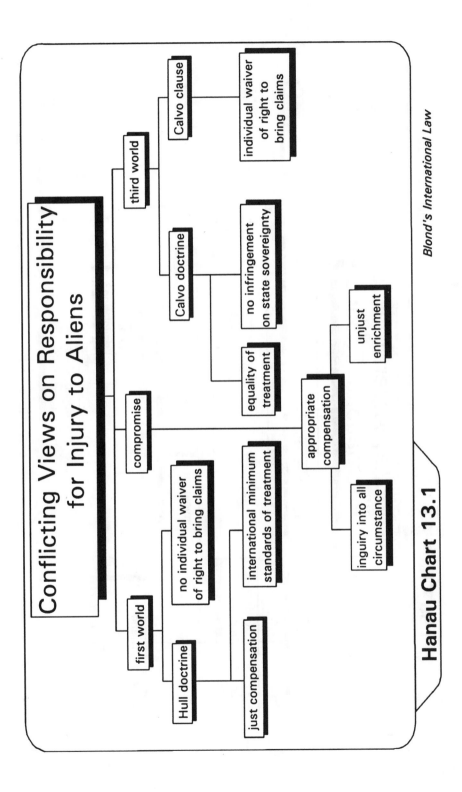

Conflicting Views on Responsibility for Injury to Aliens

first world
- Hull doctrine
  - just compensation
- no individual waiver of right to bring claims
  - international minimum standards of treatment

compromise
- equality of treatment
- appropriate compensation
  - inquiry into all circumstance
  - unjust enrichment

third world
- Calvo doctrine
  - no infringement on state sovereignty
- Calvo clause
  - individual waiver of right to bring claims

Blond's International Law

Hanau Chart 13.1

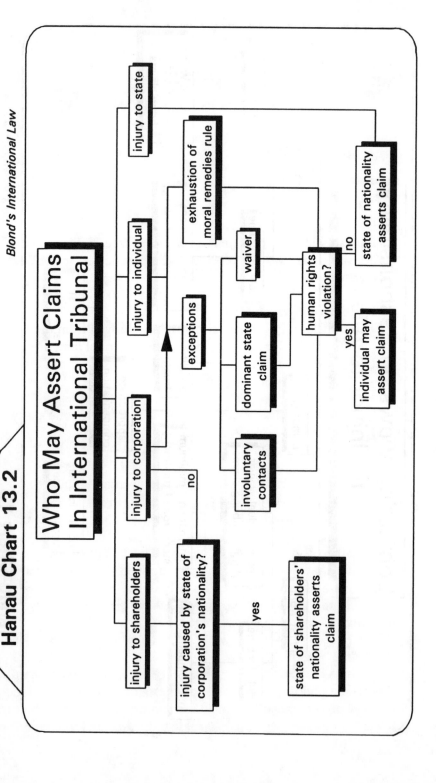

Hanau Chart 13.2

Who May Assert Claims In International Tribunal

Chapter 1

FOUNDATIONS OF INTERNATIONAL LAW

I. THEORIES

A. *Jus Naturale*

1. Natural Law - St. Thomas Aquinas
   Philosophical theory that all human laws follow, and are derived, from the law of God and are reflected in the law of nature.

2. Rationalism - Hugo Grotius
   The principles of the law of nature are derived from the law of reason. This followed the philosophy of natural law. The main principles were:

   a. Restitution
      Restitution must be made for harm done by one party to another.

   b. *Pacta Sunt Servada*
      Promises, especially those codified in treaties, must be kept.

B. *Jus Gentium* (Also called *Jus Voluntarium*)

This marked the beginning of the concept of customary law, the idea was that obligations may be derived from the customs, conduct, statements, and treaties of nations. The basic principle was that the individual ought to behave in the way that the majority of others usually behave.

C. Positivism
Positivism looked to the practice of nations rather than to theoretical philosophical truths to determine the law. This theory became prominent in the late 18th century and marked the turn toward emphasis on customary law in the determination of

international laws. Postitivism postulates that the will of the collective states of the world can be determined by the observable processes by which norms are formed between states, such as treaties.

II. INSTITUTIONS

A. League of Nations

The League of Nations was the first attempt to permanently organize most of the nations of the world. Although the goal of the League was peace through the establishment of collective security, the Covenant of the League of Nations did not provide for a supra-national authority; therefore, it could only coordinate the several actions that individual states took against an aggressor, but it could not direct states to take specific actions.

B. International Labour Organization (ILO)

The ILO was the first permanent multinational organization to concern itself with the social conditions of workers on an international level.

C. Hague Convention

The Hague Convention established principles for the conduct of war between nations. Human rights principles and principles involving the fair treatment of prisoners and protected persons were recodified in the Geneva Conventions.

D. Geneva Conventions

The Geneva Conventions are concerned with the conduct of war.

E. United Nations

The U.N. Charter created for the first time a supra-national authority that could direct nations to take specific actions, although it has no tools with which to enforce its mandates against those who refuse to obey.

III. FOUNDATIONS OF AUTHORITY OF INTERNATIONAL LAW

A. State Sovereignty

The International Court of Justice determined that the formation of international organizations could not supersede state sovereignty. However, it also determined that these formations signified that state sovereignty could no longer be considered an absolute right, as it had in a balance of power system. The Court also determined that the conclusion of international treaties does not signify a relinquishment of sovereignty, but that the right to enter into such treaties is a function of sovereignty.

B. Austin

International law is founded on the fear of provoking general hostility in other nations. Therefore, generally accepted moral principles may be enforced. Austin was known for his belief that international law is subject wholly to the whim and the will of sovereign states.

C. Hart

The mere fact that international law may not be reduced to orders backed by threats does not reduce it to only a form of morality. International law is concerned with the rights of nations to act as determined by precedents, treaties, and juristic writings, which is unconnected to whether such conduct is fair or morally just. Hart also developed the theory of formalism: the function of law is to maximize the certainty and to facilitate the proof of assessments of claims.

D. Henkin

Henkin states that, although international law may be considered only voluntary and otherwise unenforceable, most nations do observe the norms of international law, recognizing that it is in their interest to do so, and attempting to avoid undesirable consequences. International law does influence behavior and reflect international order and it responds to the changing needs of an international society. The policies served by international law are: order, stability, peace, independence, justice, and welfare. In all law, the fear of extra-legal consequences encourages obeyance; international law simply relies on such consequences (primarily economic and diplomatic sanctions) most heavily.

E. Fitzmaurice

There is a customary rule of international law that the consent of states to a rule makes the rule binding on them. The Charter of the United Nations does not do so since it is concerned only with breaches of international law that amount to acts of aggression. However, the United Nations does have censure power that induces compliance.

F. Morgenthau

The successful enforcement of international law depends on the relative political strengths of the enforcing and deviating states in each case.

G. Lissitzyn

Lissitzyn postulated that the possible rationale for compliance with U.N. directives is enforcement.

1. Unilateral Use of Force
   A state wishing to enforce a regulation may act against a breaching state. The utility of this depends on the relative balance of power.

2. Fear of Disadvantages That May Be Incurred By Breach

   a. Possible isolation from the rest of the world.

   b. The loss of good trade relations.

   c. Stronger nations have an incentive to obey, since they often have a disproportionate influence in the creation of the rules.

   d. Retaliation through sanctions (economic, diplomatic, etc.,) by other U.N. members.

IV. FOUNDATIONS OF LAW SOURCES

Since the nineteenth century, the Doctrine of Sources has been the primary means for determining rules of international law.

A. Ranking of Sources

Article 38 of The Charter of the International Court Of Justice (ICJ) delimits the sources that are used by the ICJ in determining the rules of international law. This is binding on members of the United Nations. The Restatement Of The Foreign Relations Law Of The United States § 102 is a unilateral codification of the existing state of international law by a number of American scholars.

1. Conventions
Article 38 places primary emphasis on international conventions to which the contesting states are parties because these are rules to which the parties have expressly agreed.

   a. Binding Effect
International agreements are binding only on the states that are parties to a particular agreement. Therefore, international agreements have less far-reaching effects than custom-

ary law; however, the existence of international agreements is easier to prove than customary law.

b. Customary Law Status
An international agreement may gain the status of customary law if it is intended to apply to many nations and is in fact accepted by many of those nations. This is established in the Restatement, not Article 38.

2. International Custom

a. Source of Custom
Customary law results from a general and consistent practice of states, followed by them from a sense of legal obligation. Customary law creates law for all nations, regardless of the practice or acceptance of the particular contending state. Contrary to Article 38, customary law is the primary source of international law under the Restatement.

b. Persistent Objector Exception
The exception to the binding power of customary law is: if a dissenting state that has indicated its dissent while a rule of customary law was still in formation it will not be bound by the customary law even after the custom has become a rule of international law.

c. *Jus Cogens* (Peremptory Norms)
Restatement § 702 says that the persistent objector rule should not apply to *jus cogens* that do not permit derogation (such as the rule prohibiting systematic racial discrimination).

3. General Principles of Law Common To Major Legal Systems of the World

a. Article 38 Definition
According to Article 38, these are principles that are "recognized by civilized nations." This is sometimes discredited by Third World nations, as it refers to North American and European states.

b. Restatement § 702
According to the Restatement, these principles may be invoked as supplementary rules even if they are not incorporated in customary law or international agreement.

c. Gap Fillers
These principles are generally gap-filler rules, such as estoppel and good faith.

4. Judicial Decisions and Scholarly Teachings

a. Article 38
Article 38 allows the ICJ to also refer to prior legal decisions, as well as to the opinions of scholars who are preeminent in a particular field when determining international law rules. But this may only be used as a *subsidiary* means for determination.

b. Restatement § 702
The Restatement allows judicial decisions and teachings of scholars who are preeminent in a particular area as evidence of what rules have become international law. This is a more important role than the mere subsidiary status that Article 38 allots.

5. Pronouncements of States
If states pronounce a rule of international law that is adhered to, or not opposed by other states, it may become a rule of international law.

6. *Ex Aequo et Bono* (In Justice and Fairness)
The Court also reserves the right to decide a case without regard to any of the aforementioned principles, if the parties to the case agree to such decision.

B. The International Court of Justice (ICJ)

1. Size
   The International Court of Justice is composed of fifteen judges.

2. Term
   Each judge is elected for a nine-year term. Article 3-18.

3. Qualifications
   Candidates for judge of the Court must have the qualifications required of the judges of the highest court in their countries or be "juris consultants with recognized competence in international law." Article 2.

4. Geographical Distribution

   a. The population of the court should be representative of the major geographical and political regions of the world.

   b. There may not be two judges from any one country on the court at any one time.

Chapter 2

SOURCES AND EVIDENCE OF INTERNATIONAL LAW

I.   INTERNATIONAL NORMS

International norms are rules that are legally binding on the international plane and displace the jurisdiction of domestic law. The two norms, Customary Law and Treaty Law, may be derived from many sources.

II.   CUSTOM AS A SOURCE OF LEGAL OBLIGATION

Rules of international law are based on state practice, as there is no international legislative body with the authority to declare laws. Therefore, laws that are proclaimed by states or the ICJ are merely a restatement of the existing law. The customs of nations may be used as evidence of the existence of a rule of international law.

A. Burden of Proof of Custom

States are assumed to be allowed to do anything that is not expressly prohibited; therefore, the burden of proof is on a state opposing another state's actions to show that a rule or custom prohibits such action.

B. Requirements for Legal Obligation

In order for custom to be regarded as a source of legal obligation, three factors will be looked at.

1. General Practice
   The custom must be practiced by a super majority of states
   representing each of the different economic, geographical, social
   and size categories of states, and

2. Consistent
   The custom must be systematically (as opposed to sporadically)
   adhered to by states.

3. *Opinio Juris* (Legal Obligation)
   The custom must be seen by the states as an obligatory practice
   required by law.

   a. Intent
      Opinio Juris signifies that a state regards a particular custom-
      ary rule as a norm of international law. The prerequisite for
      opinio juris is that a state *intend* its actions to be so.

   b. Permissive Rules
      Permissive rules entitle a state to act in a certain way
      without making such conduct mandatory. That a state has
      acted in a certain way in the past does not mean that it is
      obligated to do so in the future. A state must have the
      intent to bind itself to a future course of action for its
      actions to establish a rule.

C. Applicability of Customary Rule

   To determine the applicability of a rule of customary law in a
   particular circumstance, one must look to the *usage* of this rule by
   a state and the *reaction it triggers from* other states.

   1. General Rule
      When a custom satisfying the definition of Article 38 is estab-
      lished, it constitutes a general rule of international law that
      applies to every state. Customary law may arise even if some
      states object, as long as enough states do not object.

2. Binding States Who Played No Part in Formation
   Customary law binds all states who have not opposed it, even if they played no part in, or did not exist at the time of its formation.   Therefore, a state's acceptance of a custom is presumed. However, this is not true regarding local customary law (see I,E below).

3. Exceptions to Applicability

   a. Dissent
      States that, while the custom is in the process of formation, unambiguously and consistently object to its recognition as a practice of law are not bound by the customary rule. Dissent must be supported by action, not merely verbal protest.

   b. Historic or Prescriptive Rights
      If a state departs from a general rule of customary law and other states that knew, or could have known, of that departure do not object, the departing state develops a right to that departure. The theory is that, if other states accept such deviation, they must be doing so because they recognize that there are exceptional circumstances that justify it.

4. Departures as a Source of New Customary Law
   If a large number of states depart from customary law, new customary law may be created as a result. This depends on:

   a. The extent, consistency, and frequency of departures;

   b. The relation of the states concerned to the subject of the rule;

   c. The time of the process of departure; and

   d. *Opinio juris.*

D. Regional Customary Law (Limited Multi-Lateral Custom)

To become regional customary law, a custom must:

1. **Practice**
   The custom must be the subject of constant and uniform practice by the states in question;

2. **Right**
   The customary rule must have been invoked by the state exercising it as a right;

3. **Duty**
   The custom must have been respected by states against whom it has been enforced as a duty, rather than as a matter of political expediency;

4. **Burden of Proof**
   When a party state relies on regional custom, it has the burden of proving that this custom has become binding; and

5. **No Repudiation**
   It must be shown that the state against whom the custom is being enforced has not repudiated the custom through non-adherence to it.

E. Local Customary Law (Bilateral Custom)

A local customary right may be established as the result of a constant and continual practice by a nation if:

1. **Time**
   The custom has existed for a substantial period; and

2. **No Opposition**
   The custom has not been formally opposed by other affected nations. However, if a course of conduct has been subject to the approval of an affected nation in the past or such conduct has been protested by affected nations, a right has not been

established. The granting of such approval does not establish a right.

3. **No Requirement of Conformity With General International Law**
Customary law, as established by a course of conduct between two states, does not depend on general international customary law, and may differ therefrom.

4. **No Presumption of Acceptance**
The fact that a custom has been established between two or three states does not mean that it is presumed applicable to other states in the region.

III. TREATIES AS SOURCES OF CUSTOMARY LAW

A. Treaty v. Custom

Treaties and custom are always given equal weight. Treaties are not presumed to derogate custom, and custom is presumed not to alter a treaty. However, the priority of custom increases with the length of time of the existence of the custom.

1. *Lex Specialis Derogat Generali*
The generally accepted rule is that the specific prevails over the general. Therefore, if a custom is more specific than a treaty, the custom will carry greater force of law.

2. **Intent**
The intent of the parties is controlling. If the parties intend for a rule of customary law to supersede a treaty, it will do so.

B. Categories of Treaties

1. **General Multilateral Treaties**
General multilateral treaties are open to all states or to all members of a large regional group. They lay down rules of behavior and are of a norm-creating character that may be the

basis of a general rule of law. Such treaties may be codification treaties, "law-making," or both.

2. Collaboration to Regulate a Specific Area of Activity
   Treaties for collaboration may be universal, regional, or functional. Normally, they include purposes rather than rules and are effectuated through decisions of the organs that they establish.

3. Treaties Drafted in Contractual Terms
   Treaties drafted in contractual terms are usually bilateral agreements or agreements between small groups of states. They involve a mutual exchange of rights and obligations and are of a legislative type.

Note: Third world states find it in their interest to characterize treaties as *lex specialis* (contractual).

C. Multi-Lateral Conventions

Widespread and representative participation in an international convention may establish its provisions as customary law.

1. Settled Practice
   While the state practice must be extensive and virtually uniform, the passage of an extended period of time is not necessary.

2. *Opinio Juris Sive Necessitatis*
   The practice must occur in such a way as to show a general recognition that a legal obligation is involved.

3. Type of Convention
   This may be affected by whether the law, prior to a convention codifying it, is merely in a formative stage or if it is a generally accepted principle.

IV. GENERAL PRINCIPLES OF LAW

Article 38 § 1(c) empowers the court to use general principles of law when rules and customs do not suffice.

A. Definition

General principles are those that are so general that they apply within the legal systems of all states that have reached a comparative state of development in their municipal (domestic) law. (This is because municipal law has reached a greater stage of development than international law.)

B. Question of Fact

The existence or non-existence of general principles is a question of fact.

C. Examples

This rule is based on generally applicable principles, such as elementary considerations of humanity and the obligation not to knowingly allow one's territory to be used for acts that harm the rights of others. Other examples of principles referred to by the ICJ are: "no one may be a judge in his own cause," procedural rules, good faith, the obligation to repair a wrong, and estoppel.

D. Use of General Principles

General principles are used only in limited circumstances to fill in gaps left by the primary sources of treaty and custom. They are designed as an element of flexibility to allow the court more completeness.

1. Direct Importation From Municipal Law
   The terminology of private law is not likely to be adopted completely, instead it will be regarded as an indication of policy and principles. However, once an area of the law becomes a

matter of international concern (i.e., environmental law), a more positive approach in adopting select national laws will be used.

2. Reasons For Limited Use
The underlying premise behind the importation of general principles is that such rules are generally accepted. Wholesale importing of such rules would create the danger that they will become the object of dispute, thereby losing their weight and prestige.

E. Limitations on Use

The principle must be appropriate for application at the international level. For example, in the *Right of Passage Over Indian Territory Case*, the Court rejected the contention that the municipal law of easements was an international one.

V. DECISIONS OF INTERNATIONAL COURTS

A. The International Court of Justice

The International Court of Justice is a law-making body established by the United Nations Charter. All members of the United Nations have agreed to abide by its jurisdiction.

1. Decisions
The decisions of the International Court of Justice are supposed to state what the existing law is. However, the court does actually have a great amount of discretion since international cases are fact specific. This is especially true in areas where the law is broad or abstract.

2. Stare Decisis

a. No Stare Decisis
Article 38 of the Statute of the International Court is subject to Article 59, which allows the court to use prior judicial decisions merely as a subsidiary means for determining the

law. This is because the court's decisions are supposed to reflect existing law, not to create new law.

b. Weight of Past Decisions
However, past court decisions do carry weight in the court's discretionary decision making, especially in areas where the law is broad or abstract.

c. Divided Court Judgments
Divided judgments have less authority, especially when the issue is highly politicized.

3. Principles of Equity
Article 38, paragraph 2 of the Statute of the International Court of Justice authorizes the court to apply equity as distinguished from law. This is not limited by the power to decide a case *ex aequo et bono*.

a. Definition
Equity, a principle taken from contract law, means that which is reasonable and fair, and is a principle of interpretation designed to correct the insufficiencies and rigidity of law.

b. Rule of Construction
In the interpretation of legal documents and relations, equity may be used as a rule of construction of existing international laws so that states under similar circumstances will not be subject to an unjustifiable disparity in treatment.

c. Principles of Equity

i. *Intra Legem* (Within the Law)
Equitable decisions leave discretion to a law enforcement agency.

ii.   *Contra Legem* (Against the Law)
Such decisions are normally not justifiable on grounds of
equity unless the court is authorized to act *ex aequo et
bono*.   In exceptional circumstances, the court may
disregard the law if it feels it is unfair as applied to a
particular case.

iii.   *Praetor legem* (Outside the Law)
When an issue is not covered by a relevant rule.

4. *Ex Aequo Et Bono*
The court may decide cases, notwithstanding the law.

B. Arbitral Tribunals as Sources

Arbitral tribunals may be created by international agreement to
decide disputes between states. Decisions by such tribunals have
been referred to by the ICJ as subsidiary evidence of international
law, but rarely as precedent.

C. Municipal Courts

Municipal Courts are the highest national courts. They provide
evidence of customary law, as well as of the practice and *opinio
juris* of a state in question.   This is considered less weighty
evidence than that of an international body, but it is sometimes the
only pertinent case law on a subject, and cited by the ICJ.

VI. TEACHINGS OF THE MOST QUALIFIED PUBLICISTS

A. Subsidiary Source of Law

Although the writings of publicists have been responsible for the
codification of international law, the large number of treaties and
documentation of state practice has reduced the need to refer to
such writings as a source of law, unless there is a rare unanimity of
opinion in a particular area.

B. Examples of Publicists

    1. Restatement of the Foreign Relations Law of the United States
      This was prepared by a group of legal scholars and the American Law Institute.

    2. The International Law Commission
      This body is composed of thirty-five members of the U.N. General Assembly who prepare international conventions.

    3. The International Law Association
      This body has one thousand members in many national branches whose job it is to make multi-national resolutions.

    4. *L'Institut de Droit International*
      This consists of a group of 120 writers chosen on the basis of their scholarly works.

    5. Hague Academy of International Law
      The Hague Academy annually publishes scholarly writings from around the world in *Recueil des Cours*.

VII. UNITED NATIONS DECLARATIONS OF PRINCIPLES OF INTERNATIONAL LAW

United Nations declarations are made by the General Assembly. An example is the Declaration on the Protection of All Persons From Being Subject to Torture.

A. Not Legally Binding

    All nations agree that such declarations are not legally binding unless they are addressed to organs of the United Nations or to the U.N. Secretariat.

B. Evidence of Existing Law

However, most states have tried to show that a particular resolution is evidence of existing customary law, especially if it was adopted without opposition. If a resolution is found to be evidence of customary law, it would then be legally binding.

C. Absence of State Practice

1. General Rule — "No Instant Custom"
Even if a resolution is supported by the majority opinion, an absence of state practice would nullify it as evidence of customary law.

2. Custom in Absence of State Practice
A resolution may be evidence of customary law even in the absence of state practice, depending on:

a. The Type of Resolution
Resolutions are generally less binding than treaties or judgments of the court. However, a norm, which for reasons of policy is considered important, will be upheld even if state practice contradicts the resolution. For example, a resolution in an area that is considered of primary importance, such as a resolution against torture, is considered valid although its practice is negligible.

b. Intent
A vote for a resolution may not be intended to signify acquiescence to a rule of international law. The intent of states to express a rule of law is necessary for it to be evidence of a rule of customary law. However, the absence of intent at the time of adoption is not conclusive if other factors create the expectation that such resolution should be a norm.

c. Change in State Practice
A change in state practice after adoption of the resolution, is persuasive evidence of customary law.

3. Non-Unanimous Ratification
A resolution need not be unanimous if it is stating a rule of existing customary law. However, in determining the evidentiary value of a resolution, one must always take into account:

a. Size of the ratifying majority; and

b. Composition of the ratifying majority.

4. Dissenting States
Dissenting states are not bound by a resolution, unless that resolution is evidence of a pre-existing obligation on the part of the state. If the state has dissented from the customary law during its formation and continuously thereafter, it is not bound.

D. Declaratory Resolutions

Declaratory resolutions purport to state the law independent of a Charter Rule; they are claiming to state *opinio juris*, not a recommendation. However, these are neither customary law nor *opinio juris*, regardless of the size of the majority that ratified them. They are merely evidence of existing custom. If ratified by a unanimous or large majority, they are of *significant* evidentiary value.

E. Recommendatory Resolutions

Recommendatory resolutions create international obligations as opposed to restating custom. Due to principles of estoppel (i.e., other states have relied on the resolution in their actions toward the opposing state), they can be held binding on states that have agreed to them, regardless of the intent of the states that they not be binding law.

F. Purely Political Declarations

Purely political declarations, such as joint communiques or unilateral presidential declarations, are not intended to be binding law at the time of the statement. However, they are evidence of the positions taken by the states and also can become customary law through practice. Noncompliance may therefore be illegal due to a good faith principle or estoppel because other states have reason to expect compliance and rely on it.

CASE CLIPS

The Paquete Habana
(U.S. 1900) HPSS, SOL

Facts: During the Spanish-American War, the United States condemned as prizes of war two Spanish fishing vessels that were fishing in Cuban coastal waters. Fishing vessels were traditionally exempt from wartime capture.

Issue: Is the conduct of other nations under similar circumstances evidence of a rule of international law?

Rule: In the absence of a specific treaty, governmental act, or judicial decision, the customs and usages of nations may be used as evidence of the existence of a rule of international law, as may the works of jurists and scholars in the field.

"The S.S. Lotus" (France v. Turkey)
(PCIJ 1927) HPSS, SOL

Facts: A French steamer collided with a Turkish steamer on the high seas. The Turkish ship sunk and eight Turks died. When the French ship reached Turkey, Turkish authorities criminally prosecuted the French officer on watch at the time of the collision.

Issue 1: Must a state opposing jurisdiction prove the absence of customary law that permits jurisdiction?

Rule 1: Because all acts that are not expressly forbidden under international law are permitted, the burden of proof is on the state opposing an act to show that there is a rule or custom that does not allow such an act to be exercised.

Issue 2: Does customary abstention of a state from certain actions create an obligation under customary law to continue to refrain from committing those acts?

Rule 2: That most states have abstained from certain actions in particular circumstances does not prove that they are obligated to do so, only that they have chosen to do so.

Dissent: The burden of proof should be on the state seeking to show that it has jurisdiction. International law does not permit everything that is not explicitly forbidden.

Asylum Case
(Colombia v. Peru)
(ICJ 1950) HPSS

Facts: Colombia granted political asylum to a Peruvian political leader at Colombia's embassy in Peru. Peru refused to allow the political leader to leave the country.

Issue: May a government unilaterally invoke regional customary law against another state?

Rule: A state may unilaterally rely on regional custom, but it has the burden of proving that this custom has become binding. To do so, a state must prove that the custom is the subject of continuous and uniform practice by the states in question, that such rule was invoked by the state exercising it as a right, and that the rule is respected by the states against whom it has been enforced as a duty. After the existence of a custom is established, it must be shown that the state against whom the custom is being enforced has not repudiated the custom through non-adherence to it.

Case Concerning Right of Passage Over Indian Territory
(Portugal v. India)
(ICJ 1960) HPSS

Facts: India obstructed the right of passage claimed by Portugal through Indian territory that surrounded Portuguese enclaves located on the Indian Peninsula.

Issue: In the absence of an express recognition of a claimed right, may such a right be established on the basis of a long-standing constant and continual course of dealings between nations (local custom)?

Rule: A local customary right may be established as the result of a constant and continual practice by a nation if, over a substantial period of its existence, it has not been formally opposed by other affected nations. However, if a course of conduct has been subject to the approval of an affected nation in the past or such conduct has been protested by affected nations, a right has not been established. The granting of approval does not establish a right.

Note: Customary law as established by a course of conduct between two states does not depend on general international customary law.

North Sea Continental Shelf Cases
(Federal Republic of Germany v. Denmark)
(Federal Republic of Germany v. Netherlands)
(ICJ 1969) HPSS

Facts: The Netherlands and Denmark claimed that the boundaries between their continental shelf territories and West German territories should be determined by the principle of equidistance set forth in Article 6 of the Geneva Convention of 1958. Germany was not a party to the Convention.

Issue 1: May the provisions of a ratified, multi-national convention become customary law that is binding on non-party states?

Rule 1: In order for a provision of a multi-national convention to be considered customary law that is binding on non-party states, state practice must be extensive and virtually uniform and must show a general recognition that a legal obligation is involved.

Issue 2: May a decision of international law be influenced by equitable principles?

Rule 2: Equity may be used as a rule of construction of existing international laws so that states under similar circumstances will not be subject to an unjustifiable difference in treatment.

Dissent: Many different states participate in the process of forming the provisions of an international convention, and subsequent acceptance or acquiescence to those provisions by other states should be seen as a ratification of general rules of international law sufficient to make them customary law.

The Diversion of Water From The Meuse
(Netherlands v. Belgium)
(PCIJ 1937) HPSS

Facts: The Netherlands submitted a complaint stating that construction of certain canals by Belgium violated an agreement not to alter the flow of the Meuse River.

Issue: May the principle of equity be used as a principle of international law?

Rule: Article 38, paragraph 2 of the Statute of the International Court of Justice authorizes the court to apply equity as distinguished from law.

Corfu Channel Case
(United Kingdom v. Albania)
(ICJ 1949) HPSS, SOL

Facts: Albania mined a channel that was part of Albanian territorial waterways. The mines damaged British vessels and killed Britons.

Issue: Does a nation have an obligation to warn other nations of dangers within its territorial waters?

Rule: Nations have an obligation to warn other nations of dangers in their territorial waters that are used for international navigation.

Advisory Opinion on the Western Sahara
(ICJ 1975) HPSS, SOL

Facts: The United Nations General Assembly requested an advisory opinion on claims asserted by Morocco and Mauritania to the former Spanish colony of Western Sahara.

Issue: Do declarations and resolutions of the United Nations General Assembly constitute binding international law?

Rule: A United Nations Resolution that interprets the United Nations Charter and is adopted by the General Assembly may become a legally binding norm of international law if it is generally accepted by member nations.

Texaco Overseas Petroleum Et Al. v. Libyan Arab Republic
(1977) HPSS, SOL

Facts: In violation of a contractual agreement, Libya nationalized the property of two American oil companies.

Issue: Is a General Assembly resolution that is supported by a majority of states binding international law?

Rule: A General Assembly Resolution is binding when accepted by a majority of nations only if that majority includes members of all various political, geographical, and economically developed groups.

Filartiga v. Pena-Irala
(U.S. 1980) HPSS, SOL

Facts: Jurisdiction was asserted under the U.S. Alien Tort Statute, which granted jurisdiction to the U.S. for acts in violation of the law of nations. Two Paraguayans brought a wrongful death action in an American court for acts committed in Paraguay by the Paraguayan chief of police.

Issue: Can a United Nations declaration that was not intended to be binding on the parties at the time of its adoption become binding as customary law?

Rule: A United Nations declaration that was not initially intended to be binding on the parties may become customary law provided (1) it is adopted by a large majority of states, (2) it creates an expectation of adherence to its rules, (3) state practice justifies that expectation.

Trendtex Trading Corporation v. Central Bank of Nigeria
(England 1977) SOL

Facts: The Central Bank of Nigeria sought to invoke sovereign immunity in a suit brought in England. The applicable rule of customary international law did not require the court to grant the immunity.

Issue: Are the rules of international law incorporated into, and considered to be part of, English law?

Rule: Under the doctrine of incorporation, the rules of international law are considered to be part of English law.

The Over the Top
Schroeder v. Bissell
(U.S. 1925) SOL

Facts: The U.S. sought a judgment decreeing the forfeiture and sale of a ship and her cargo, claiming that the sale of whisky on board the ship to a special agent of the Internal Revenue Department violated the Tariff Act of 1922. The owner of the ship asserted that, under recognized principles of international law, the acts complained of could not constitute offenses against the U.S. when committed by foreign nationals on the high seas beyond the territorial jurisdiction of the U.S.

Issue: May a district court refuse to enforce an act of Congress when the act is inconsistent with recognized principles of international law?

Rule: Unless it is clear that a congressional act was intended to disregard an established principle of international law, a court will presume that the congressional act was intended to be in conformity with international law.

Attorney General of Israel v. Eichmann
(Israel 1961) SOL

Facts: Eichmann was tried in Israel under a law punishing Nazis for their crimes against the Jewish people during World War II. D claimed that Israel had no jurisdiction over him and that Israeli law conflicted with international law.

Issue: If international law and national law conflicts, which law is to be preferred?

Rule: While a court must attempt to avoid a conflict between the municipal law and the obligations incumbent on the state by virtue of international law, a court must adhere to municipal law when the law exists in the form of written statutes.

Administration des Douanes v. Société Cafes Jacques Favre
(France 1975) SOL

Facts: Ps sued the French Customs Administration, claiming that the imposition of a consumption tax on imported coffee at a higher rate than the domestic product was in violation of the Rome treaty of 1957, establishing the European Economic Community. The French Constitution provided that treaties have a superior authority to international laws.

Issue: Do statutes enacted subsequent to a treaty prevail over a treaty's provisions?

Rule: Because a treaty is integrated into the legal order of the member-States and is binding on their courts, treaty provisions shall prevail over statutes enacted subsequent to a treaty.

Re Draft Ordinance Modifying Law 6/61 Governing Expropriation
(Gabon 1970) SOL

Facts: The Supreme Court of Gabon was asked to give an opinion on the constitutionality of a draft ordinance amending legislation on expropriation. Contrary to a prior treaty, the proposed legislation introduced discrimination between nationals, French citizens and the subjects of almost all citizens of the Organization Commune Africaine et Malgache.

Issue: Is a law that conflicts with a prior international treaty unconstitutional if the constitution establishes the treaty as the superior authority?

Rule: A law that conflicts with the principles embodied in a treaty is unconstitutional where the provisions of a prior international treaty have a superior authority over the laws of a state.

Norwegian State v. Carlile
(Norway 1964) SOL

Facts: Carlile, a British subject, was arrested and indicted for swindling in Norway. Denmark and Sweden requested the Norwegian authorities indict Carlile for similar acts performed in their countries.

Issue: Does the prohibition against applying one country's law to acts committed in other countries apply to an indictment for infractions punishable under the laws of all countries where the acts were committed?

Rule: Even though international law prohibits the application of one country's law to acts committed in other countries, the prohibition does not apply at the stage of indictment.

The Red Crusader
(1962) SOL

Facts: The British trawler *Red Crusader* was impounded by Danish authorities. A commission of inquiry was set up between the governments of Denmark and the United Kingdom to investigate the incidents relating to the impound.

Issue: May two states involved in a dispute establish a commission of inquiry to investigate and make a finding of the facts leading to the dispute?

Rule: The governments of two states involved in a dispute may set up a commission of inquiry to assist in resolving the dispute.

Case of Certain Norwegian Loans
(France v. Norway)
(ICJ 1957) SOL

Facts: When a dispute concerning the method of payment of Norwegian loans arose between the governments of France and Norway, the French government referred the matter to the ICJ. The French asserted that Norway was bound to settle the dispute in that court because it had accepted the compulsory jurisdiction of the court. Norway claimed that, since the French Declaration accepting the compulsory jurisdiction of the ICJ excepted matters within the national jurisdiction, they were not bound to resolve the matter in the ICJ because the issue was governed by municipal law.

Issue: Is a government entitled to rely on the reservations made by another government in its Declaration accepting the compulsory jurisdiction of the ICJ?

Rule: If one government has limited its acceptance of the compulsory jurisdiction of the court, other governments are entitled to rely upon any reservations made.

Case Concerning Military and Paramilitary
Activities In and Against Nicaragua
(Nicaragua v. United States of America)
(ICJ 1984) SOL, HPSS

Facts: The Secretary of State of the U.S. sent to the Secretary-General of the U.N. a letter stating that the U.S.'s acceptance of the compulsory jurisdiction of the ICJ shall not apply to disputes arising out of, or related to, events in Central America and that such proviso would take effect immediately. Three days later, the Government of Nicaragua instituted proceedings in the ICJ against the U.S. concerning its military activities in Nicaragua.

Issue: May a state invoke the principle of reciprocity in order to be excused from compliance with the terms set forth in its declaration of acceptance of the compulsory jurisdiction of the ICJ?

Rule: As the notion of reciprocity is concerned only with the scope and substance of the commitments entered into and not with the formal conditions of their creation or extinction, reciprocity cannot be invoked to excuse departure from the terms of a state's own acceptance.

Chapter 3

THE RELATION OF INTERNATIONAL LAW TO MUNICIPAL LAW

I. MUNICIPAL LAW IN INTERNATIONAL LAW

Municipal law is the domestic law of a nation.

A. Municipal Law Must Allow Compliance

States must ensure that their constitutions and laws enable them to comply with their international obligations.

B. Internal Law Not An Excuse for Non-Compliance

A state cannot use its internal law as an excuse for non-compliance with the requirements of international law. See Vienna Convention on the Law of Treaties, Article 46; Restatement (Revised) § 311(3).

C. Equality of Force

Generally, international law has the same binding force on a nation as domestic law.

D. Interpretations of Municipal Law

When international tribunals are called on to interpret municipal law, they usually comply with interpretations made by the courts of that state unless the interpretation is obviously erroneous or fraudulent.

II. INTERNATIONAL LAW IN MUNICIPAL LAW

A. General

1. Customary International Law
    Customary international law is binding on all states; they are, therefore, under an obligation to conform their domestic law to its standards.

2. Misapplication of International Law
    An international court does not have the power to set aside the provisions of a national court that has misapplied international law; however, it may award damages based on the misapplication.

3. Monist Theory
    This school of thought regards international and municipal law as part of the same legal system in which international law is supreme. Therefore, international law cannot be subject to constitutional limitations.

4. Dualist Theory
    This school of thought regards international law and municipal law as two distinct systems; therefore, international law can be applied only after it has been incorporated into a domestic legal system. After incorporation, international law is subject to constitutional limitation and repeal.

B. International Law in the Municipal Law of European States

1. Practice

    a. Monist States
        France, Luxembourg, Belgium, England, and the Netherlands follow the monist tradition and are more likely to concede the supremacy of international law in the case of a conflict.

b. Dualist States
Italy and Germany have strong dualist traditions. Neither treaties nor international law are subject to greater protection than domestic statutes.

c. European Economic Community Law (EEC)
EEC law must be applied by the municipal courts of all member states and, in the case of a conflict with municipal law, EEC law will take precedence.

C. International Law in the Municipal Law of the United States

1. Incorporation into United States Law

a. Self Executing
Customary international law is treated as automatically incorporated into the laws of the United States from the time the norm is established, and courts are allowed to give it effect over legislative provisions. Both state and federal courts treat international law as incorporated.

b. Constitutional Provisions

i. The General Rule
Article III, § 2 states that cases arising under the treaties of the United States are within the judicial power of the United States.

ii. Offenses Against the Law of Nations
Article I, § 8 gives Congress the power to define and punish offenses against the law of nations. In *United States v. Arjona*, the Supreme Court declared that Congress has the power to create and define any law that is necessary and proper to guarantee a right secured by the law of nations and to provide remedies. In 1791, the Alien Tort Act 28 U.S.C.A. § 1350 gave the district courts original jurisdiction for any tort committed against an alien in violation of the law of nations.

2. Federal Common Law (Restatement (Revised) § 132)

   a. Rule
   Customary international law is considered federal common law, despite the fact that it is not expressly incorporated into the laws of the land. Thus, not only do federal courts have original jurisdiction, but they need not follow state interpretations and their decisions are binding on state courts.

   b. Arising under International Law
   Federal district courts have original jurisdiction over any action arising under international law. An action does not arise under international law if the rule of international law enters into the case only as a defense.

   c. Creation of International Law
   Unlike federal common law, federal courts find international customary law by looking to the practice of other states and the opinions of jurists; they have no power to make it.

3. Application of International Law

   a. Constitutional Limitations
   International law is considered to be subject to constitutional limitations and may not be applied in the case of a conflict with a provision of the Constitution. In such a case, however, the United States may be in default of its international obligations and, thereby, face sanctions.

   b. Status in Relation to Internal Law

      i. Custom versus Treaties
      Although the status of domestic law as customary law in relation to treaties has not been determined, it has roughly equal weight.

ii.   Supreme Law of the Land (Restatement (Revised) § 131)
Article VI of the Constitution states that treaties are the
supreme law of the land. Both treaties and customary
law are considered to have this stature under this provision. This means that they have equal status to an act of
Congress.

iii.   Conflict Between Custom and Domestic Law
In the case of a conflict between a treaty or a rule of
customary law with an act of Congress, the most recent
law will be given effect. The United States has accepted
customary law to modify earlier treaties and statutes.

4. Executive Branch as Law Maker

a. Violation of International Law
The executive branch has the duty of legislating customary
law through its actions with other nations (and the duty,
under Article II, § 2 of the Constitution, to ensure that the
laws are faithfully executed). It may, therefore, violate
international law, and the courts will give effect to constitutional acts that violate international law. This is how new
rules of custom are forged.

b. Violation of Existing Legislation
The president may also create a treaty that is inconsistent
with a prior act of Congress.

c. Binding International Law
A determination of international law by the Supreme Court
would bind the United States in an action in which the
United States was a party.

5. Sovereign Immunity
Every sovereign state is bound to respect the independence of
every other sovereign state, and the courts of one country will
not sit in judgement on the acts of another state's government.
States are immune to submission to the courts of another state
unless they consent to suit.

6. The Act of State Doctrine (see also Chapter 13, § IV)

  a. Defined
     United States courts will not scrutinize the actions of foreign governments that are alleged to be in violation of international law.

  b. Self Restraint
     The act of state doctrine is not a rule of international law, but a rule of self-restraint. Therefore, the United States is not obligated to apply the doctrine and may give the doctrine effect even if the foreign state's action does not really fall under it.

  c. Invocation
     The courts will apply the act of state doctrine in cases where the executive branch has *not* indicated that it should not apply.

  d. Exceptions

    i. Commercial Transactions
       The United States considers commercial transactions excepted from the act of state doctrine. This includes actions by branches of governments that possess only commercial rather than governmental authority.

    ii. Takings
        The doctrine does not encompass takings of property outside of the taking state's jurisdiction.

    iii. Treaty Violation
         The act of state doctrine is not applicable to violations by a foreign state of a treaty between it and the United States.

    iv. Counterclaims
        The doctrine does not apply to bar a counterclaim.

e. Applicability to Takings of Property Inside the United States
The judicial branch will not examine the validity of a taking of property within its own territory by a foreign government in the absence of a treaty or other legally controlling principles. To determine the situation of debt (as property), courts will look to the intent of the parties, the jurisdiction of the debtor, and the currency in which the debt is to be paid.

f. General Application
There is evidence to support the application of the act of state doctrine in cases involving unsettled issues of international law or sensitive national interests, unless the executive has taken a position.

g. Waiver
Although the doctrine may not be waived, if a foreign state agrees to submit to American courts, the reasons for applying the doctrine is weaker.

h. Application to The United States President
Although this doctrine does not apply to acts of the executive branch, under the political question doctrine, the courts usually refuse to question executive acts involving the president's relations with foreign governments.

i. Conflicts of Law
This doctrine overrules the principle that a court may refuse to apply foreign law if it is found contrary to the public policy of the forum and requires the court to apply such law without question.

7. Bernstein Exception to the Act of State Doctrine
A court may admit evidence of wrongdoing on the part of a foreign government if the foreign acts are particularly heinous. However, it may not declare the foreign government's acts invalid on that ground.

8. Second Hickenlooper Amendment
   This amendment bars application of the act of state doctrine to cases involving claims to property.

   a. Rule
      No court in the United States shall decline, on the ground of the federal act of state doctrine, to make a determination on the merits of a claim to title to property asserted by any party, including a foreign state, based upon a confiscation or other taking by an act of that state in violation of international law.

   b. Requirements

      i.   Expropriated property must come within the court's territorial jurisdiction.

      ii. The act of the expropriating nation must be in violation of international law.

      iii. The asserted claim must be a claim of title or other right to property (22 U.S.C. § 2370 (e)(2).

   c. Presumption
      The courts should presume that the act of state doctrine should not be applied unless the president has stated that it is needed to protect foreign policy interests in a particular case.

   d. Exceptions
      The amendment is not applicable in cases where:

      i. Not Contrary
          The act is not contrary to international law;

      ii. Claim
          The foreign state has a claim to property pursuant to an irrevocable letter of credit; or

    iii. Presidential Determination
The president has determined that the act of state doctrine is required.

D. Law of the United States Regarding Treaties

1. Treaty Power

a. Power to Make
Article II, § 2 of the Constitution states that the president has the power to make treaties if two-thirds of the Senate concur.

b. Supreme Law of the Land
Article VI of the Constitution states that all treaties shall be the supreme law of the land, and that judges in every state shall be bound thereby, anything in the constitutions or laws of the states notwithstanding.

c. Ratification
After the Senate has given favorable advice and consent, the president may ratify a treaty at his discretion.

d. Reservation
The Senate may condition its consent on whether the president enters a reservation to a treaty.

e. State Power
Article I, § 10 of the Constitution states that no state shall, without the consent of Congress, enter into any agreement or compact with a foreign power.

2. Restraints on Treaty Power

a. Applicability of Constitutional Restraints
The Constitution does not expressly impose restraints on the treaty power, and no provision of any treaty has ever been held unconstitutional. However, the executive and legisla-

ture cannot extend their power beyond the limits of the Constitution in the making of treaties.

b. The Bill of Rights
While the Bill of Rights protects aliens, these rights may be subordinated to strong public policy interests.

   i. Foreign Governments
Foreign governments are not granted the protection of the Bill of Rights. However, foreign states or organizations are granted procedural due process and treated as persons for the purpose of jurisdiction and suit under American law.

   ii. Diplomats and Representatives
Full constitutional protection is extended to diplomats and representatives of foreign governments.

   iii. Civil Rights for Aliens
The Civil Rights Acts, 18 U.S.C. §§ 242-43, and 42 U.S.C. §§ 1981 et. seq., provide both civil and criminal remedies for violations of the rights of all persons within the United States, including aliens.

   iv. Scope of the Treaty Power
The federal government cannot broaden its powers under the treaty making authority nor may it alter the distribution of powers between the branches of government.

   v. The Tenth Amendment
Although the treaty power is usually invoked to deal with matters of international concern, the tenth amendment will not preclude treaties that involve the regulation of an important national interest even if they touch on relations that are customarily left to the control of the states.

c. Other Restrictions

   i. The Hughes Doctrine
The Constitution limits the treaty power to matters of international concern or relations. This doctrine presents an obstacle to the ratification of international human rights treaties.

   ii. Restatement Abolishes Hughes
The Restatement (Revised) § 302 states that it is no longer a requirement that a matter addressed under the treaty power be of international concern.

3. Treaties as Law of the Land

a. Self Executing Treaties
A treaty that declares that a rule is established is self-executing and must automatically be given effect by the courts as if it were an act of the legislature.

b. Non-Self-Executing Treaties
A treaty that instructs the legislature to enact implementing legislation is a non-self-executing political contract and cannot be given effect by the courts in the absence of an act by the legislature.

c. Constitutional Restraints on Self-Execution
If a treaty deals with subject matter that is within the exclusive legislative power of Congress, such as the making of war, the treaty cannot take effect in the absence of specific implementing action by Congress.

d. Intent
The intent of the government determines whether a treaty is self-executing.

e. Restatement of a Principle of Law
   If a treaty merely restates a principle of international law, it is self-executing and needs no implementing legislation, notwithstanding the terms of the treaty.

f. Omissions
   Treaties that involve the duty to refrain from committing certain acts are usually considered self-executing.

g. Presumption in Favor of Self-Execution
   In the event that the government takes no actions to implement a treaty, there is a strong presumption that the treaty is self-executing, unless there is a clear indication to the contrary.

h. Obligation to Create Implementing Legislation
   A treaty that contains provisions mandating the enactment of implementing legislation is not automatically considered a non-self-executing treaty. Various self-executing human rights treaties contain such provisions.

4. Conflict Between Treaties and Legislation (see Restatement (Revised) § 135)

   a. Act of Congress with Treaty
      An act of Congress supersedes an earlier treaty or rule of international law if:

      i. Purpose
         The clear purpose of the act is to supersede earlier rules and treaties; or

      ii. Non-Reconcilable
          The act and the earlier rule cannot be fairly reconciled.

   b. Treaty with Treaty
      The United States may modify or repeal a treaty as it may any other legislation. If a treaty contradicts an earlier treaty

or legislation, the courts will try to interpret them in a manner that gives effect to both. If this is not possible, the most recent law will control.

c. Treaty With Domestic Law (Including State Law)
A treaty that becomes effective as law supersedes any preexisting, inconsistent provisions of domestic law.

d. Supersession of Preexisting Treaty
If the United States enters into a treaty or legislates in a manner inconsistent with its obligations under a prior treaty, the United States remains under international obligation under the prior treaty. The offended state may seek remedy from the executive, from international law, or may institute sanctions.

5. Suspension or Termination of Treaties

a. Power to Terminate
The constitution does not specify which branch of government has the power to terminate treaties.

  i. The President
  The president may terminate treaties through international acts or treaties that contradict prior treaties. This power has never been questioned by Congress.

  ii. Congress
  Congress may also terminate treaties by enacting legislation that contradicts prior treaties or by refusing to enact implementing legislation.

  iii. Courts
  Courts do not have the power to terminate treaties, although they may interpret treaties as having been terminated by acts of other branches of government.

E. Executive Agreements in United States Law

1. Congressional-Executive Agreements

a. Power to Create
Although the Constitution does not specifically grant the power to create executive agreements, they have now become an accepted alternative to treaties. The Restatement (Revised) § 303 states that "The President, on his own authority, may make an international agreement dealing with any matter that falls within his independent powers under the Constitution."

b. Creation
The president can create an executive agreement with the joint approval of both houses of Congress. Therefore, Congress controls executive agreements to the same extent that it controls treaties.

c. Legal Status - Supreme Law of the Land
Executive agreements have the same legal status as treaties and supersede any inconsistent prior legislation or treaties.

d. Advantages over Treaties
Executive agreements take less time to promulgate. They can be submitted to both houses of Congress simultaneously and become effective on the date that the president signs them.

e. When Used
Executive agreements are used in lieu of treaties in cases where the treaty process may be unlikely to produce the desired result or ratification.

f. National Commitment Agreements
The president is required to obtain the approval of Congress for any agreement that involves the financial or military resources of the United States.

2. Executive Agreements
The president can make some agreements without the approval of either house of Congress. Generally, these are agreements that deal only with powers that are exclusively incident to the executive power. Only the executive is empowered to conduct foreign relations. This includes the resolution of international claims, establishment of diplomatic relations, and determination of public policy with regard to acts of foreign governments.

F. European Law Regarding Treaties

1. The Netherlands
In the Netherlands, self-executing agreements may not be contradicted by either prior or subsequent legislation.

2. The United Kingdom
In the United Kingdom, no treaty is self-executing. No treaty is valid until Parliament implements it.

3. France
France requires that treaties have authority that is superior to domestic laws, but it is not clear whether treaties may be superseded by subsequent legislation.

4. Italy
Italian law, under general rules of international law, overrides domestic legislation. However, subsequent domestic legislation overrides prior treaties.

5. Germany
German law, under general rules of international law, overrides domestic legislation. However, subsequent domestic legislation overrides prior treaties.

CASE CLIPS

Banco Nacional de Cuba v. Sabbatino
(S.Ct. 1964) HPSS, SOL

Facts: Cuba nationalized a Cuban sugar company owned by United States nationals in retaliation for the United States' reduction of a sugar import quota. An American company contracted to buy sugar from the Cuban government, but after receiving the shipment, paid the former American owners.

Issue 1: Does the act of state doctrine apply to acts of state that violate international law?

Rule 1: (Harlan, J.) The judicial branch will not examine the validity of a taking of property by a foreign government within its own territory in the absence of a treaty or other legally controlling principles even if the taking is alleged to be a violation of international law.

Issue 2: Is the act of state doctrine applicable in the absence of its specific invocation by the executive?

Rule 2: The act of state doctrine applies in cases where the executive branch has not indicated that it should not apply.

Dissent: (White, J.) The courts have a duty to resolve controversies in accordance with international justice and are therefore obligated to inquire into all cases where there is a possible violation of international law, even if there is no clear consensus in the international community on the issue at hand.

Missouri v. Holland
(S.Ct. 1920) HPSS, SOL

Facts: Missouri brought suit to stop the enforcement of a treaty between the United States and Canada that gave protected status to migratory birds, claiming the treaty violated the tenth amendment that reserved certain rights to the states.

Issue: Does the treaty power of the federal government extend to matters that occur within the territory of a state?

Rule: (Holmes, J.) Treaties that involve the regulation of an important national interest do not infringe upon the tenth amendment powers reserved to the states, even if they concern matters that are usually left to the control of the states.

Foster and Elam v. Neilson
(S.Ct. 1829) HPSS

Facts: Ps sued to recover land in the Louisiana Territory that was granted to them by the Spanish governor, but the possessor of the land claimed that the grant was made after the land had been transferred from Spain to the United States. Ps relied on a treaty that stated that all grants of land made by Spain would be confirmed by the United States.

Issue: Must a court give effect to all treaties made by the United States as the supreme law of the land?

Rule: (Marshall, C.J.) A treaty that instructs the legislature to make a rule is a non-self-executing political contract, and cannot be given effect by the courts in the absence of an act of the legislature.

Whitney v. Robertson
(S.Ct. 1888) HPSS

Facts: A treaty between the Dominican Republic and the United States stated that no higher duty would be assessed upon goods from the Dominican Republic than were assessed upon those of any other country. P claimed this was violated when the United States allowed sugar from the country of Hawaii to be imported duty free in return for special privileges.

Issue: If legislation is inconsistent with a treaty, which will prevail?

Rule: (Field, J.) If legislation is inconsistent with a treaty the most recent one will control the other.

Charlton v. Kelly
(S.Ct. 1913) HPSS, SOL

Facts: P, a U.S. citizen, brought a writ of habeas corpus to prevent his extradition to Italy. He claimed that the Italian government's refusal to extradite Italian nationals to the United States invalidated an extradition treaty between the United States and Italy, thus, P was not extraditable.

Issue: Does violation of a treaty obligation by one party to a treaty automatically invalidate that treaty?

Rule: (Lurton, J.) The violation of a treaty obligation by one party to the treaty makes the treaty voidable by the other party to the treaty.

United States v. Belmont
(S.Ct. 1937) HPSS

Facts: The U.S. brought suit against D to recover sums deposited by a Russian corporation. After the Soviet Union nationalized the corporation, it assigned to D all amounts due to the United States.

Issue: Must a state policy yield to an international agreement made by the executive without the approval of Congress?

Rule: (Sutherland, J.) The Executive has the sole authority to represent the government in matters regarding diplomatic relations; therefore, international agreements made by the executive in this area must be complied with, whether or not they amount to a ratified treaty.

Alfred Dunhill of London, Inc. v. Republic of Cuba
(S.Ct. 1976) SOL

Facts: The Cuban government nationalized the cigar industry that previously had been operated by Cuban corporations. When Dunhill, a cigar importer, sued the Cuban government seeking restitution for sums paid to the Cuban government, the Cuban government repudiated the debt, justifying its action as an act of state.

Issue: Does the act of state doctrine include the repudiation of a purely commercial obligation owed by a foreign government?

Rule: (White, J.) The act of state doctrine should not be expanded to include the repudiation by a foreign government of purely commercial debts and, thus, such acts may be subject to the scrutiny of the U.S. courts.

First National City Bank v. Banco Nacional de Cuba
(S.Ct. 1972) SOL

Facts: Banco Nacional de Cuba sued First National City Bank when First National refused to return the surplus on a sale of collateral following satisfaction of a loan. First National defended its action on the ground that it was entitled to counterclaim for the nationalization of its branch in Cuba.

Issue: May the courts exercise jurisdiction over counterclaims where the executive has advised the court that the act of state doctrine should not apply.

Rule: Majority opinion not provided.

Concurrence: (Powell, J.) The act of state doctrine does not preclude the courts from adjudicating claims where the executive has advised the court that the act of state doctrine should not apply.

Kalamazoo Spice Extraction Co. v. Provisional Military Government of Socialist Ethiopia
(U.S. 1984) SOL

Facts: D nationalized Kalamazoo's interest in its Ethiopian subsidiary. The nationalized Ethiopian corporation sued Kalamazoo in federal district court for withholding payments owed to it for spices supplied to Kalamazoo. Kalamazoo counterclaimed for uncompensated nationalization of property, claiming that the existence of a treaty between the U.S. and Ethiopia requiring compensation in the event of a taking of property created an exception to the act of state doctrine.

Issue: Does the existence of a treaty requiring just compensation in the event of a taking of property compel an exemption to the act of state doctrine?

Rule: The U.S. may, consistent with the act of state doctrine, exercise jurisdiction over claims against a foreign sovereign involving the taking of property without compensation if the foreign sovereign has, by treaty, agreed to compensate.

International Association of Machinists v. OPEC
(U.S. 1981) SOL

Facts: International Association of Machinists sued OPEC and its member nations, alleging that their price-setting activities violated U.S. antitrust laws.

Issue: Does the act of state doctrine preclude the U.S. courts from exercising jurisdiction over claims concerning another state's commercial activity when doing so would require the courts to judge the legality of the sovereign acts of a foreign state?

Rule: The act of state doctrine precludes the U.S. courts from exercising jurisdiction over claims concerning another state's commercial activity when doing so would entail the adjudication of a politically sensitive dispute.

West v. Multibanco Comermex, S.A.
(U.S. 1987) SOL

Facts: The Government of Mexico nationalized the entire private banking industry and established exchange control regulations that granted Mexico's Central Bank the right to approve the rate of exchange for repayment of all deposits. Ps, U.S. investors who purchased certificates of deposit from Mexican banks, claimed that the exchange rate approved resulted in a reduction of principal thereby effecting a taking of their property in violation of international law.

Issue 1: Is the establishment of exchange controls, a legitimate exercise of a state's power and, thus, considered an act of state?

Rule 1: Because a state has a strong interest in its monetary policy, the imposition of exchange controls is a legitimate exercise of a state's power in the regulation of its internal affairs.

Issue 2: Does the Hickenlooper Amendment apply to claims of expropriation of certificates of deposit owned by citizens of foreign states even though certificates of deposit are characterized as intangible property?

Rule 2: Although certificates of deposit are characterized as intangible property, rights arising from a certificate of deposit are "rights to property" within the meaning of the Hickenlooper Amendment; "tangibleness" of property is not the dispositive factor.

Compania de Gaz de Nuevo Laredo, S.A. v. Entex, Inc.
(U.S. 1982) SOL

Facts: P, a Mexican corporation, claimed that D conspired with the Government of Mexico to take control of its assets in Mexico after the Mexican government appointed an intervenor to take over its operations.

Issue: May U.S. courts exercise jurisdiction over claims of another government's act of expropriation?

Rule: Under the act of state doctrine, an act of expropriation by a foreign government is not a commercial action but a governmental action and, thus, such actions may not be scrutinized by the U.S. courts.

Hunt v. Coastal States Gas Producing Co.
(U.S. 1979) SOL

Facts: In 1957, the Government of Libya granted Hunt the right to explore and extract oil from the Sarir field. In 1973, the Government of Libya nationalized Hunt's rights. The proceeds realized by Coastal States from the oil purchased from a company owned by the Libyan Government formed the basis of Hunt's suit for conversion.

Issue: Does a claim for the conversion of a contractual right come within the exception to the act of state doctrine created by the Hickenlooper Amendment?

Rule: As the Hickenlooper Amendment, by its express terms, applies only to a claim of title or other right to property, the exception to the act of state doctrine created by the Hickenlooper Amendment does not apply where only a contractual right has been expropriated.

Buttes Gas and Oil Company v. Hammer
(United Kingdom 1981) SOL

Facts: Buttes Gas and Oil sued Armand Hammer in the U.K. for slander after Hammer accused Buttes of conspiring with the ruler of Sharjah (a minor Arab emirate). To counter D's assertion of truth as a defense, P claimed actions performed in Sharjah were not subject to the scrutiny of the British courts.

Issue: Is there a general principle similar to the American "act of state" doctrine in English law?

Rule: English law embraces the general principle that the courts in England will not adjudicate the sovereign acts of foreign sovereign states.

Anglo-Iranian Oil Co. Ltd. v. S.U.P.O.R. Co.
(Italy 1953) SOL

Facts: The Anglo-Iranian Oil Co. claimed ownership to certain oil purchased by S.U.P.O.R. in Persia and shipped to Venice, alleging that the Persian Law nationalizing the petroleum industry had not affected the ownership of the particular shipment of oil.

Issue: May a court exercise jurisdiction over a claim concerning the expropriation of property when doing so would require the court to apply the law of a foreign state?

Rule: A court may examine a claim of expropriation of property even when doing so would entail the application of a foreign state's law.

Decision On Expropriation
(Federal Republic of Germany 1959) SOL

Facts: A claim was brought against a German-Indonesian trading company that shipped to Bremen tobacco grown on the plantations of two Netherlands firms expropriated by the Indonesian State.

Issue: Where a foreign state expropriates property contrary to the *jus gentium* (law of nations) is a court automatically required to treat the expropriation as null and void?

Rule: Where a foreign state expropriates property contrary to the *jus gentium*, a court has complete discretion to recognize either the claims of the confiscating party or those of the former owner.

Republic of Iraq v. First National City Bank
(U.S. 1965) SOL

Facts: When Faisal II, the King of Iraq, was killed in 1958, the new government confiscated all property belonging to the dynasty. The Republic of Iraq sued First National, the administrator of the King's estate, to recover the King's New York assets.

Issue: Does the act of state doctrine, require U.S. courts to give effect to foreign confiscation decrees affecting property within the U.S.?

Rule: The United States will respect foreign confiscation decrees confiscating property within the U.S. only if they are consistent with the policy and law of the U.S.

Chapter 4

STATES

I. DETERMINATION OF STATEHOOD

A. State Defined

A state is an entity that has a permanent population, a defined territory, is under the control of its own government, and has the capacity to engage in formal relations with other states.

B. When the Question of Statehood Arises

1. Admission to International Organization
   An international organization must determine whether an entity is a state if that entity wishes to participate in an organization which is open only to states.

2. Multilateral Treaties
   The parties to a treaty must jointly determine whether an entity is a state if that entity wishes to participate in a treaty that is open only to states.

3. Bilateral Treaties
   A government of an independent, sovereign state must first determine whether an entity is a state if that entity wishes to enter into a treaty with the state. Normally, this determination is made by the executive branch.

4. Adjudication of Claims
   National courts must settle questions of statehood, especially in respect to entities that have not been recognized as states by the executive branch. Determining whether an unrecognized entity should be regarded as a state is important in issues involving property disputes, questions of nationality, and the validity of official acts.

C. The Effect of Recognition on Statehood

1. Constitutive View (see Restatement (Revised) § 202)
The acts of recognition of statehood by other nations confers international statehood on an entity.

2. Declaratory View
The status of international statehood depends on whether an entity factually possesses the criteria to meet the standards of international law for statehood.   The weight of authority supports this position.   See *L'Institut de Droit International*, the Inter-American Convention of the Rights and Duties of States, and the Charter of the OAS.

3. Practice
In practice, the determination of the facts relevant to whether a state meets the international law criteria for statehood often depends on whether states have agreed or refused to recognize the entity.   In addition, it is generally accepted that states are obligated to recognize entities that meet the criteria for statehood.

D. Requirements for Statehood

1. Permanent Population
An entity must have a permanent population in order to qualify as a state.   However, there is no minimum population size, as states with fewer than 500 people have been recognized.   In addition, all inhabitants need not be permanent.

2. Defined Territory
The entity must have some area of land over which it exercises exclusive control.   However, the borders of this area need not be precisely demarcated.   There is no minimum size requirement.

3. Government
The entity must be a stable and functioning political entity.

  a. Strength
  The government must be strong enough to assert itself without the aid of foreign troops.

  b. Effective Internal Administration
  The government must be able to establish order and normal social and political life.

  c. Firmly Established Governmental Institutions

    i. There must be an established seat of government; and

    ii. The majority of the population must accept the legality of the government.

4. Capacity to Enter into Relations with Other States
A state must have the financial and political capability to engage in international relations.

E. Duty of Recognition

Recognition of another state is an optional political act. However, if an entity satisfies all of the requirements for statehood, other states may subject themselves to a legal risk if they ignore the entity's existence.

F. Duty of Nonrecognition

1. Unlawful Intervention
It is common practice to withhold recognition from a revolutionary force until it is successful in its conflict with the parent state.

2. Illegal States
Even when an entity meets all of the traditional conditions for statehood, it may be viewed as illegal or illegitimate by the

United Nations or other international organizations.   See
Resolution Concerning Southern Rhodesia.

II.   RECOGNITION OF GOVERNMENTS

A. Criteria for Recognition

1. The criteria for recognition of a new regime is the assurance
   that the regime does in fact control the state's government.

2. In the twentieth century, the United States has withheld
   recognition from governments that have taken power without
   consent of the people governed or in violation of the state
   constitution.   However, these criteria for recognition often
   prove to be politically impractical.

B. Unrecognized Governments

1. Power to Bind the State
   Generally, agreements made by unrecognized *de facto* govern-
   ments that exercise authority throughout the country, are valid.
   See *Tinoco*.

2. Insurgent Authority in Part of State
   De facto authorities may perform ordinary governmental
   functions but are rarely seen as subjects of international law or
   parties to treaties.

C. Governments-In-Exile

Unlike *de facto* governments, these governments have legal
recognition but lack actual authority in the state.   While able to
obtain various legal rights and recognitions, these governments are
often powerless to serve practical aims.

D. Termination of Recognition

A state cannot be "derecognized" if it continues to meet the qualifications of statehood. (See Restatement (Revised) § 202, Comment g.) A state derecognizes one regime when it recognizes another regime as the government. (See Restatement (Revised) § 202, Comment g.)

III. STATE SUCCESSION

A. Effect on the Internal Legal System

Traditionally, private law survives a transfer of power, while public law does not. However, in practice if there is no continuity between the internal legal system of the old and new regimes, no succession will occur.

B. Succession to Public Debts

1. National Debts
   If the debtor entity retains fiscal independence, then national debtor-creditor relationships are unaffected. If the debtor entity is liquidated or absorbed into a larger state, debts may not be assumed by the succeeding power.

2. Local Debts
   Local debts are generally assumed by the successor state.

C. Succession to Contracts

If the predecessor state remains in existence, all rights and obligations under its contracts will generally remain with that state. See Restatement (Revised) §209.

D. Succession to State Property

When one state acquires part of the territory of another state, the property of the predecessor state located within this territory becomes the property of the successor state.

E. Succession to Penalties for International Law Violations

In general, successor states have no responsibility for the international law violations of their predecessor.

IV. TERRITORIAL ENTITIES OTHER THAN STATES THAT HAVE INTERNATIONAL STATUS

A. Dependent Entities as Parties to Treaties

Members of composite states, "dependent states", colonial dependencies, territories administered under mandates, and entities subject to other forms of international supervision are all examples of non-states that possess treaty-making or other international powers.

B. Associated States

Some states pass through this status after being subordinate colonies, but before becoming independent states. Associated states status allows an entity to maintain complete internal independence yet depend on its parent state in matters concerning international relations.

C. Mandated, Trust, and Other Internationalized Territories

1. Mandated and Trust Territories
   These territories, established in the twentieth century, were designed to promote "well-being and development" and eventually independence of the peoples involved.

2. Other Internationalized Territories
   These territories are typically created as part of a multinational plan to make an entity "open and free" to people of all nations and still preserve the autonomy of the territory.

D. Entities *Sui Generis*

These are unique internationally recognized entities that do not fit into any of the preceding categories. Examples include: The State of the Vatican City and the Holy See, and Taiwan.

V. INTERNATIONAL STATUS OF "PEOPLES" AND THEIR RIGHT OF SELF-DETERMINATION

A. Equal Rights and Self-Determination

The United Nations and the International Covenants on Human Rights have declared that all peoples have the right to freely determine their political, economic, social, and cultural development.

B. Giving Effect to Self-Determination

1. The United Nations
   The U.N. uses a variety of methods, ranging from efforts to ascertain the "will of the people" to using military forces, to effectuate the right of self-determination.

2. The Will of the People
   Popular opinion is most commonly gauged by internationally supervised, secret ballots.

3. Recognizing National Liberation Movements
   National liberation movements are sometimes granted access to the United Nations and other international organizations before they are independent states. This is a controversial measure in that it speeds the undermining of existing sovereign states.

VI. ACQUISITION OF TERRITORIAL SOVEREIGNTY

A. Basic Principles

See the *Island of Palmas, Legal Status of Eastern Greenland and Western Sahara* case clips.

B. Contiguity

1. The theory behind title by contiguity is that the sovereign state nearest a territory that is not part of an independent state may make a claim of acquisition due to geographical proximity.

2. Title by contiguity was largely discredited when the United States lost its claim in the *Island of Palmas Case.*

C. Title by Prescription

While this mode of acquiring title is better suited to personal property, the "long and peaceful possession" of a territory is often viewed as determinative in acquiring sovereignty.

D. Consolidation

Some scholars suggest that all modes of acquiring territorial title be subsumed under the notion of a "process of consolidation." Proof of long use, similar to prescription, is the foundation of a process of consolidation.

E. Other Methods of Acquiring Territorial Sovereignty

1. Accretion
Accretion occurs when a state's territory is expanded by natural forces, e.g., shifting river courses, receding of the sea.

2. Cession
Cession involves the transfer of sovereignty by means of an agreement between the ceding and the acquiring states.

3. Conquest
Conquest is the acquisition of an enemy's territory by the enemy's total surrender and an accompanying declaration of annexation. However, a treaty of cession is the more common method of annexing territory at the end of a war.

F. Extent of Territorial Sovereignty

1. Land Territory
   a. Boundaries separating the land areas of two states are determined by acts of the states.

   b. When two states are separated by a river or a lake, the boundary's location is the middle of the river or lake.

2. Airspace

   The Convention on International Civil Aviation grants every state the complete and exclusive sovereignty over the airspace above its territory.

CASE CLIPS

League of Nations Commission of Jurists
on Aaland Islands Dispute
(1920) HPSS

Facts: A dispute arose concerning the Aaland Islands following the Finnish Civil War of 1917-18.
Issue: What criteria must be met for a country to achieve statehood?
Rule: Statehood can not be achieved until a stable political organization has been created or until the public authorities have the strength to assert themselves throughout the territories of the state without the assistance of foreign troops.

Resolution Concerning Southern Rhodesia
(U.N. 1965) HPSS

Facts: Illegal authorities seized power in Southern Rhodesia and proclaimed independence from Great Britain and Northern Ireland.
Issue: Does a country automatically become a recognized sovereign state upon meeting the traditional criteria for independence, i.e., an authoritative government and capacity to enter into foreign relations?
Rule: The Security Council of the United Nations may renounce a new state that violates the principle of self-determination as a

"minority regime" even if it meets the traditional criteria for independence.

The Tinoco Claims Arbitration
(Great Britain v. Costa Rica)
(U.N. 1923) HPSS

Facts: Great Britain entered into contracts with the Tinoco regime of Costa Rica, a government not recognized by many leading powers, including Britain. When the Tinoco regime fell, the restored government in Costa Rica nullified all of the Tinoco agreements.

Issue: Do the acts of an unrecognized, predecessor government bind the existing government?

Rule: Contracts entered into by a previous government with *de facto* sovereignty are binding on subsequent regimes even if the predecessor government was unrecognized by its bargaining partners.

Salimoff & Co. v. Standard Oil of N.Y.
(U.S. 1933) HPSS, SOL

Facts: The Soviet Government confiscated all oil lands in Russia and sold some of the extracted oil to D. P, the former owner of the property, claimed that the confiscatory decrees of the unrecognized Soviet government amounted to theft.

Issue: Does a government with *de facto* authority, but without widespread legal recognition, have legal force within its borders?

Rule: Domestic decrees of a government that maintains internal peace and order and provides for general national welfare are generally authoritative even if the government is not legally recognized.

Upright v. Mercury Business Machines Co.
(U.S. 1961) HPSS

Facts: P was paid for the sale and delivery of typewriters manufactured by an East German corporation. D claimed that the transaction was invalid since the corporation was the instrument of an unrecognized government.

Issue: What effect is given to acts that occur under the administrative rule of an unrecognized government?

Rule: The acts of a *de facto* government that does not have lawful recognition are generally seen as valid, provided that they do not violate public or national policy.

Island of Palmas Case
(United States v. The Netherlands)
(1928) HPSS

Facts: The Island of Palmas (Miangas) was situated within the boundaries of the Philippines as ceded by Spain to the United States in 1898. For more than two hundred years, the Netherlands had possessed the island and exercised sovereignty. The United States claimed title to the island based on its succession to the rights of Spain.

Issue: Does occupation of a territory lead to the establishment of territorial sovereignty by the occupying state?

Rule: The continuous and peaceful display of territorial sovereignty as shown by physical occupation is sufficient to establish title.

Legal Status of Eastern Greenland Case
(Denmark v. Norway)
(PCIJ 1933) HPSS, SOL

Facts: In 1931, Norway proclaimed sovereignty over portions of Eastern Greenland. Denmark urged that the Nordic occupation was invalid due to the history of Danish sovereignty in the territory.

Issue: How must an effective occupation be shown in order to prove acquisition of territorial sovereignty?

Rule: A claim of sovereignty based not upon some particular act or title, but merely upon continued display of authority, involves (1) the intention and will to act as sovereign and (2) some actual exercise or display of such authority.

Advisory Opinion on the Western Sahara
(ICJ 1975) HPSS, SOL

Facts: Spain, Mauritania, and Algeria each asserted sovereign rights to the Western Sahara. Spain claimed that, despite the presence of tribes of nomadic farmers, no nation could claim sovereign power at the time of its colonization of the area.

Issue: What constitutes "legal ties" between a nation and a territory sufficient to demonstrate the acquisition of territorial sovereignty by the nation?

Rule: A nation seeking sovereign power must be able to show that it is in such a position that it possesses rights that it is entitled to ask the local inhabitants to respect.

In re Citizenship of X
(Fed. Rep. of Germany 1978) SOL

Facts: After acquiring citizenship in the Duchy of Sealand, X sought to have his German citizenship revoked. The Duchy of Sealand was a man-made island with a population of 40.

Issue: Can an entity formed out of man-made territory be considered a state under international law?

Rule: Under international law, an entity must possess three essential attributes to qualify as a state: territory, population, and government. The territory must consist of a naturally created portion of the earth's surface and not a man-made island.

The Arantzazu Mendi
(England 1939) SOL

Facts: Both the Republican and Nationalist Spanish Governments requisitioned the *Arantzazu Mendi*, a Spanish ship. The Republican Spanish government sought a writ of requisition. The Nationalist Spanish government, recognized by England, contested the jurisdiction of the writ based upon sovereign immunity.

Issue: Does the recognition of a government entitle it to sovereign immunity?

Rule: The recognition of a government as a sovereign state enables that entity to claim sovereign immunity.

In re Harshaw Chemical Co.'s Patent
(England 1970) SOL

Facts: Harshaw applied for an extension of their patent pursuant to section 24 of the British Patents Act, which entitles the patentee to an extension of the term of the patent for any loss or damage resulting from hostilities between the government and any foreign state. Harshaw's opponents contended that the application should be denied because North Korea lacked the necessary qualifications of a foreign state.

Issue: Is the recognition of an entity as an independent sovereign state an essential element of statehood?

Rule: Recognition of an entity's claim as an independent sovereign state is an essential element of statehood.

In re Al-Fin Corporation's Patent
(England 1969) SOL

Facts: Al-Fin applied for an extension of their patent pursuant to the British Patents Act, claiming that losses due to hostilities between Britain and North Korea entitled it to an extension of the patent term. Al-Fin's application was opposed on the grounds that North Korea is not a state because it is not recognized.

Issue: Is governmental control over a defined territory sufficient to qualify it as a state regardless of recognition?

Rule: The qualifications of statehood are not limited to recognition there must be control of a defined area of territory.

Clerget v. Banque Commerciale Pour L'Europe du Nord
and Banque du Commerce Exterieur du Vietnam
(France 1969) SOL

Facts: P obtained a default judgment against D and sought to execute the judgment by garnishing funds held by banks for D. D contested jurisdiction, claiming sovereign immunity.

Issue: Is a state not recognized by the forum state entitled to sovereign immunity?

Rule: If the state effectively exercises the functions of a state within a defined territory and its government is obeyed by the majority of the population, recognition is unnecessary. Immunity from jurisdiction is derived from the independence and the sovereignty of a State, not from recognition.

Russian Socialist Federated Soviet Republic v. Cibrario
(U.S. 1923) SOL

Facts: P brought an action in a U.S. court. D contested the jurisdiction, asserting that P's unrecognized status denied it access to the U.S. courts.

Issue: Is a government permitted to bring suit in the domestic courts of a state that does not recognize it?

Rule: The right of a foreign government to bring suit in another country is based upon comity. Until a government is recognized no comity exists and it is denied the right to sue.

Capacity of an East German Juridical Person
To Be a Party In a Trial Hearing For
Nullification of a Trademark Registration
(Japan 1973) SOL

Facts: P, an East German corporation, brought suit to nullify a trademark held by D. P's request was denied because it was a juridical person of a country not recognized by Japan.

Issue: Are the reciprocal rights granted to nationals of a foreign country dependant upon the recognition of that country's statehood?

Rule: A citizen is entitled to reciprocal rights if the unrecognized country has specific territory and people and its legal system is sufficiently developed to ensure the enjoyment of reciprocal rights.

Bank of China v. Wells Fargo Bank & Union Trust Co.
(U.S. 1952) SOL

Facts: In a suit brought by P to recover a sum of money, D expressed its willingness to pay, but asserted that it was unable to do so because both the Nationalist and the Peoples Governments of China claimed ownership.

Issue: Are courts required to give conclusive effect to the acts of a recognized government, to the exclusion of an unrecognized government, regardless of the facts?

Rule: Courts are not required to give conclusive effect to the acts of a recognized government; recognition is not intended to condone every act of a recognized government.

A.M. Luther v. James Sagor & Co.
(England 1921) SOL

Facts: P brought suit to establish its right to a quantity of wood sold to D by the Soviet government after it had nationalized P's assets.

Issue: In the domestic courts of one country, are the acts of a foreign *de facto* government treated in a similar manner as those of a *de jure* government?

Rule: The acts of a *de facto* government are treated by domestic courts in the same manner as the acts of a state with *de jure* recognition.

Attorney General v. Solomon Toledano
(Morocco 1963) SOL

Facts: Toledano requested that the court give executory force to a document notarized in Israel, a state not recognized by the Moroccan government.

Issue: Are the consequences of the nonrecognition of a state greater than those of the nonrecognition of a government?

Rule: Because the legislation of an unrecognized state and all the rules that regulate its functioning are nonexistent in the eyes of the unrecognizing country, the nonrecognition of a state has more extensive consequences than the nonrecognition of a government.

Warenzeichenverband Regekungstechnik E.V. v.
Ministero Industria, Commercio E Artigianato
(Italy 1975) SOL

Facts: P, an East German association, requested the registration of a trademark. The Italian government denied the request because it did not recognize East Germany as a state.

Issue: What is the effect of nonrecognition in matters of private law?

Rule: Private law is not effected by nonrecognition.

Banco Nacional de Cuba v. Sabbatino
(S.Ct. 1964) HPSS, SOL

Facts: Cuba nationalized an American sugar company in retaliation for the United States reduction of a sugar import quota. An American company contracted to buy the sugar from the Cuban government, but after receiving the shipment, paid the former American owners.

Issue: Does the severance of diplomatic relations with a recognized foreign government bar access by that government to a country's domestic courts?

Rule: The severance of diplomatic relations with a recognized government should not inevitably result in the withdrawal of that governments's privilege of bringing suit.

Chapter 5

ORGANIZATIONS, COMPANIES, AND INDIVIDUALS IN INTERNATIONAL LAW

I. INTERNATIONAL ORGANIZATIONS

A. Public International Organizations

Most members of public international organizations, such as the United Nations and its constituent bodies, are states.

B. Nongovernmental Organizations

Nongovernmental organizations are made up of individuals representing particular interests, such as human rights, trade union associations, and professional associations. The original nongovernmental organization is the International Committee of the Red Cross. Nongovernmental organizations play a consultative role at the United Nations, under article 71 of the United Nations Charter, the Human Rights Committee and the special rapporteur system. They generally do not have the status of international legal persons.

C. Multinational Public Enterprises

These are organizations created by groups of states to govern their behavior in a commercial or economic area. They are governed by municipal law, generally of the state of their headquarters. An example of a multinational public enterprise would be an organization that coordinates mail delivery in a certain area of the world.

II.   LEGAL PERSONALITIES AND ORGANIZATIONS

A. International Legal Personality

An entity has international legal personality if it is capable of possessing international rights and duties and has the capacity to take international action, such as making treaties, bringing claims for breaches of international law, and enjoying privileges and immunities from municipal jurisdiction.   International legal personality involves the capacity to perform acts in international law in addition to municipal law.

B. Test for International Legal Personality

If an organization was intended to have international legal personality and this is expressly stated or implied, because the organization may make binding recommendations to its members, has legal capacity, privileges, and immunities within the territories of its members, has become a party to international agreements, or exhibits other characteristics normally assumed by states, the organization has international legal personality.

C. International Organizations

International organizations are generally recognized to have international legal personality, largely because they distinguish between the legal capacity of their members and themselves. However, there is a dispute whether the personality and inherent legal rights and duties derived from this depend on the characteristics of the organization under its charter or are inherently derived from the fact it is an international legal organization.

D. Capacity to Bring Claims Against States

1. International Personality
   The capacity of an international organization to bring an international claim is based on the organization possessing international personality.

2. Necessity
The capacity of an international organization to bring a *particular type* of claim is based on the particular function and characteristics of the organization, as stated in its constitution.

3. Objective Legal Personality
Theoretically, organizations that possess objective legal personality have the capacity to perform any acts, subject only to the limitations of their own constitution and the consent of members. However, courts generally rely on the necessity test to determine whether an organization has the capacity to act in a certain matter.

4. Concurrent Authority of Member States
Member states may not act independently of an organization on matters that are covered by the scope of the organization's charter.

5. Representatives of International Organizations
Acts of authorized agents of the organization and agents with apparent authority are binding on the organization, as well as its members. Even *ultra vires* acts (acts beyond the scope of power granted) may be binding if they merely violated an internal rule, or were relied on by a third party.

E. Capacity to Make Treaties

1. General (See Chapter 6, § II,B,1)
International organizations have the capacity to make agreements with states, subject to the internal rules of the organization. This is the main characteristic of international personality.

2. Particular Scope
An organization's capacity to make a particular type of agreement with a state depends upon the scope of the organization's mission as defined by the particular functions and purposes articulated in the organization's charter.

F. Standing

1. Before International Tribunals
Whether an international organization has standing before a particular international tribunal depends on the internal rules governing the tribunal.

2. Before the International Court of Justice
Only states may appear before the ICJ. Advisory opinions may be requested only by states, the United Nations General Assembly, or the Security Council.

G. Responsibility

1. Of Organizations
International organizations are responsible for torts committed by their agents or those acting under the guidance of the organization. International organizations are also responsible for contractual obligations.

2. Of Member States
Member states are not individually liable for the acts of an organization, although they may be responsible for contributing to pay for financial damages incurred.

H. Internal Jurisdiction

Regarding internal matters, international organizations have general jurisdiction and compulsory judicial power over its members, agents, and departments.

1. Inherent
This jurisdiction is a power of the organization regardless of whether it is expressly authorized in the rules of the organization.

2. Organic
This jurisdiction is binding on members and agents of the organization in their capacity as members and agents of the organization only.

3. Exclusive
This jurisdiction is exclusive of all other judicial and arbitral bodies.

III. INTERNATIONAL ASSOCIATIONS

A. Inter-Governmental Corporations and Consortia

These companies have a public purpose, although they are created in the form of a private corporation. Examples of such organizations are the *instruments* used to implement common market or other interstate economic agreements, such as international banks.

B. Intergovernmental Producer Associations

The United Nations has recognized the right of states to form producer associations. Generally, these associations are formed by developing countries that are the producers of a single or a few agricultural or natural resource commodities. Producer associations allow countries to control the market prices of commodities through practices such as price fixing and export limitations

IV. TRANSNATIONAL CORPORATIONS UNDER INTERNATIONAL LAW

A. Private Corporations

Private corporations that have their headquarters in one state, although they may carry out their operations in several states, are subject to national law and are generally not international legal persons.

1. Nationality
   The state of nationality of a private corporation may be any of the following.

   a. *Siège Social*
      The nationality of the state in which it maintains its head-quarters.

   b. Principle Place of Business
      The state in which it maintains its principle place of business.

   c. State of Incorporation
      The state in which it was incorporated.

2. Capacity to Enter Into International Agreements
   Private corporations may enter into agreements with governments of other countries, under which circumstances public international law would govern.

3. Capacity to Bring International Legal Claims
   Private corporations may not bring claims against states. They must rely on the state of their nationality to protect their international legal rights.

B. Multinational Corporations (MNCs)

1. Definition
   Multinational corporations are corporations that control or own manufacturing plants or offices for the sale of services in countries other than the country of their nationality. These include both private and government-run corporations.

2. Problems of Nationality of Multinational Corporations
   One country cannot effectively control the behavior of an MNC due to the MNC's ability to transfer assets internationally using channels within the corporation itself and to effect national economies by moving production facilities from plants located in one country to those located in another.

a. Country of Nationality
Countries in which MNCs are based fear the negative effect that movement of production facilities to other countries may have on domestic employment, as well as the decrease in wages that the threat of such movement may necessitate. In addition, they fear that trade and redistribution of profits within the MNC network may effect the country's balance of payments, without a corresponding favorable trade impact on the country itself.

b. Foreign Countries
Countries in which the MNC conducts operations fear control of economic sectors important to the national economy by foreigners, the negative effect this may have on political sovereignty, and the excessive costs to the domestic economy that a corporation not concerned with the welfare of the nation may exact to meet its profit goals.

c. Labor Concerns
Employees fear that employment by a foreigner, upon whom the local economy may have become dependent, will result in a decrease in union control over employee welfare and in union bargaining power.

d. MNCs' Concerns
MNCs themselves fear that their substantial investment will be subject to nationalization without appropriate compensation.

3. Possible Solutions to MNC Control Problem
Countries may be able to control and monitor MNCs by creating supranational citizenship and a corresponding law specifically to control multinational corporations. This may be done either by international treaty or by slowly expanding the existing international law norms. The United Nations is currently considering a Code of Conduct for Transnational Corporations.

V. INDIVIDUALS IN INTERNATIONAL LAW

A. Status of Individual Under International Law

International law is applicable to individuals in their relationships to states and is also sometimes applicable to relationships between individuals if they encompass subjects of international concern.

1. Exhaustion of Local Remedies
   An individual must exhaust local (national) remedies of the state with which it has a dispute before suit can be brought under international law.

2. Who Has the Right to Bring an International Claim

   a. General International Law
      Only aliens can make a claim under traditional international law. A claim by an individual against the state of which he is a national is considered a matter of national law.

   b. Human Rights Law
      With the development of human rights law, international law is beginning to recognize the right of all individuals to bring suit against any state.

3. Who May Bring an International Claim
   An individual, in areas other than human rights law, may not bring a claim in an international tribunal. He must have the state of which he is a national bring the claim for him.

B. Status of the Individual Under the European Community

There are three types of treaty provisions that effect an individual within the community.

1. State
   Traditional treaties are addressed to, and create rights and obligations between, states only.

2. Institutional
Institutional treaties are addressed to community institutions only. Individuals are effected by the secondary implementing legislation, which may apply to member states or to individuals directly. This category has developed in order to protect individuals against bodies that have a great deal of law making power, but are not subject to political control by an elected body.

3. Individual
This legislation applies directly to relations between individuals and states and affords the individual a direct remedy against a state in court. This category developed to preserve an individual's rights derived from membership in the community that a state may be in a position to suppress if the expression of these rights conflict with an interest of the state.

C. The Legal Responsibility of Individuals in International Law

Individuals are generally not held responsible for their acts under international law. But, the nation under whose rule they live is responsible for promulgating and enforcing laws that comply with international law.

1. The Development of International Responsibility

a. Traditional Law
There are some areas, such as piracy, spying, and sabotage, that have traditionally been considered violations of "the law of nations" and, although international law has traditionally left punishment for the violation of these laws to states, any state was allowed to punish the individual for such crimes. This is the basis under which individual legal responsibility has developed.

b. The Geneva Conventions
The Geneva Conventions permit states to punish individuals for violations of the enumerated rules of international conduct.

c. Hijacking Conventions
Hijacking conventions generally require that states bring individuals to trial for their crimes, or that they extradite them in order to allow other states to do so.

2. Trials of Individuals as War Criminals

a. Trial of Individuals
The Nuremberg Charter, which was entered into after the Second World War, established a tribunal to try Nazi war criminals as individuals, regardless of whether they had acted in their individual capacity or as members of organizations.

b. Acts of States
Nuremberg established that individuals are responsible for acts committed in their capacity as heads of state. Since violations of international law are committed by people, international law cannot be enforced without punishing the individuals who committed the crimes.

c. Superior Orders
Individuals may not use the defense that they were merely following orders and did not personally intend to commit war crimes if moral choice was in fact possible. The essence of the Nuremberg Charter is that individuals have duties that transcend the national obligations imposed by states.

d. Acts Committed Against Fellow Nationals
Although international law does not traditionally extend to acts committed within a state against fellow nationals, it has traditionally been a duty of the state to punish the individuals who committed these acts. In the case of a state that no longer has an operating government, these acts may be punished under international law.

e. *Nullum Crimen Sine Lege*
Individuals who commit war crimes may be punished in the absence of a codified international rule of law that prohibits

those crimes. The initiation of war is in itself a crime under international law. Therefore, individuals who breach this rule are on sufficient notice that their acts are criminal.

D. Terrorists in International Law

State sponsored terrorism has increased dramatically in recent decades.

1. State Responsibility in Cases of Terrorism
   International law does not clearly require states to prosecute or extradite international terrorists in the absence of a treaty. However, international law does prohibit a state from allowing its territory to be used as a base for terrorist activities (the traditional rule prohibits use by armed bands).

2. Terrorism as an International Crime
   The Convention to Prevent and Punish the Acts of Terrorism Taking the Form of Crimes Against Persons and Related Extortion That Are of International Significance and the Bonn Declaration on Hijacking unequivocally condemn all acts of terrorism and call upon all states to refrain from organizing or assisting terrorists. U.N. Security Council Resolution No. 579 declares that all states are required to prevent hostage taking.

3. Political Offense Exception to the Obligation to Extradite
   Many countries have been reluctant to extradite terrorists due to the strong international law principle that asylum should be provided for those accused of political offenses. However, there have been two European conventions that have placed some limits on this exception: The European Convention on the Suppression of Terrorism and the Agreement on the Application of the European Convention for the Suppression of Terrorism.

4. International Sanctions Against Terrorism
   Neither international law nor any anti-terrorism conventions require sanctions against nations that aid terrorists. However, under the Bonn Declaration on Hijacking, member nations have

agreed to discontinue airline flights to countries that will not extradite or prosecute hijackers. It is hoped that this will provide a model for future sanctions.

VII. NATIONALITY OF INDIVIDUALS

A. Definition

Nationality is a legal bond having as its basis a genuine connection of interests and sentiments, together with the existence of reciprocal rights and duties between the nation and the national. The national should generally be more closely connected with the nation conferring nationality than with any other nation.

B. Determination

Generally, it is up to each state to determine, according to its own laws, whether an individual possesses the nationality of that state.

C. Limits

1. No Extension Without Consent
   No state may forcibly extend its nationality to any individual. The foreigner's consent is necessary to legalize his nationalization. However, there are few other limitations placed on a state's power to determine nationality by international law.

2. Implied Consent
   Consent may be inferred from marrying a national, but not from habitual residence.

3. Minimum Contacts
   Generally, in order for other states to be required to recognize a conferral of nationality, some minimum contacts between the individual and the state of his nationality are necessary. These include habitual residence, family ties, and business connections.

D. Factors Effecting Determination of Nationality

When determining nationality, states usually look for a bond between an individual and the state, such as place of birth, domicile, or nationality of family. There are two predominant bases on which states make their determinations, although most states use a combination of both. These are:

1. *Jure Sanguinis*
An individual is considered a national if he has descended from nationals.

2. *Jure Solis*
An individual is considered a national if he was born in the territory of the nation.

E. Dual Nationality

Individuals with dual nationality are considered to be nationals of each of the two states.

1. Extending Diplomatic Protection
Only the state with which an individual has effective (dominant) nationality may afford diplomatic protection to a national in a conflict of nationality case.

2. Bringing Claims
A dual national may bring claims against a state of his nationality in an international tribunal only if that state was *not* the state of dominant nationality when the dispute arose.

3. Determining Dominant Nationality
The state that has dominant nationality is the state in which the individual habitually resides or with which, under the circumstances, the individual appears to be the most closely connected (considering economic, social, political, civic, and family life).

CASE CLIPS

Reparation For Injuries Suffered
In the Service of the United Nations
(ICJ 1949) HPSS

Facts: Not provided.

Issue 1: What factors need be present to confer international personality on an organization?

Rule 1: If an organization was intended to have international legal personality and this is expressly stated, or is implied by the fact the organization may make binding recommendations to its members, has legal capacity and privileges and immunities within the territories of its members, has become a party to international agreements, or exhibits other characteristics normally assumed by states, the organization has international legal personality.

Issue 2: Does an organization with international legal capacity possess the totality of rights and duties available under international law?

Rule 2: Whether an organization with international legal capacity possesses the totality of rights and duties depends on the purposes and functions of the organization as specified in documents or developed in practice.

Issue 3: May the United Nations bring international claims against a state for reparation on behalf of an agent of the United Nations for injury suffered in performance of his duties?

Rule 3: An international organization may seek reparations for injuries caused to its agents in the performance of their duties when it is essential to ensure the independence of the agent in his actions on behalf of the organization that he need not rely on the state of his nationality for protection.

Issue 4: May the United Nations bring an international claim against a state that has injured an agent of the United Nations in the performance of his duties?

Rule 4: An international organization possessing international legal personality always has the capacity to bring claims for injuries suffered by the organization itself, including its agents, even if the injuring state is not a member of the organization.

Mavrommatis Palestine Concessions
(Jurisdiction)
(Greece v. Great Britain)
(PCIJ 1924) HPSS

Facts: The British government refused to recognize the rights of a Greek citizen arising out of contracts held between him and the previous government of Palestine. The Greek government brought suit against Britain under international law.

Issue: May a case concerning a dispute between an individual and a state (of which that individual is *not* a national) be governed by international law?

Rule: International law may govern cases concerning the rights of an individual because a state's interest in protecting the rights of an individual is really the state's interest in protecting its own right to ensure that its subjects receive the respect due them under international law.

Nottenbohm Case
(Liechtenstein v. Guatemala)
(ICJ 1955) HPSS, SOL

Facts: In 1939, after living in Guatemala for thirty-four years, a German national went to Liechtenstein for a few months and requested citizenship. He then returned to Guatemala and had his nationality changed in the Guatemalan Register of Aliens. In 1941, when Germany went to war with Guatemala, he was arrested, detained, and subjected to the confiscation of his property on the basis of his German nationality.

Issue: Does the act of conferring nationality upon an individual by one state impose an obligation on another state to recognize that state's right to exercise its protection with respect to the naturalized citizen?

Rule: A state has no obligation to recognize the effect of another state's act of conferring nationality by naturalization unless the legal bond of nationality is based upon a genuine connection between the individual and the state. A legal bond is established by a genuine connection of existence, interest and sentiments, together with the existence of reciprocal rights and duties.

Iran-United States, Case No. A/18
(1984) HPSS, SOL

Facts: A claims settlement agreement between the U.S. and Iran allowed citizens of either country to bring claims for reparation.

Issue: May dual nationals bring claims against one of their countries of nationality in an international tribunal?

Rule: A dual national may bring claims against a state of his nationality in an international tribunal if that state was not the state of dominant nationality during the period in which the dispute arose.

Judgment In Case of Lieutenants Dithmar and Boldt
Hospital Ship "Llandovery Castle"
(Germany 1921) SOL

Facts: In 1918, a German U-boat sunk the steamer *Llandovery Castle*, a steamer used by the British government to carry wounded soldiers home to Canada. Dithmar and Boldt, who were the first and second officers of the watch, conducted a look-out for the captain as he proceeded to fire at the lifeboats of the *Llandovery Castle*. International law forbade firing upon hospital ships.

Issue: May a subordinate officer, be punished for executing an order of his superior, that is universally understood to be a violation of the law?

Rule: A subordinate officer who, in executing an order of his superior, commits a violation of the law is liable to punishment if it was known to the him that the order of his superior was universally known as a violation of civil or military law.

United States v. Calley
(U.S. Court of Military Appeals 1973) SOL

Facts: First Lieutenant Calley was convicted for the premeditated murder of civilians in the village of My Lai in the Republic of South Vietnam. Calley attempted to justify his actions by claiming that he had been taught the doctrine of obedience throughout his military career and that he was merely following the orders of his superior.

Issue: Is the proper standard for determining whether an officer may be held criminally liable for illegal acts committed in compliance with the orders of his superior whether a man of ordinary sense and understanding would know the order was illegal?

Rule: The acts of a subordinate done in compliance with an unlawful order given to him by his superior are excused and impose no criminal liability upon him unless the superior's order is one that a man of ordinary sense and understanding would, under the circumstances, know to be unlawful, or if the order in question is actually known to the accused to be unlawful.

Dissent: The standard adopted by the majority is too severe. The standard should be that an officer may be held criminally liable for his acts committed pursuant to the order of his superior if: (1) almost every member of the armed forces would have immediately recognized that the order was unlawful, and (2) the officer should have recognized the order's illegality as a consequence of his age, grade, intelligence, experience, and training.

Matter of Demjanjuk
(U.S. 1985) SOL

Facts: Israel requested the extradition of Demjanjuk, a Ukrainian who became a naturalized American citizen, charging him with the murder of tens-of-thousands of Jews and non-Jews while operating the gas chambers at a concentration camp in Poland in 1942.

Issue 1: Does a civilian court have subject matter jurisdiction over an extradition proceeding where the crimes alleged occurred during wartime?

Rule 1: Congress has not provided exclusive jurisdiction over military matters or crimes related to the conduct of war to military tribunals, thus, a civilian court may exercise jurisdiction over an extradition proceeding where the crimes alleged occurred during wartime.

Issue 2: Does international law require that trials of military personnel for war crimes take place before a military tribunal exclusively?

Rule 2: International law does not prohibit the trial of alleged war criminals before national civil tribunals.

United States v. Von Leeb (The High Command Case)
(American Military Tribunal 1948) SOL

Facts: Defendants, members of the armed forces, were indicted on four counts: (1) crimes against peace; (2) war crimes; (3) crimes against humanity; and (4) a common plan or conspiracy to commit the crimes charged in counts one, two, and three.

Issue: May a member of the armed forces be held criminally liable for waging an aggressive war?

Rule: Under international common law, a member of the armed forces who participates in the preparation, planning, initiating, or waging of an aggressive war on a policy making or policy influencing level may be held criminally liable for war crimes.

Handel v. Artukovic
(U.S. 1985) SOL

Facts: Ps brought a class action suit against D seeking compensatory and punitive damages for alleged war crimes during World War II.

Issue: May an individual seeking relief for war crimes committed in violation of international law bring a civil suit in a municipal court?

Rule: While international law may provide the substantive rule of law in a given situation, the enforcement of international law is left to individual states, thus, the courts may not imply a private right of action for an individual to sue in a municipal court for alleged war crimes in violation of international law.

United States v. Mitchell
(Ct. App. 1966) SOL

Facts: D was convicted of wilful failure to report for induction into the armed forces. He claimed that the war in Vietnam was being conducted in violation of various treaties to which the U.S. was a signatory and that the selective service operated as an adjunct to this military effort.

Issue: May a defendant standing trial for failure to report for induction into the armed forces justify his actions by claiming that the selective service is aiding a war conducted in violation of a treaty?

Rule: The congressional power to raise and support armies is a separate matter from the use that the executive makes of those who have been inducted into the armed forces, thus, that the selective service aids the execution of an illegal war is not grounds to reject conscription.

Mitchell v. United States
(S.Ct. 1967) SOL

Facts: Same as above. The Supreme Court denied a writ of certiorari.

Issue: May a defendant standing trial for the wilful failure to report for induction into the armed forces justify his actions by claiming that the selective service is aiding an aggressive war (a violation of the Nuremberg Principles)?

Rule: Majority opinion not provided.

Dissent: (Douglas, J.) This case presents several extremely sensitive and delicate questions that should be answered; the Nuremberg Treaty established a standard of future conduct for all the signatories.

United States v. Samas
(U.S. Board of Review (Army) 1967) SOL

Facts: To challenge the legality of the Vietnam war, D filed suit in federal court seeking an injunction to prevent his deployment to Vietnam.

Issue: May an inducted member of the armed forces justify his refusal to obey a deployment order on the grounds that the war effort is illegal?

Rule: The legality of the war effort is to be decided by the law officer; no military organization could exist if each man were free to decide in which wars he would participate.

Randall v. Commissioner of Internal Revenue Service
(U.S. 1984) SOL

Facts: D refused to pay income taxes, claiming, among other things, that military spending violated his religious beliefs and international treaty obligations.

Issue: May a taxpayer justify his nonpayment of income taxes on the ground that U.S. military spending is in violation of international treaty obligations?

Rule: Since the act of paying taxes does not amount to complicity in any war crime committed by the government, a taxpayer may not justify his nonpayment of income taxes on the grounds that the government's military spending violates international treaty obligations.

United States v. Montgomery
(U.S. 1985) SOL

Facts: D and others broke into the Martin-Marietta Aerospace Corporation's defense plant to protest the U.S. nuclear military policy and were found guilty of destroying U.S. army property. At trial, D offered the affirmative defenses of necessity and international law, claiming that the U.S. nuclear military policy was in violation of international law.

Issue: May a defendant justify conduct that is a violation of domestic law as necessary to avoid liability under international law?

Rule: A defendant may not justify conduct that is a violation of domestic law as necessary to avoid liability under international law where the domestic law does not impose upon the defendant a duty or responsibility to act. The Nuremberg Principles apply only where an individual, having an affirmative duty under domestic law, must violate that law to avoid liability under international law.

United States v. Linnas
(U.S. 1981) SOL

Facts: The U.S government instituted proceedings to revoke Linnas' certificate of naturalization and U.S. citizenship. Documents admitted into evidence established that Linnas had served in a supervisory role in the management of a German concentration camp in 1941; however, Linnas failed to disclose this information in his visa application to the U.S.

Issue: May the U.S. revoke the citizenship of a person who was naturalized under the Displaced Persons Act if his citizenship was procured by a willful misrepresentation of material facts?

Rule: The U.S. may revoke a citizenship procured by a willful misrepresentation of material facts.

Linnas v. Immigration and Naturalization Service
(U.S. 1986) SOL

Facts: The Board of Immigration Appeals ordered Linnas deported to the Soviet Union under § 241(a) of the Immigration and Nationality Act (INA), commonly referred to as the Holtzman amendment, because of his active participation in the Nazi persecution of Estonian Jews during World War II. The Holtzman amendment required the deportation of persons shown to have participated in the Nazi's persecution of Jews and others.

Issue: Does the Holtzman amendment constitute a bill of attainder?

Rule: The deportation of a noncitizen from the U.S. does not constitute punishment, thus, the Holtzman amendment does not constitute a bill of attainder.

Attorney General of Israel v. Eichmann
(Israel 1962) SOL

Facts: Eichmann was found guilty of the gravest offenses under the Nazi and Nazi Collaborators Punishment Law. At the time the offenses were committed, the state of Israel was not in existence.

Issue: Does a state have jurisdiction over extraterritorial offenses, that is, offenses that were committed outside the territory of that state by a citizen of a foreign state?

Rule: Pursuant to the principle of universal jurisdiction, a state has jurisdiction to try a citizen of a foreign state for offenses that were committed outside the territory of the prosecuting state.

Demjanjuk v. Petrovsky
(U.S. 1985) SOL

Facts: Demjanjuk, a naturalized citizen of the U.S., challenged Israel's right to extradite him and try him for war crimes.

Issue 1: Is a naturalized citizen extraditable to face charges for a crime not specifically provided for in a extradition treaty?

Rule 1: A naturalized citizen may be extradited to faces charges for a crime not specifically provided for in a extradition treaty if it is the natural and logical interpretation of the treaty.

Issue 2: Does a state have jurisdiction to try nonterritorial crimes when the crime committed is universally condemned?

Rule 2: Universal condemnation classifies the perpetrator as an enemy of all people and enables any state who has custody of the perpetrator to punish him for nonterritorial crimes.

Issue 3: Does a state have jurisdiction to try a crime if it was nonexistent at the time the crime was committed?

Rule 3: The universality principle permits a state to try a universally condemned crime even if the state did not exist at the time the crimes were committed.

Re Immigration Act and Hanna
(Canada 1957) SOL

Facts: Hanna, a "stateless" person, claimed that an immigration order issued by Canadian immigration officials was illegal. The order did not specify the place of his deportation, but rather listed four alternative places to which he could be deported.

Issue: Is a deportation order that fails to specify the place of deportation valid?

Rule: A deportation order that fails to specify the place of deportation or that is too vague for the place of deportation to be ascertained without further inquiry is invalid.

Mergé Case
(1955) HPSS, SOL

Facts: P, a twenty-four-year-old American citizen, married an Italian and acquired dual citizenship. P then lived in Italy and Japan for the next thirteen years. When the U.S. submitted a claim to Italy for compensation for losses incurred by its nationals due to World War II, Italy rejected P's claim on the basis that she was an Italian national.

Issue: May a state, in behalf of one of its nationals, bring a claim against another state that also considers the claimant as one of its nationals?

Rule: A state may bring a claim in behalf of one of its nationals against another state that also considers the claimant a national only when the nationality of the state bringing the claim is the "effective" (dominant) nationality. The state that has dominant nationality is the state in which the individual habitually resides or with which, under the circumstances, he appears to be the most closely connected (considering economic, social, political, civic, and family life).

Joyce v. Director of Public Prosecutions
(England 1946) SOL

Facts: D, a naturalized American citizen by birth, went to England as a young man and obtained a British passport after presenting himself as a British subject by birth. He was arrested in Germany for acts of treason against the Crown.

Issue: May an alien residing within a state be held guilty for acts of treason against the sovereign committed outside the state?

Rule: In reciprocation for the protection of the sovereign, one owes a duty of allegiance to the state, thus, an alien residing within a state may be held guilty for acts of treason against the sovereign committed outside the state if the individual retains the protection of the sovereign while abroad.

D'Aquino v. United States
(U.S. 1951) SOL

Facts: D, a U.S. citizen residing in Japan during World War II, was convicted of treason against the U.S. D claimed the charges against her were arbitrary, because, under U.S. law, a person, like herself, could be lawfully naturalized to an enemy belligerent and, under the Government's naturalization policy, transfer their allegiance to Japan and provide aid and comfort to the enemy with impunity.

Issue: May an individual who fails to transfer his allegiance to a state to which he provides aid and comfort during time of war be convicted of treason?

Rule: If an individual fails to transfer his allegiance to a state to which he provides aid and comfort during time of war, it is not unconstitutional to convict him of treason.

Rex v. Neumann
(South Africa 1946) SOL

Facts: Neumann, a German national by birth, resided in South Africa with his family and enlisted in the armed forces there. He was charged with having enlisted in the military forces of Germany and obtaining information from the military forces of South Africa while those two nations were at war with one another; he was indicted for high treason.

Issue: Does an alien resident domiciled in a foreign sovereign state owe any allegiance to that state when that state and his own are at war with one another?

Rule: An alien resident domiciled in a foreign sovereign state owes a qualified allegiance to that state even when that state and his own are at war with one another; this allegiance does not terminate even when the alien resident is not physically present within the state.

United States v. Rexach
(U.S. 1977) SOL

Facts: The U.S. sought to tax Lucienne D'Hotelle, who became a naturalized U.S. citizen in 1942, for her one-half share in her husband's income. In 1946 Lucienne established residence in France and remained there until 1952. According to the Nationality Act of 1940, naturalized citizens who returned to their country of birth and resided there for three years lost their American citizenship, nevertheless, Lucienne continued to travel abroad using her U.S. passport.

Issue: May the government collect income taxes for periods during which an involuntarily expatriated person affirmatively exercises a specific right of citizenship?

Rule: The government may collect income taxes for periods of time during which an involuntarily expatriated person affirmatively exercises a specific right of citizenship.

Di Portanova v. United States
(U.S. 1982) SOL

Facts: P, a dual U.S.-Italian citizen by birth who renounced his U.S. citizenship, claimed that he was entitled to a refund for taxes paid to the U.S. for income received from a trust. P alleged that he was not engaged in a trade or business and, thus, he should not have been taxed at the higher rates imposed on business income.

Issue: May an expatriate's income be taxed at the rate imposed upon a nonresident alien who is engaged in business in the U.S. if the nonresident alien is not engaged in a trade or business in the U.S.?

Rule: An expatriate may be taxed upon income derived from the U.S. at the rate imposed by the Internal Revenue Code on income of a nonresident alien who is not engaged in a trade or business in the

U.S., provided that the principle reason for his expatriation was not the avoidance of taxes.

United States v. Rumsa
(U.S. 1954) SOL

Facts: In an Application for Immigration Visa and Alien Registration, D, a Lithuanian national, expressed his intent to reside permanently in the U.S. D was indicted for refusing to submit to induction into the armed forces of the U.S., claiming that he had the right to be deferred from military service by waiving the right to become an American citizen.

Issue: May Congress require that all aliens admitted for permanent residence into the U.S. be subject to induction into the armed forces under the same conditions applicable to citizens?

Rule: All aliens admitted into the U.S. for permanent residence may be subject to induction into the armed forces, regardless of the alien's personal intentions with respect to his residence in the U.S.

In re M.M. and X.M.
(Greece 1934) SOL

Facts: Petitioners were born in England of a Greek father. According to the Greek Law of Nationality, the children of a Greek father are Greek, regardless of where they are born, and nationality may only be lost by naturalization with the consent of the Greek government. Petitioners, however, had declared themselves to be British subjects but did not seek the consent of the Greek government.

Issue: May an individual effect the loss of nationality of a state without complying with the laws of the state regarding the loss of nationality?

Rule: In order to effect the loss of nationality, an individual must comply with the laws of that state regarding the loss of nationality.

Chapter 6

TREATIES

I. INTRODUCTION

A. Title

Other names designating a treaty include: protocol, charter, covenant, declaration, agreement, convention, exchange of notes, act, statute, or communique. The particular name does not affect the legal status of the treaty.

B. American Definition

According to the United States Constitution, Article II, § 2, a treaty is an international agreement made by the president with the advice and consent of the Senate. Two-thirds of the Senate must vote in favor of the agreement.

C. Registration

Article 102 of the United Nations Charter requires that every treaty that a member state becomes part of be registered with the Secretary-General.

D. Nonbinding Agreements

Whether an agreement has legally binding force as a treaty depends on the *intent* of the parties. Nonbinding agreements create moral or political commitments only.

II. THE VIENNA CONVENTION ON THE LAW OF TREATIES

The Vienna Convention, concluded in 1969, is the authoritative source of international treaty law. The ambit of the Convention has developed largely through customary application of its provisions, rather than through legal adoption.

A. Scope

1. Between States
The Convention is limited to treaties between states. It does not include treaties with international organizations or multinational corporations.

2. Written
The Convention applies only to treaties that are written.

3. Non-Retroactive
The Convention does not apply to treaties concluded before its ratification in 1969. In addition, the rules of customary law continue to govern issues not addressed by the Convention.

B. Definition of Treaty

Whether an international agreement constitutes a treaty must be determined by the circumstances of each case.

1. Between Two or More Subjects of International Law Having International Personality
Treaties were originally required to be between states only. An agreement between a state and a private company could not have the character of a treaty, even if a state owned a greater than fifty-percent share in a foreign corporation. However, this definition has expanded, as treaties with and between international organizations become the norm. It now includes agreements between states and international organizations that are subjects of international law.

2. Governed by International Law
For an international agreement to be a treaty, international law must govern the entirety of its whole formation and execution.

a. Intent
An agreement must be intended by the parties to be governed by international law. The terms of the contract and parties' statements are indicative of intent.

b. Nature and Object of Agreement
The nature and object of an agreement may also determine whether an agreement may be governed by municipal law. For example, an agreement for the cessation of land can not be governed by municipal law; whereas, a contract for the purchase of goods or a loan is usually governed by municipal law.

C. Binding Agreements

An agreement need not be a treaty to be binding. The parties need only have the intent to create legal rights and obligations or to establish relations governed by international law.

1. Intent to be Bound
States rarely express their intent not to be bound by an agreement. Therefore, to determine whether a state intended to be bound, one must look to:

a. Amount of Precision or Generality in Terms
Broad declarations of principles or general goals are too indefinite to create legal obligations. However, this is not dispositive of intent, as certain treaties, due to their nature, are purposefully vague despite their binding character (e.g., the Yalta Treaty and the United Nations Charter);

b. Published
Whether the agreement is published in national treaty collections;

c. Registered
Whether the agreement is registered under Article 102 of the United Nations Charter;

d. Description
Whether it is described as a treaty or a legal agreement when submitted to each party's national government; and

e. The Level of Authority of Government Representatives Who Signed or Approved Treaty
Generally, officials of higher authority conclude binding agreements.

2. Reciprocity
Based on the principles of good faith and estoppel, a state may be bound by its unilateral statement in the absence of a reply or reaction from other states under the following conditions:

Mnemonic: PIN

a. Publicly
The statement must be made publicly;

b. Intent
The state making the statement must intend to be bound; and

c. Negotiations Unnecessary
The statement need not have been made in the context of negotiations.

D. Nonbinding Agreements

States may conclude agreements that entail an expectation of compliance but that are not intended to be legally binding. Again, the intent of the parties is decisive. An example of such an agreement is a "gentlemen's agreement" concluded between heads of state.

1. Responsibility of Parties

a. Internal
An internal response is expected by both the legislature and administrative agencies of the state to give effect to the agreement.

b. External
By entering into an international pact with other states, a party may be presumed to have agreed that the matters covered are no longer exclusively within its concern.

2. Not governed by International Law
Nonbinding agreements generally are not covered by customary international law or the Vienna Convention. However, principles of international law or custom that do not conflict with the nonbinding character of the agreement may be used to interpret and apply a nonbinding agreement.

3. Breach

a. Without Legal Effect
An injured state may not claim judicial remedy or reparation in case of breach. However, it may impose its own diplomatic or economic sanctions.

b. Legal Effect
The injured party may demand restitution on the basis of estoppel or reliance.

III. CONCLUSION OF TREATIES

A. Capacity to Enter into Treaties

Entities generally have the capacity to enter into treaties if they possess international personality.

1. International Organizations
According to the U.N. Special Rapporteur on the Law of Treaties, international organizations have the capacity to enter into treaties.

2. Constituent States in a Federal Country
The capacity of constituent states within a federal country to enter into agreements with foreign states is governed by the

constitutional law of the country of which the state is a part. Where authorized, it is not clear whether constituent states are acting on the basis of independent legal capacity or as agents of their federal government.

3. Self-Governing Territories
Self-governing territories, such as commonwealths, have independent capacity to make treaties subject only to the consent of the territory that exercises control over it.

B. Full Powers (Article 7)
A "full power" is a document by which a state grants a named representative the power to execute a treaty. According to Article 7 of the Vienna Convention, a person is considered to have full powers if one of the following criteria is met:

1. Documentation
The person produces a full powers document;

2. Intent
It appears from the practice of the state or from the circumstances that the state's intention was to consider the person as representing the state.

3. Head of State
The person is a head of state or a minister of foreign affairs.

4. Confirmation (Article 8)
An act is performed by a person without full powers, but is afterwards confirmed, expressly or impliedly, by the state.

C. Adoption of the Text of a Treaty [Article 9(1)]
Adoption consists of the formal acts by which the parties accept the text of a treaty. The general rule is that adoption occurs by the consent of the drafting states.

1. Bilateral Treaties
   The adoption of the text of a bilateral treaty must be unanimous. Disagreement of a party with any part of the treaty constitutes a counterproposal.

2. Restricted Multilateral Treaties
   These treaties involve a limited number of states in the exchange of a series of interconnected rights, e.g., treaties of economic integration. Due to their nature, restricted multilateral treaties also require unanimity.

3. Multilateral Treaties [Article 9(2)]
   Adoption of the text of a multilateral treaty is accomplished by a two-thirds vote of the drafting states, unless otherwise provided.

D. Expression of Consent to be Bound

1. Signature (Article 12)
   The Signature by a named representative is an expression of a state's consent to be bound if:

Mnemonic: TIF

   a. Treaty Provides
      The treaty provides that this is to be the effect of a signature;

   b. Intent Established
      The intention of the parties that signature should indicate consent is otherwise established; or

   c. Full Powers Express Intent
      The full powers express intent of the state that signature indicates consent.

2. Initialling (Article 12(2)(a))
   Initialling is the equivalent of signature if the parties so agree.

3. Signature Subject to Confirmation (Article 12)
   If a signature is subject to the confirmation of a state, once it is confirmed it constitutes a full signature.

4. Ratification (Article 14)
   Ratification subjects a treaty to legislative or parliamentary control. When a treaty is subject to ratification, it does not become binding until after it is approved by the legislature.

5. Acceptance or Approval (Article 14)
   Acceptance is a term used to mean either ratification (signature subject to acceptance) or accession (acceptance without a prior signature). Acceptance is normally used when a treaty is not of the type that would require ratification or when the state wishes to use a simplified ratification procedure. *Approval* is used interchangeably with *acceptance*.

6. Accession (Article 15)
   Accession is the means by which a state becomes a party to an existing treaty to which it is not an original signatory.

7. Exchange of Instruments Constituting a Treaty (Article 13)
   States may be bound by an exchange of instruments that constitutes a treaty between them, if the instruments so provide, or it is the intent of the states that the instruments should have that effect.

8. Any Other Means So Agreed (Article 11)
   States may be bound by any means that they all expressly agree to (e.g., unsigned notes verbales).

E. Obligation not to Defeat the Object of the Treaty (Article 18)

Once a state agrees to be bound by a treaty, it has an obligation not to commit any acts contrary to the object of the treaty, even if the treaty has not yet come into force, unless unduly delayed, or the state has signed the treaty subject to ratification and its intention not to become a party prior to ratification is clear.

F. Reservations

1. Definition
A reservation is a unilateral statement by which a state excludes or varies the legal effect of certain terms of the treaty. Reservations may not be made to bilateral treaties. (See section III,C,1, above.)

2. When Made
Reservations may only be made at the time of expression of consent to a treaty. An act manifesting a party's intent to be bound by a treaty that contains a reservation is effective as soon as one other party to the treaty accepts the reservation.

3. Acceptance
Whether reservations may be made to a treaty depends on the intent of the parties. If the parties to a multilateral treaty intend to allow reservations, the reservation need not be approved by all of the parties. Unless expressly or impliedly prohibited, the reservations are assumed permissible.

   a. Acceptance by a Party
   If a party accepts the reservation of another state, the treaty is in force as between those two states, but not as between the reserving state and other states of the convention who do not accept the reservation.

      i. Reservation that Omits Provisions
      Neither the reserving state nor the state accepting the reservation are bound by the reserved provisions.

      ii. Reservation that Modifies Provisions
      The state that accepts the modifications is bound by the changed provisions.

   b. Nonacceptance by a Party
   If a party does not accept the reservation of another state, the treaty is still in effect between them, except for the

clauses effected by the reservation, unless the objecting state clearly expresses a contrary intention.

3. Compatible with the Object and Purpose of the Treaty
   A party may not make a reservation contrary to the object and purpose of a treaty.

4. Interpretive Statements
   These statements are made to indicate how a state interprets the provisions of a treaty. These are not obligatory and need not be accepted by the other states unless they constitute reservations.

5. Legal Consequences of Reservations

   a. Permissibility
      The compatibility of a reservation with the object and purpose of a treaty is a matter of treaty interpretation and subject to judicial review.

   b. Opposability
      However, acceptance of a reservation by another party to a treaty is a matter of policy not subject to judicial review.

6. Importance of Reservations
   Most reservations do not deal with substantive treaty provisions, but rather with procedural or jurisdictional provisions. The significance of reservations is that they may allow states to participate in certain multilateral treaties where they otherwise would not.

G. Entry Into Force (Article 24)

A treaty enters into force at the time and in the manner that the contracting parties agree. If the treaty does not provide for entry into force, the treaty comes into force as soon as all parties consent to be bound.

H. Provisional Application (Article 25)
A treaty provisionally applies to its parties prior to its entry into force if it so states or the parties so agree. However, a party can always terminate provisional application by indicating its desire not to become a party to the treaty before the treaty enters into force.

IV.   OBSERVANCE APPLICATION AND INTERPRETATION OF TREATIES

A. Observance

1. *Pacta Sunt Servada*
Treaty obligations must be honored in good faith. The breach of a treaty involves an obligation to make a reparation in some form.

2. Internal Law (Article 27)
A state may not invoke its internal law as a justification for failure to perform a treaty. Domestic law should be construed, as far as possible, to avoid violating a state's international obligations.

B. Application

1. Nonretroactivity (Article 28)

a. Situations Prior to Treaty
A treaty may expressly or impliedly apply to a situation that had occurred or ceased to exist prior to the entry into force of the treaty. However, in the absence of such a provision, treaties are nonretroactive.

b. Changed Meaning Over Time
If legal terms or other concepts have changed in meaning with time, an interpreting court should use the meaning of the term at the time of its interpretation, not at the time of its adoption. States may, however, agree that the definition

of a term at the time of a treaty's adoption should be used by courts.

2. Territorial Application
A treaty is presumed to apply to all the territories of a contracting party, including airspace and territorial waters, unless it states or implies otherwise.

3. Successive Treaties Relating to Same Subject Matter

a. Strict Interpretation of Same Subject Matter
Two treaties are not considered to relate to the same subject matter if general provisions in one treaty disagree with a specific provision in an earlier treaty.

b. Incompatible Treaties
Article 30 of the Vienna Convention states that if states are parties to two incompatible treaties, the later treaty will prevail in the absence of an express treaty provision. The relevant date is the date of the adoption of the text of the treaty, not the date of its entry into force. If there are two incompatible treaties and one state is a party to both while the other state is a party to only one of them, the treaty to which they are both parties will prevail in their relations.

C. Interpretation of Treaties

1. Interpretation by Courts
One state may not be subject to the interpretation by courts of another state in the absence of express agreement. Treaties will generally provide for interpretation by an international court or through international arbitration. See *Jesse Lewis Claim.*

2. Interpretation By The Parties

a. Unilateral Interpretation
A unilateral interpretation of an international agreement is not binding on other states to the agreement, although it may have an advisory effect.

b. Authentic Interpretation

An interpretation of a treaty made by all the parties to the treaty, such as through the exchange of notes, has the effect of adding a clause to the treaty.

3. Problems and Methods of Treaty Interpretation

a. Objective of Treaty Interpretation

There are two schools of thought regarding the primary objective of treaty interpretation.

i. Real Intent

This school strives to ascertain the common or real intent of the parties. This places the text and the diplomatic history on the same level.

ii. Textualism

This school attempts to determine the plain meaning of the text. This subordinates the diplomatic history to the text itself.

b. Vienna Convention Article 31 on Interpretation

This gives greatest weight to the plain meaning of the text itself in the absence of a clear contrary intent by the parties.

i. Intrinsic Materials

The Convention allows intrinsic materials, which are materials that the parties have agreed to, to supplement the meaning of the text and act as gap fillers, as long as they agree with the basic meaning of the text. Examples of intrinsic materials are: related agreements, subsequent practice, subsequent agreements, and rules of international law.

ii. Extrinsic Materials

Extrinsic materials are those materials not subject to the parties' express agreement. They are supplementary means of interpretation that may be used when recourse to intrinsic materials leave the meaning obscure or unreasonable. Examples of extrinsic materials are: the preparatory work of a treaty and the circumstances of its conclusion.

c. Principle of Maximum Effectiveness
Texts are presumed to have a definite force and effect and should be interpreted in the manner that gives the greatest value to this force and effect consistent with the other parts of the text.

4. Treaties in Multiple Languages
Where each language version of a text has been authenticated, they are equally authoritative and should be interpreted so as to give corresponding provisions a common meaning.

D. Treaties and Third States

1. Third States
A third state is any state that is not a party to the treaty in question.

2. *Pacta Tertiis Nec Nocent Nec Prosunt*
Treaties do not confer on third states any rights or obligations without their consent.

3. Obligations of Third States (Article 35)
A third state may be bound by a treaty if:

a. Intent of Parties
The parties intended the provision to establish obligations for third states; and

b. Express Agreement
The third state expressly agreed to be bound to the provision.

4. Rights of Third States (Article 36)
A third state may have rights under a treaty if:

a. Intent
The parties intended the provision to grant rights to third states;

b. Assent
The third state assented to the rights; and

c. Compliance
The third state complied with the conditions established to attain the right in the treaty.

5. Modification of the Rights and Obligations of Third States
The rights and obligations of third states cannot be modified without the express consent of all the parties, including the third state, unless the parties have otherwise agreed.

V. AMENDMENT AND MODIFICATION OF TREATIES

A. Amendment of Multilateral Treaties (Article 40)

Most multilateral agreements contain specific rules for amendment, generally by a two-thirds majority. The U.N. Charter states that amendments shall come into force for all members when they have been adopted by two-thirds of the members.

1. Notification
All parties to a treaty must be notified of any proposed amendment to the treaty.

2. Participation
All parties to a treaty must be given the opportunity to participate in the negotiation of an amendment, as well as the right to become a party to the amendment.

3. Party to Amendment
Each state that becomes a party to an amendment is a party to the amended, and a party to the unamended, treaty *vis-à-vis* any party to the treaty not bound by the amendment.

B. *Inter Se* Agreements (Article 41)

Inter se agreements are made when a small group of parties to a treaty agrees to modify a treaty as between themselves only. An example of an inter se agreement is a regional agreement. In order for an inter se agreement to be concluded:

1. Treaty Provision
   The treaty must provide for such modification;

2. Not Incompatible
   The modification proposed must not be incompatible with the treaty;

3. No Adverse Affect
   The modification must not adversely affect the rights of other parties to the treaty; and

4. Notice
   Other parties to the treaty must be given notice of the agreement.

C. Modification

A treaty may be modified by the subsequent practice of parties, but not if it is the consequence of an inter se agreement.

VI. INVALIDITY OF TREATIES

A. General Provisions Relating to Invalidity

1. Separability (Article 44)
   A provision that is declared null or invalid may be severed from the treaty, rather than causing the nullification of the entire treaty, if the omission of the provision does not materially upset the balance of interests that was the basis of the parties' consent to be bound.

2. Fraud

In the case of fraud or corruption, only the victim may invoke invalidity and invalidate part or all of the treaty.

3. Prohibition of Invalidity

A state may not claim invalidity if, after becoming aware of a ground for invalidity, it agrees or acquiesces to the treaty's continued force.

B. *Ultra Vires* Treaties (Article 46)

Although a state may not invoke internal law as a ground for invalidity of a treaty, an exception exists if its consent to be bound was expressed in violation of a provision of internal law regarding competence to conclude treaties. This can only be done if the violation is manifest and concerns a law of fundamental importance.

1. Who May Invoke

Only the state whose consent was expressed in violation of its internal law may invoke it.

2. Manifest

A violation is manifest if it would be objectively evident to any state dealing with the matter in accordance with normal practice and good faith. Thus, there is some question as to whether this could be invoked in the United States, because it is unclear exactly when the ratification of the Senate is needed.

3. Reluctance of Tribunals

No treaty has ever been declared invalid because it has been entered into in an unconstitutional manner. International commentators aver that there is a practice that holds constitutional provisions not directly relevant in international law.

C. Error, Fraud, Corruption, and Coercion

1. Error (Article 48)
   Most errors in the past were map errors that were either remedied by treaty or were considered to effect not the treaty, but its application, and were remedied by arbitration. Error does not usually make a treaty voidable.

   a. Essential Error
      If the error regards a matter that formed an essential basis of the consent of a party to a treaty, the party whose consent was based on the error has the right to void the treaty.

   b. Contributory Error
      If the party contributed to the making of the error, or should have known of the error, the treaty is not voidable.

2. Fraud (Article 49)
   Fraud also makes a treaty voidable by the victim. Fraudulent conduct encompasses false statements, misrepresentations, or other deceitful proceedings by which a state is induced to give consent to a treaty that it would not otherwise have given.

3. Corruption (Article 50)
   Corruption encompasses acts calculated to exercise a strong influence on the representative of a state to enter into a treaty, i.e., bribery. A corrupt representative is not alone sufficient, but rather, the corrupt acts must be imputable to the other negotiating state. Corruption also makes a treaty voidable by the state whose official has been corrupted.

4. Coercion

   a. Coercion of a Representative (Article 51)
      Consent to be bound by a treaty that was procured through the use of threat is without legal effect.

b. Coercion of a State (Article 52)
Consent of a state to be bound by a treaty that was produced by threat of force makes the treaty automatically void. This is a principle of customary law, applicable to all treaties concluded after the entry into force of the U.N. Charter. Although there have been proposals to include more subtle forms of coercion, such as threats to withdraw economic aid, this was not included for fear that it would harm the stability of treaties.

D. Conflict with a Peremptory Norm (*Jus Cogens*)

1. Definition (Article 53)
A peremptory norm (also called a norm of *jus cogens*) is recognized by the international community, as a whole, as a norm from which no derogation is permitted. This recognition need not be by every state in the international community, but neither can it be accepted by a mere majority. It must be accepted by all or most states of different social and economic systems.

2. Examples of Peremptory Norms
The prohibition of unlawful force or aggression, the prohibition of genocide, any act that is criminal under international law, and the violation of certain human rights, such as the prohibition against torture or arbitrary deprivation of life, are examples of peremptory norms.

3. Treaty in Conflict With *Jus Cogens*
Any treaty that constitutes a derogation from, or conflicts with, a peremptory norm is void.

4. Retroactivity
This rule is not retroactive, and any treaty that came into force before the emergence of a new peremptory norm remains valid.

VII. TERMINATION OR SUSPENSION OF TREATIES

Although there is no absolute right to termination, there are few restraints. If a claim to termination is disputed, the procedural and notification requirements of Articles 65 and 66 exhausted, and the party has submitted to the compulsory conciliation procedure of Annex V of the Vienna Convention, the results of the conciliation are not binding on the party. Therefore, it remains possible for the party to maintain its right to terminate as long as it has satisfied the procedural and notification requirements.

A. Termination by the Terms of a Treaty (Article 54)

1. Termination Generally
   Treaties may be terminated by their own terms. Most treaties contain clauses addressing the date, circumstances, or right to termination. Any treaty may also be terminated, at any time, by the consent of all the parties.

2. Revocation of Termination (Article 68)
   Termination of a treaty may be withdrawn at any time before the date that the termination is to become effective.

3. Quorum for Multilateral Treaties (Article 55)
   If the termination of a treaty by a party to a multilateral treaty lowers the number of parties below that necessary for the treaty to enter into force, the treaty is not terminated unless it so states.

B. Termination of a Treaty Containing No Provisions Therein

A party to a treaty that contains no provisions for withdrawal may withdraw only if:

1. Intent
   The parties intended to allow withdrawal; or

2. Nature of the Treaty
   The nature of the treaty is such that withdrawal should be implied.

C. Termination of a Treaty Implied by Conclusion of a Subsequent Treaty (Article 59)

The conclusion of a second treaty that is incompatible with a first is considered to have terminated the first, if:

1. All Parties
   All the parties to the first treaty are also parties to the second treaty;

2. Provisions

   a. The second treaty is incompatible with a major or essential provision of the first; or

   b. The whole matter that was the subject of the first treaty is governed by provisions of the second; and

3. Intent
   The parties to the second treated intended to terminate rather than suspend the operation of the first treaty.

D. Termination By Breach (Article 60)

Breach of a treaty, however serious, does not itself terminate a treaty.

1. Material
   The breach must be material for the treaty to be voidable by the injured party. A material breach is the breach of a provision that is essential for the accomplishment of the object and purpose of a treaty.

2. Breach of Bilateral Treaty
The injured party may terminate or suspend operation of the treaty in whole or in part. This right is without prejudice to the injured party's right to present an international claim for reparation.

3. Breach of Multilateral Treaty

 a. All Parties Affected By Breach
 By unanimous agreement other parties may terminate or suspend the treaty in whole or in part as between themselves and the breaching party or all parties.

 b. Party Specially Affected By Breach
 An individual party may alone react to the breach by another party to a multilateral convention if the breach effects it in particular. In this case, the individual party may only suspend operations as between itself and the breaching state. Its relations with the other parties remain unaffected.

 c. Breach that Undermines Treaty Regime
 Where a breach undermines the treaty as a whole and materially changes the position of all parties to a treaty, any party to the treaty may revoke the treaty without first consulting the other parties.

4. Waiver of Termination
The parties to any treaty may choose not to terminate a breached treaty.

5. Humanitarian Treaties
Breach may not be invoked as an excuse for the termination of humanitarian treaties.

6. Jurisdiction
Breach or unilateral suspension of a treaty does not render its jurisdictional clauses inoperative, since the very purpose of such clauses is to test the validity of a state's actions under these circumstances.

7. Countermeasures During Arbitration
An aggrieved state is not required to continue performance while awaiting the results of arbitration concerning a breach. The aggrieved state may suspend performance and take any other countermeasures that are not disproportionate to the breach.

E. Fundamental Change of Circumstances (*Rebus Sic Stantibus*) (Article 62)

Although the majority of modern treaties are short term or are renewable at yearly intervals, there are some long-term treaties to which this doctrine would apply. However, international courts generally do not admit that this doctrine applies to the facts of a case at hand.

1. Rule
The fundamental change of circumstances rule is formulated in the negative to indicate that it is a rule that may only be invoked under exceptional circumstances. The rule may be invoked when:

a. Unforeseen
The possibility of the change was unforeseen by the parties;

b. Essential Basis
The circumstances before the change were an essential basis for entering into the treaty;

c. Radically Alter
The change in circumstances must radically alter the duties to be performed under the treaty; and

d. Not Performed
The obligations under the treaty must have not yet been performed.

2. Fundamental Change of Circumstances May Not be Invoked When:

    a. Establishes a Boundary
    The treaty establishes a boundary; or

    b. Breach
    The change is due to a breach by one of the parties. However, if the change is caused by actions of a party that do not amount to breach, the other parties may claim the change as a reason for termination of the treaty.

3. Equity and Justice
If to one party's detriment, a change of circumstances not contemplated by the parties may severely strain the relations of the parties and increase the likelihood of breach. However, allowing the fundamental change to trigger renewal of negotiations is calculated to induce compromise.

4. Remedies
Fundamental change of circumstances may be invoked as a reason for terminating, withdrawing from, or suspending operations of, a treaty.

F. War between Contracting Parties

Not all treaties between countries become void due to war. Treaties whose execution is not incompatible with a state of war will remain in effect, unless expressly terminated. Such treaties may only be disregarded to the extent and time required by war. Treaties that remain in effect during war are those referring to boundaries or the rules of war. Treaties dissolved by war are treaties of peace, alliance, or commerce. However, a treaty designed to regulate commerce would not necessarily be voided.

VIII. STATE SUCCESSION AND TREATIES

A. Succession Obligations and Rights Generally

1. Succession of States
   The succession of states is the replacement of one state by another in the responsibility over a territory, such as the emergence of independent rule in a former colony or the joining of two states. This is not the same as a change of government within a state.

2. Devolution Agreements
   Devolution agreements are agreements between a former and present government regarding the transfer of treaty rights and obligations from the former to the present government.

   a. Successor States
      Successor states are not automatically bound by devolution agreements.

   b. Third Parties
      Other parties to a treaty are not bound to accept the successor state as a party.

3. Unilateral Declarations by Successor States

   a. Generally
      A successor state may unilaterally declare that it intends to continue the treaties of the former state. Generally, the new state declares that it will continue the treaties for a trial period while it decides which treaties it will honor and which it will terminate. No party is bound by these declarations, except by grounds of estoppel.

b. The Restatement (Revised) § 201

   i. Transfer of Territory (Moving Treaty Frontiers Rule)
When a territory passes from the hands of one sovereign state to another, the treaty obligations of the first state over the territory cease to have effect and those of the second state come into force.

   ii. Absorption of Entire State
When a state is lawfully absorbed by another state, the absorbed state's agreements are terminated and supplanted by the absorbing state's treaties.

   iii. Territory Gains Independence
The new state does not become a party to a former government's treaties without its consent and the assent of the parties to the treaties.

   iv. Preexisting Boundaries
Preexisting boundaries remain the same.

c. The Vienna Convention on the Succession of States
This treaty, while not adhered to formally by many states, often regulates the transition from colony status to statehood.

B. Treaties Not Affected by the Succession of States

This type of treaty occurs when a state grants a foreign state(s) the right to use its territory, or restricts the use of its own territory for the benefit of foreign state(s). Examples of such treaties are territorial treaties, rights of transit, international waterways, and demilitarization treaties.

C. The Newly Independent States

1. Clean Slate Rule
Newly independent states do not acquire the obligations of their predecessor states. The only obligations they maintain are territorial treaty obligations.

2. Right of Consent
The new state has the right to notify its prospective treaty partners of its consent to enter into the treaties of its predecessor, but not the absolute right to enter into them. More often than not, the new state is given the option as if it were a right.

a. Multilateral Treaties
The new state does, apparently, have a right of option as regards general multilateral treaties. This absolute right to join does not officially extend to multilateral treaties that are of a more restricted character.

b. Bilateral Treaties
Accession of new states to bilateral treaties is consensual and voluntary on the part of both parties. However, most states agree to maintain treaties for the purposes of immigration, travel taxes, and other technical matters.

D. Uniting and Separation of States

1. Uniting of States
This includes any form of unity whether it leads to the creation of a single state, a federal system, or two joined states retaining individual personality. The treaties of both states remain in force.

2. Separation of States
This deals with the separation of independent parts of a state, for example, federal states, as opposed to dependent territories. Treaties in force at the time of the dissolution remain in force with respect to each newly separated part.

CASE CLIPS

Decision of June 30, 1953
(Germany 1953) HPSS

Facts: The German state of Baden entered into an agreement with a French public river control agency, by which they would set up a joint agency to control a German port.

Issue: Is an agreement between a state within a federal republic and a government entity a treaty?

Rule: An agreement between the agencies or subdivisions of two different nations is not a treaty unless these constituents are acting on behalf of the state as a whole. The authorization of a state to allow its constituent parts to act on behalf of the state as a whole must be express.

Reservations to the Convention on Genocide
(ICJ 1951) HPSS

Facts: Not provided.

Issue 1: May a reserving state remain party to a convention if the reservation is objected to by some of the other parties to the convention?

Rule 1: A state may not make a reservation to a convention that was intended by the parties to be universal in scope. However, if the parties to a multilateral treaty intend to allow reservations, the reserving party will be a party to the convention even if the reservation is not approved by all of the parties, as long as the reservation is not contrary to the object and purpose of the treaty.

Issue 2: What is the effect of a reservation as between the reserving state and the parties that object to a reservation?

Rule 2: No state can be bound by a reservation to which it has not consented. Therefore, a convention may not be in force between a state that makes a reservation and a state that does not accept that reservation, unless the state objecting to the reservation does not object on the grounds that the reservation is contrary to the object and purpose of the treaty and consents to allow the treaty to be in effect between them except for the clauses effected by the reservation.

Issue 3: What is the effect of a reservation as between the reserving state and the parties that accept the reservation?

Rule 3: If a party accepts the reservation of another state, the convention is in force as between those two states, with the exception of the clause that was reserved.

Dissent: A reservation to a treaty should be required to be unanimously accepted unless the treaty expressly provides for reservations.

Advisory Opinion on Reservations
(1982) HPSS

Facts: Two states ratified the American Convention on Human Rights with reservations. The Vienna Convention on Treaties, Article 20(5) required that, in the absence of an express acceptance of the reservation, acceptance could be implied only after a year in which there were no objections.

Issue: Must a reservation by a state that ratifies a multinational human rights convention be accepted by other parties to the convention in order for the convention to come into force between them?

Rule: The principles of acceptance and reciprocity do not apply to a human rights treaty. Reservations may be considered compatible with a human rights treaty unless they are contrary to the purpose of the treaty. Since this treaty represents a collective of unilateral commitments, reciprocity is inapplicable.

Advisory Opinion on Restriction to the Death Penalty
(1984) HPSS

Facts: Guatemala made a reservation to Article 4(4) of the American Convention on Human Rights, stating that, although it did not oppose the restriction on the application of the death penalty to political crimes, its Constitution did not exclude the application of the death penalty to common crimes related to political crimes.

Issue: May a reservation to a certain article of a treaty apply by implication to another article?

Rule: A reservation may not be construed to limit treaty rights to a greater extent than is provided in the reservation.

Jesse Lewis (The David J. Adams Claim)
(United States v. Great Britain)
(1921) HPSS

Facts: A Canadian court condemned an American ship because it determined that the ship had violated a bilateral American-Canadian treaty and Canadian implementing legislation.

Issue: Is an interpretation of a treaty by the courts of a party to the treaty binding on other parties?

Rule: The principle of the sovereign equality of states does not allow one state to be subjected to the unilateral interpretation of a treaty by another party.

Legal Status of Eastern Greenland Case
(Denmark v. Norway)
(PCIJ 1933) HPSS

Facts: In a property dispute between Norway and Denmark, Norway claimed that its foreign minister did not have the authority to make certain oral representations binding.

Issue: Are a foreign minister's statements binding in the absence of constitutional approval by the executive?

Rule: A court will not look behind the authority of a foreign minister to commit his state; it is sufficient that the minister acted within his province under international law.

Advisory Opinion on the Continued Presence of
South Africa in Namibia (South West Africa)
(ICJ 1971) HPSS, SOL

Facts: In 1966 the General Assembly adopted a resolution that terminated South Africa's mandate in Namibia, but South Africa refused to leave.

Issue: Does a material breach of a mandate agreement that does not expressly provide for termination on account of breach justify termination of the mandate?

Rule: Breach does not automatically terminate a treaty but creates the right to invoke breach as a ground for termination. This rule is presumed to exist in all treaties except those of a humanitarian nature. The failure of a treaty to include this right cannot be interpreted as its exclusion.

Appeal Relating to the Jurisdiction of the ICAO Council
(India v. Pakistan)
(ICJ 1972) HPSS

Facts: India suspended flights to Pakistan in violation of an international civil aviation treaty, but claimed the right to do so because Pakistan, India argued, had terminated the treaty in regards to India by acquiescing to the demands of hijackers.

Issue: Does a breach or a corresponding unilateral suspension of a treaty render the jurisdictional clauses of that treaty inoperative as regards the breaching or suspending parties?

Rule: Breach or unilateral suspension of a treaty does not render its jurisdictional clauses inoperative as the very purpose of such clauses is to test the validity of a state's actions under these circumstances.

The Fisheries Jurisdiction Case
(United Kingdom v. Iceland)
(ICJ 1973) HPSS

Facts: Iceland and the United Kingdom agreed by exchange of notes that the U.K. would recognize an extension of Iceland's fishery limit to twelve miles if Iceland would agree to submit any disputes to the ICJ. Subsequently, when the customary law of territorial fishery limits extended beyond twelve miles, Iceland refused to allow the U.K. to fish at the twelve mile limit or recognize the court's jurisdiction, claiming fundamental change of circumstances.

Issue: May a change in international law constitute a fundamental change of circumstance that is an obligatory ground for revocation of a treaty?

Rule: For a fundamental change of circumstances to constitute a ground of revocation of a treaty, the change must have increased the burden of the obligations to be executed to the extent of rendering the performance something essentially different from that which was originally undertaken.

Techt v. Hughes
(U.S. 1920) HPSS

Facts: An Austro-Hungarian had a claim to an inheritance in New York based on a treaty between the United States and Austria-

Hungary. War broke out between the two countries just before the inheritance could take effect.

Issue: Are all treaties between warring nations voided due to war?

Rule: Treaties whose execution is not incompatible with a state of war will remain in effect, unless expressly terminated. Such treaties may be disregarded only to the extent and time required by war.

Free Zones of Upper Savoy and the District of Gex
(France v. Switzerland)
(PCIJ 1932) SOL

Facts: France claimed that the Treaty of Versailles, to which Switzerland was not a signatory, abolished certain tariff-free areas near France's border with Switzerland. Switzerland claimed that her rights in these areas had been created by various treaties stemming from the Congress of Vienna.

Issue: May rights that a country acquired as a nonparty to a treaty be nullified by a subsequent treaty to which that country was not a participant?

Rule: It must be ascertained on a case-by-case basis whether states who are parties to a treaty intended the nonparty state to acquire the right that it is claiming and if such rights may be nullified by a subsequent treaty to which the claiming state was not a party.

Case on Interpretation of the Austrian State Treaty
(1959) SOL

Facts: Pursuant to the prohibitions in the Austrian State Treaty, the Federal Ministry denied the request of an Austrian glider club for licensing a glider of German construction. The glider club claimed that there was an inherent contradiction in the German language version of the treaty since one article used the German word meaning "aircraft" and another used the German word meaning "airplane."

Issue: Where there exists doubt as to the interpretation of a regulation, how ought the ambiguity be resolved?

Rule: According to international law, the existence of diverging authentic texts of a state treaty results in adopting that version that infringes least on a state's sovereignty.

James Buchanan & Co. Ltd. v. Babco Forwarding & Shipping Ltd.
(England 1977) SOL

Facts: A shipment of whiskey valued at £7,000 was stolen. If it was sold in England a £30,000 excise tax would be added. The shipment was tax exempt because it was intended for export. After the theft, P had to pay the added tax. D, the carrier, claims it is only responsible for the actual value of the whisky and not tax. The European Road Convention provides that charges incurred in respect of the carriage of goods are refundable; but the interpretation of carriage charges was ambiguous.

Issue: When a situation arises that is not within the letter of an international agreement but is within the spirit of the law, what rule of interpretation should be applied?

Rule: A judge should go beyond the literal meaning of the law and look to the design and purpose of the legislation, filling any gaps to reach its intended goal.

Note: The House of Lords affirmed the holding of this case but rejected the interpretive approach.

Nederlandsche Rijnvaartvereeniging v. Damco
Scheepvaart Maatschappij
(Netherlands 1954) SOL

Facts: In 1936, Germany abolished the Rhine Navigation Court, which effected a unilateral suspension of treaties adjudicated there. During 1946-47, the court was reinstated. In 1946, a collision occurred at a point on the Rhine that was the boundary between the United States and the French Occupation Zones. In 1948, a claim was brought in the Rhine Navigation Court regarding that collision.

Issue: What are the legal consequences of a unilateral suspension of a treaty that cannot be denounced unilaterally?

Rule: There are no legal consequences stemming from a unilateral denunciation of a treaty that cannot be denounced unilaterally.

Bremen (Free Hansa City of) v. Prussia
(Germany 1925) SOL

Facts: A treaty entered into in 1904 provided for an exchange of territory between Bremen and Prussia. To compensate Prussia, because the territory received by it was less valuable, Bremen assured

Prussia that the territory would be used for navigation purposes exclusively. Prussia claims that World War I changed the circumstances that formed the basis of the Treaty.

Issue: Is a fundamental change of circumstances (*rebus sic stantibus*) a valid excuse for the non-compliance termination of the restrictive clauses of a treaty?

Rule: International law recognizes the doctrine of *rebus sis stantibus* as a defense for the termination of a treaty. However, where the party would not have entered into the treaty without the restrictive clauses, they may not be abolished without consent.

Ware v. Hylton
(S.Ct. 1796) SOL

Facts: D refused to pay a debt owed to P, claiming that a law passed by the Commonwealth of Virginia allowed any citizen of Virginia owing money to a subject of Great Britain to pay any part of the debt to the loan office and receive in exchange a receipt discharging the debt. P asserted that Article 4 of the Definitive Treaty of Peace between Great Britain and the U.S. provided that creditors must be able to recover the full value of all bona fide debts without legal interference. (P and D were subjects of Great Britain when the debt was incurred.)

Issue: May a state enact a law governing the seizure of private debts that supersedes a treaty requiring that there be no legal impediments to the recovery of all bona fide debts?

Rule: (Chase, J.) Where state law and a treaty that is constitutionally valid conflict, the treaty is supreme, therefore, a state may not enact a law that is inconsistent with a treaty.

Missouri v. Holland
(S.Ct. 1920) SOL

Facts: The United States and Great Britain entered into a treaty for the protection of certain migratory birds. Pursuant to the agreement, Congress enacted a statute that prohibited the killing of migratory birds. Missouri sued to prevent the game warden from carrying out the treaty, alleging that it was an unconstitutional interference with the rights reserved to the states by the tenth amendment.

Issue: May Congress, pursuant to its treaty-making power, regulate a subject area otherwise reserved to the states by the tenth amendment?

Rule: (Holmes, J.) A statute enacted pursuant to Congress' treaty-making power which purports to regulate a subject-matter of national interest does not interfere with the rights reserved to the states under the tenth amendment.

Reid v. Covert
(S.Ct. 1957) SOL

Facts: Mrs. Covert was tried by a court-martial for the murder of her husband, a sergeant in the United States Air Force, who was stationed at an airbase in England. Mrs. Covert was not a member of the armed services. The Government claimed that a court-martial was a necessary and proper means of carrying out the United States' obligations under an international agreement made with Great Britain.

Issue: May Congress authorize the court-martial of civilian dependents accompanying servicemen overseas?

Rule: (Black, J.) Since treaties and laws enacted pursuant to them must comply with the Constitution, a civilian defendant may not constitutionally be tried by military authority since a court-martial does not meet the requirements of the fifth and sixth amendments.

Edwards v. Carter
(U.S. 1978) SOL

Facts: The President of the United States returned the Panama Canal Zone to the Republic of Panama through the treaty process in accordance with Article II, § 2 of the Constitution. Plaintiffs (members of the House of Representatives) claimed that Article IV, § 3, clause 2 gives Congress the exclusive power to convey to foreign nations any property owned by the U.S.

Issue: Does the Constitution give Congress the exclusive authority to dispose of U.S. property so as to prohibit the disposition of such property by self-executing treaty?

Rule: Article IV, § 3 does not give Congress the exclusive authority to dispose of U.S. property and, thus, U.S. property may be transferred to foreign nations through self-executing treaties.

United States v. Pink
(S.Ct. 1942) SOL

Facts: Incidental to the U.S. recognition of the USSR, the Soviet Union assigned to the U.S. amounts owed her by U.S. nationals. Consequently, the U.S. sued the New York Superintendent of Insurance, who had seized the assets of the New York branch of a Russian insurance company.

Issue: Does the president's power to recognize foreign nations include the power to determine the public policy that is to govern the question of recognition?

Rule: (Douglas, J.) In conducting foreign relations, the president has the power to remove any obstacles to full recognition, including the settlement of claims of U.S. nationals.

United States v. Guy W. Capps, Inc.
(U.S. 1953) SOL

Facts: The U.S. and Canada entered into an executive agreement that required any Canadian potato exporter contracting with a U.S. importer to include in the contract a clause stipulating that the potatoes would not be sold on the market as food. Defendant, a U.S. importer, purchased an order of potatoes from a Canadian exporter that he then sold to a retail grocery organization.

Issue: May the U.S., in the absence of action by Congress, sue for breach of a contract that was based upon an executive trade agreement regulating foreign commerce?

Rule: As the power to regulate foreign commerce is vested in Congress, the executive may not enter into executive agreements to regulate foreign commerce or sue for breach of a contract entered into pursuant to such agreements.

Dames & Moore v. Reagan
(S.Ct. 1981) SOL

Facts: Pursuant to an agreement between the U.S. and Iran releasing the Americans held hostage at the American Embassy in Teheran, the President issued an executive order that nullified the attachment of all Iranian assets and suspended all legal proceedings involving U.S. parties against Iran. Dames & Moore, who had contracted with the Atomic Energy Organization of Iran and was owed money for services performed under that contract, sought injunctive relief, claiming that the President's actions were beyond his constitutional powers.

Issue: May the president issue an executive order that authorizes the suspension of claims in American courts?

Rule: (Rehnquist) While there is no statutory provision that expressly authorizes the president's suspension of claims in American courts, it is established practice that the president may extinguish claims of U.S. nationals against foreign countries by executive agreement.

Goldwater v. Carter
(Ct. App. 1979) SOL

Facts: Without seeking the Senate's advice, President Carter gave notice of termination of the Mutual Defense Treaty with the Republic of China.

Issue: May the president unilaterally terminate a treaty that contains an explicit provision for termination by either party?

Rule: When the Senate, when consenting to a treaty, does not include a provision requiring the Senate's consent to a notice of termination, the president is empowered to unilaterally terminate the treaty in accordance with its terms.

Goldwater v. Carter
(S.Ct. 1979) SOL

Facts: See above. The Supreme Court granted a writ of certiorari. In a memorandum decision, the Court vacated the judgment of the court of appeals and remanded to the district court with directions to dismiss the complaint.

Issue: May the Court consider the issue presented by Congress' claim that congressional approval is required in order to effectuate the president's decision to terminate the Mutual Defense Treaty?

Rule: Omitted.

Concurrence 1: (Powell, J.) A dispute between Congress and the president is not ripe for judicial review until each branch has acted to assert its constitutional authority. If this case were ripe for judicial review, the Court would not be prevented from considering the issue as the case does not involve a nonjusticiable political question, but rather concerns only the constitutional division of power between Congress and the president.

Concurrence 2: (Rehnquist, J.) Because this case involves the authority of the president in the conduct of our country's foreign relations and the extent to which Congress is authorized to negate the action of the president, this case presents a "political question," and therefore, is nonjusticiable.

United States v. Percheman
(S.Ct. 1833) SOL

Facts: In 1819, Spain ceded Florida to the U.S. by a peace treaty that included a provision that private rights previously granted would be respected. Percheman (P), who claimed title to land in Florida under a grant to his predecessor by the Spanish governor in 1815, sought to quiet title in the land.

Issue: May one claim, directly under a treaty, title to land even though Congress has failed to enact any legislation to implement a provision in the treaty safeguarding prior grants?

Rule: (Marshall, C.J.) Where a treaty involving the cessation of land contains an express provision for the protection of preexisting private property rights, government action is not required in order to give validity to titles that, under the law of nations, are already valid.

Asakura v. City of Seattle
(S.Ct. 1924) SOL

Facts: Seattle passed a city ordinance that made it unlawful to engage in the business of pawnbroker without a license and provided that only citizens of the U.S. could apply for such a license. P, a Japanese citizen residing in the U.S., claimed that the ordinance violated a treaty between the U.S. and Japan that established the rule of equality between Japanese subjects residing in the U.S. and native citizens in all facets of life, including trade.

Issue: May a city enforce an ordinance that violates a provision of a treaty?

Rule: (Butler, J.) Since a treaty made under the authority of the U.S., much like the provisions of the Constitution and laws of the U.S., is the "supreme law of the land," the provisions of a treaty may not be nullified by a municipal ordinance or state law.

Sei Fujii v. State
(1952) SOL

Facts: P, a Japanese alien, challenged the validity of the California alien land law that prohibited Japanese aliens from owning land, claiming that it was a violation of the provisions of the U.N. Charter.

Issue 1: Does a treaty automatically supersede local laws that are inconsistent with it where the provisions of the treaty are not self-executing?

Rule 1: The provisions of the U.N. Charter only state the general purposes and objectives of the Charter and do not purport to impose legal obligations on the individual member nations. Where future legislative action is contemplated in order to carry out the objectives of a treaty, the provisions of the treaty do not supersede existing domestic legislation.

Issue 2: Does the alien land law violate the due process and equal protection clauses of the fourteenth amendment?

Rule 2: A law that discriminates against a class of individuals on the basis of race is invalid as a violation of the fourteenth amendment unless the state can show that such individuals are injurious to legitimate state interests.

Chapter 7

INTERNATIONAL RESPONSIBILITY AND REMEDIES

I. GENERAL PRINCIPLES OF RESPONSIBILITY

International responsibility arises whenever there is a breach of an international obligation. Under some circumstances, the harmed state may take measures of self-help or countermeasures short of using force.

II. THE "ACT OF STATE"

A. Subdivisions of the State

Conduct of an official state subdivision is considered to be an act of the state under international law.

B. Other Public or Private Organizations

The conduct of nongovernmental public or private organizations are considered "acts of the state" if it is established that the group was in fact acting on behalf of the state.

C. Subdivisions of Another State

Conduct by a subdivision of a state that takes place in the territory of another state is not considered to be an act of the "host" state.

D. Factions of an Insurrection Movement

The conduct of a faction of an insurrection movement within an established state will not be considered an act of that state unless the movement becomes the new government of the state.

III.   OBJECTIVE RESPONSIBILITY AND "LEGAL INTEREST"

States have an international responsibility for acts committed by their officials or their subdivisions despite the absence of fault on the part of the actor.

IV.   THE REQUIREMENT OF INJURY

The breach of an international obligation gives rise to responsibility, irrespective of injury caused, to other states unless the specific obligation requires an injury as a condition for breach.

V.   CRIMES AND DELICTS

A. International Crimes

An international crime results from the serious breach of an international duty that is essential to the maintenance of international peace, security, self-determination, human rights, or environmental protection.

B. International Delicts

Any wrongful act on the international stage that is not an international crime constitutes an international delict.

VI.   CIRCUMSTANCES PRECLUDING WRONGFULNESS

A. Consent

The valid consent given by one state to another state, for what would ordinarily be an act not in conformity with international law, precludes the wrongfulness of the act.

B. *Force Majeure* and Fortuitous Events

When the state subdivisions are involuntarily put in a position that makes it impossible for them to act in conformity with the requirements of international obligations the wrongfulness of the act is precluded.

C. Distress

In cases where acting in accordance with an international duty is possible, but would result in the loss of human life, the wrongfulness of the act is precluded when the act was not likely to cause a comparable or greater danger.

D. Necessity

In cases where acting in accordance with an international duty is possible, but would result in endangering an essential state interest, the wrongfulness of the act is precluded when the act was not likely to cause a comparable or greater danger.

E. Self-Defense

Where acting in accordance with an international obligation poses a threat created by the state acted against, self-defense precludes wrongfulness of the act if the danger avoided was greater than the foreseeable results of the act committed.

VII. COUNTERMEASURES AND SELF-HELP

A. Reprisals

Reprisals are countermeasures that would be unlawful if not for the preceding illegal act of the state against which they were taken.

1. Necessity
   The reprisal must be necessary to terminate the violation or prevent further violation.

2. Proportionality
   The reprisal must not be out of proportion to the violation and the injury suffered.

B. Reciprocal Measures

A state injured by a breach of a multilateral treaty may suspend its performance of obligations toward the state that acted wrongfully when such obligations correspond to, or are directly connected with, the obligations breached.

C. Retorsion

1.Definition of Retorsion
Retorsion refers to countermeasures taken by the harmed state against the offending state that are generally permissible in international law regardless of the prior breach. Examples include suspending diplomatic relations or bilateral aid.

2. Limits on Retorsion
Retorsion may not be used to coerce another state to give up its sovereign rights.

D. Collective Sanctions

1. Definition of Collective Sanctions
The joint or parallel action of several aggrieved states in response to an offending state's violation of an international duty.

2. The United Nations Security Council
If the collective sanctions are of a nonmilitary nature, they may be adopted by the Security Council under Chapter VII of the U.N. Charter as mandatory enforcement measures. The Council may require U.N. members to sever economic or diplomatic relations with the offending state.

VIII. REPARATION

Reparation is the term describing the various methods by which a state can discharge its responsibility for the breach of an international obligation.

1. Restitution
   Restitution puts the harmed state in the position it would have been in had the breach not occurred. The offending state performs the obligation that it previously failed to discharge.

2. Indemnity
   Indemnity is the monetary compensation that must, as far as possible, wipe out all the consequences of the illegal act. It is the most common form of reparation.

3. Satisfaction
   When the damage done is nonmaterial or the injury involved is moral, the reparation may come in the form of official apologies or punishment of the guilty officials involved.

IX.   IMPLEMENTING REPARATION

A. Procedural Requirements

1. Standing
   A state must have the requisite legal interest to present claims through diplomatic channels or to tribunals.

2. Laches
   Some requests for reparation have been denied because the claim was not made in a timely fashion.

3. Negotiation
   Generally, negotiation or consultation must be attempted before a claim may be submitted to a tribunal or other settlement procedure.

4. Exhausting Other Remedies
   A state seeking reparation through an international tribunal must generally show that it has exhausted all avenues of relief in its national court system.

5. Consent to Third Party Settlement
An international tribunal can only hear claims for reparation in which all states concerned have consented to the international tribunal's jurisdiction.

B. Enforcement and Execution of Awards

1. Execution Against Assets of Noncomplying State
Although rare, a state may, in some cases, enforce an award for money damages by taking assets of the offending state within the territory of the collecting state.

2. Execution Through Domestic Courts
Sometimes a court within the creditor nation will attempt to attach funds of the debtor nation.

3. Multilateral Treaty Enforcement Provisions
Although seldom used, the U.N. Charter provides that the Security Council may enforce awards granted by the International court.

4. A Common Fund for Payment of Awards
A few treaties have arranged for a bank account to be maintained in a neutral country for the possible payment of reparations arising out of debts, contracts, expropriations, and other measures affecting property rights.

C. Claims Settlement by the United States

"Foreign Claims Settlement Commissions" have been created in the United States to distribute funds from foreign governments to U.S. nationals entitled to them.

X. REMEDIES OF PRIVATE PERSONS IN DOMESTIC COURTS FOR VIOLATIONS OF INTERNATIONAL LAW

A. Obligation to Provide a Remedy to Injured Persons

While there is no general duty in international law for a state to grant a remedy to an injured individual, there may be an obligation arising under specific requirements of international agreements.

B. Limitations on Individual Remedies in Domestic Courts

Remedies in municipal courts are limited by sovereign immunity, the act of state doctrine, and jurisdictional requirements.

CASE CLIPS

Case Concerning The Barcelona Traction, Light and Power Co. (Belgium v. Spain), Second Phase (ICJ 1970) HPSS, SOL

Facts: Belgium brought suit on behalf of Belgium nationals working for a corporation in Spain who claimed that they were damaged by conduct of the Spanish state contrary to international law.

Issue: May a state bring a claim in behalf of its nationals for violations of international obligations?

Rule: In order for a state to bring a claim on behalf of its nationals, the state must show that the defendant state has broken an obligation towards it in respect of its nationals. Only the party to whom an international obligation is due can bring a claim in respect of its breach.

Case Concerning Air Services Agreement Between France and the United States (1978) HPSS

Facts: France refused to allow Pan Am to use smaller aircraft in its flights between Paris and London. The United States countered by suspending French air traffic into Los Angeles.

Issue: Does a state have the right to take retaliatory counter-measures to what it deems a breach of an international agreement?
Rule: If one state perceives an act by another state to be a violation of an international obligation, the first state is entitled to affirm its rights through the use of "reasonably equivalent" countermeasures.

Chapter 8

PEACEFUL SETTLEMENT OF DISPUTES

I. THE DUTY TO SETTLE DISPUTES PEACEFULLY

A. Charter Obligations

Articles 2 and 33 of the U.N. Charter state that all members must settle their international disputes by peaceful means.

B. Treaty Obligations

1. The General Act of 1928
   Sometimes called the Geneva Act, this act is the most ambitious effort to establish a duty of peaceful settlement. The Act originally had twenty-two members, but today it has only seven. The United States has never acceded to the Act.

2. Other Settlement Treaties
   Regional and bilateral treaties are the most common forum for conciliation and arbitration agreements.

3. Dispute Clauses in Other Treaties
   Treaties on a wide range of topics include obligations to settle disputes using judicial settlement, there is arbitration, conciliation, or negotiation.

C. The Meaning of "Dispute"

"Dispute" has developed into a term of art for specifically contested differences. The disagreement must be on a point of law or fact, a conflict of legal views or interests between two persons.

II. NONADJUDICATORY PROCEDURES

A. Negotiation

Negotiation is the first stage of settlement. Where an obligation to negotiate exists, there is not necessarily any duty to reach an agreement, only a duty to sit down with your negotiating partner.

B. Mediation and Conciliation

1. Mediation
   A third party enters the negotiation with the purpose of inducing the original parties to settle their dispute on their own.

2. Conciliation
   Conciliation is the process of settling a dispute by referring it to a commission whose task it is to determine the facts and to develop potential settlement proposals. While seemingly attractive, this procedure has been seldom used in practice.

C. International Organizations

1. Dispute Settlement Through the United Nations

   a. Primary Objectives
      The U.N., through Chapters VI and VII of its Charter, endeavors to stop armed conflict in specific situations and to assist the parties of a conflict in achieving peaceful solutions to their difficulties.

   b. Fact Finding
      U.N. fact-finding in international disputes ranges from gathering witness testimony to organizing and authorizing military observer groups to monitor cease fires, armistices, and disarmament zones.

III.   ARBITRATION

A. The Role of Arbitration in Settlement

Unlike conciliation, arbitration results in a binding settlement of a dispute on the basis of law. The states involved in the dispute select the arbitration judges, but can not subject the judges to their instructions.

B. The *Compromis d'Arbitrage*

When specifications on the method by which the arbitral tribunal will be constituted, the questions it will answer, and the procedures it will use are not given in the instrument creating the arbitration, these decisions are made using a *compromis d'arbitrage*. The *compromis* typically gives the arbitrating tribunal the authority to resolve any questions of procedure not answered by the *compromis* itself.

C. Some Substantive Problems of Arbitration

1. Procedural Problems
   The validity of an arbitration award may be challenged if one party charges that the tribunal has exceeded its mandate, there was corruption on the part of the tribunal, or the award was not adequately justified. These challenges have proven to be the rule rather than the exception.

2. Fraud
   Where there is clear evidence of impropriety or mistake of law by the tribunal, the arbitration may be reopened and the decision corrected.

D. The Iran-United States Claims Tribunal

Located in The Hague, this tribunal, which has jurisdiction over all private claims of U.S. nationals against Iran and nationals of Iran against the United States, is the most active arbitral body in the world today. The tribunal uses the arbitration rules of the United

Nations Commission on International Trade Law. All Decisions of the tribunal are final and binding and may be enforced in the courts of any nation in accordance with its laws.

IV. THE INTERNATIONAL COURT OF JUSTICE (ICJ)

A. General Formulation

The court consists of fifteen judges selected by the Security Council and the General Assembly of the U.N. The judges may include no more than one national of any state. The judges serve for nine years, with five judges rotating off every three years. If a party in a case does not have a judge of its nationality on the court, it may designate an *ad hoc* judge.

B. Recourse to the Court

Many of the court's decisions since its creation in 1946 have had a major impact on the development of international law. But, states have not chosen to submit most of their legal disputes to the court. The most general reason for avoiding the court is that litigation is often uncertain, time consuming, and troublesome.

C. Jurisdiction

1. Two Kinds of Jurisdiction
The court decides cases between states and it renders advisory opinions. For cases, the jurisdiction of the court arises out of the consent of both parties involved. For advisory opinions, the case need only be categorized as a "legal dispute."

2. Compulsory Jurisdiction under the Optional Clause
Article 36 of the Statute allows states to recognize the court's jurisdiction as compulsory in matters of treaty interpretation, specific questions of international law, the existence of facts that would constitute breach of an international agreement, and the nature or extent of reparation for specific breaches of an international agreement.

3. Objections to Jurisdiction

Preliminary objections allow states to contest the jurisdiction of the ICJ before the court has made a decision, or even held a hearing on the merits of the case. See *Nuclear Tests, Aegean Sea Continental Shelf* and *U.S. Diplomatic and Consular Staff in Tehran* Cases.

4. Intervention

A state may intervene in a case between other states under two sets of circumstances:

a. A state may intervene when it has an interest of a legal nature in the case.

b. A state may also intervene if it is a party to the convention that is before the Court.

D. Advisory Opinions

An advisory opinion may be requested by the U.N. or by any of the specialized agencies that have been authorized to request advisory opinions by the Statute of the ICJ, which establishes the court's jurisdiction. States may not request an advisory opinion.

CASE CLIPS

Nuclear Tests Case
(Australia v. France)
(ICJ 1974) HPSS, SOL

Facts: Australia argued that France had promised to stop conducting atmospheric testing of nuclear weapons and that this created a binding international obligation.

Issue: Does the International Court of Justice (ICJ) have the authority to decide whether a public promise by a nation creates an international obligation?

Rule: Determining whether a public statement by a nation constitutes an international duty is directly within the authority of the ICJ.

Aegean Sea Continental Shelf Case
(Greece v. Turkey)
(ICJ 1976) HPSS

Facts: Turkey, while exploring for oil in the Aegean Sea, set off explosive depth charges in an area that Greece claimed as part of the continental shelf of certain Greek islands. Greece sought an injunction banning these explorations.

Issue: May the ICJ refuse to grant an injunction when the result will not irreparably prejudice the rights of the parties?

Rule: The ICJ may refuse any form of interim protection when it feels that the potential prejudice to the parties involved will not be severe.

Case Concerning United States
Diplomatic and Consular Staff in Teheran I
(U.S. v. Iran)
(ICJ 1979) HPSS, SOL

Facts: The U.S. charged Iran with violating several treaties by allowing U.S. citizens to be taken hostage in the United States Embassy in Teheran. Iran claimed that the ICJ was acting out of its jurisdiction since the matter at hand was not about hostage taking but rather about U.S. historical interference with the Iranian state.

Issue: Does the ICJ have jurisdiction over situations involving consular property and the taking of hostages?

Rule: The ICJ may decide cases where internationally protected persons have been detained within consular or diplomatic territory.

Case Concerning United States
Diplomatic and Consular Staff in Teheran II
(U.S. v. Iran)
(ICJ 1980) HPSS, SOL

Facts: Iran refused to attend the hearing of the ICJ involving allegations by the United States of Iran's support of the illegal taking of hostages in the United States Embassy in Teheran.

Issue: In a case between two states, where one state fails to appear to protest the jurisdiction, may the Court still render a judgment?

Rule: If the ICJ finds that the party before it has presented a convincing claim, it may render judgment even in the absence of the other party involved.

Case Concerning Military and Paramilitary
Activities In and Against Nicaragua
(ICJ 1979) HPSS, SOL

Facts: After the Sandinista regime took power in Nicaragua, the United States allegedly began a series of acts of aggression against it. Nicaragua brought this case to the ICJ. The United States did not attend the proceedings, but defended their actions under the auspice of "collective self-defense."

Issue: May a state justify interfering with another state's internal affairs as "collective self-defense" where there has been no verified use of force?

Rule: Collective self-defense is not a viable justification for active intervention in another state's internal affairs where there has been no use of force by that state.

Chapter 9

THE USE OF FORCE

I. THE USE OF FORCE BETWEEN STATES

A. The Traditional Law

1. **Definition**
   The traditional law was the law governing uses of force before the U.N. Charter. It is uncertain whether the traditional law has survived the Charter.

2. **Intervention**
   Intervention is a term subsuming all invasions of a state's independence or territory. Prohibiting intervention in the quest for the ideal of completely independent and equally sovereign nations is an illusory goal since any act of a state may have "intervening" repercussions in another state.

3. **Permissible Interventions Short of War**
   A variety of non-war measures fall under the term *retorsion*. They include the severance of diplomatic relations, closing ports to ships of the offending state, or the display of naval forces near the waters of the offending state.

   a. **Reprisal**
      An act of reprisal must be preceded by an act contrary to international law and must be proportional in effect to the preliminary act.

   b. **Self-Defense**
      Self-defense may be a justification for countermeasures when the necessity of the actions is "instant, overwhelming, and leaving no choice of means or moment for deliberation." See *The Caroline*.

4. War in International Traditional Law

    a. War as a Lawful Instrument of National Policy
    Prior to the establishment of international organizations to enforce the law, war was a means of self-help to give effect to claims allegedly based on international law.

    b. The State of War in International Law
    In the nineteenth century, it was debated whether a state of war existed when only one party formally declared war or when there was evidence of large-scale fighting. The U.N. Charter ignored this issue by seeking to eliminate the use of force whether it was called war or not.

    c. Neutrality
    A state adopting an attitude of impartiality toward fighting states could assume the legal status of neutrality. The choice of neutrality, absent a specific treaty obligation, is a matter of international politics rather than international law.

B. Pre-United Nations Efforts to Outlaw War

    1. Hague Convention II
    This 1907 convention tried to make arbitration a mandatory alternative to the use of armed forces for the recovery of international contract debts.

    2. The League of Nations
    Proposed in 1919, the League was created to promote international peace through collective security. War was illegal only when begun in breach of the Covenant of the League. The League failed when the member states ignored their obligations during the rapidly building military activities of the 1930s.

    3. The Nuremberg Charter and Trials
    The United States, France, the United Kingdom and the Soviet Union established this International Military Tribunal for the trial of war criminals whose offenses have no particular geographical location whether they be accused individually or in

their capacity as members of organizations or groups or in both capacities. See *Judgment of the International Military Tribunal.*

C. The Law of the United Nations Charter

1. Purposes
   The purposes of the U.N. include the maintenance of international peace, the development of friendly relations among nations, and international cooperation in solving social, economic and humanitarian problems.

2. The Organization of the United Nations

   a. General Assembly
      All members of the U.N. are members of, and have one vote in, the General Assembly. The General Assembly may make recommendations on any matters within the scope of the Charter.

   b. Security Council
      The Security Council is made up of five permanent and ten nonpermanent members. The five full-time members are China, France, the U.S.S.R., the United Kingdom and the United States. The nonpermanent members are elected by the General Assembly for two-year terms. The council's primary duty is to maintain international peace and security. The council may authorize both measures that do not involve the use of force and those that do.

   c. Secretariat
      This is the administrative body of the United Nations, headed by the Secretary-General.

   d. International Court of Justice
      The Court is the principal judicial organ of the U.N.

3. The Prohibition of the Use of Force
   Article 2(4) provides: "All Members shall refrain in their international relations from the threat or use of force against the territorial integrity or political independence of any state, or in any other manner inconsistent with the Purposes of the United Nations."

   a. "Use of Force"
      While there is no universally agreed upon definition for this nebulous phrase, it may be understood as "any infringement upon national sovereignty and international order."

   b. "Threat of Force"
      Most often in the form of an ultimatum, this occurs when a state forces its will on another state by threatening coercive measures, such as blockade, bombardment, or occupation of a given territory.

   c. Definition of Aggression
      In 1974, the General Assembly adopted the Definition of Aggression Resolution, which defines aggression as "the use of armed force by a state against the sovereignty, territorial integrity or political independence of another state." Article 3 of the Resolution lists several types of acts that qualify as acts of aggression.

   d. Indirect Aggression
      These "ideological" attacks range from propaganda and psychological warfare by radio or aerial leaflets to the organizations of subversive, political movements within another state.

   e. Intervention

      i. Intervention by Invitation
         Interventions are deemed legal if the intervening army is invited by the government to help put down an attempted coup or to restore law and order. However, problems arise when an "invited intervention" interferes with the

choice of a population in respect to the composition of their government or the policies it should follow.

    ii.   Humanitarian Intervention
        A state is generally seen as having the right to intervene by the use or threat of force to protect its nationals suffering injuries within the territory of another state. This is also the theory by which the Red Cross intervenes upon a state's territory.

    iii. Nonintervention
        The U.N. declared, in 1965, "No State has the right to intervene, directly or indirectly, for any reason whatever, in the internal or external affairs of any other State. Consequently, armed intervention and all other forms of interference or attempted threats against the personality of the State or against its political, economic and cultural elements, are condemned."

  f. Limited Threat or Use of Force: The Cuban Missile Crisis
     President Kennedy ordered the interdiction by U.S. forces of the delivery of offensive weapons to Cuba. There is debate over whether a blockade of this nature constitutes a threat or a use of force.

4. Article 51: The Self-Defense Exception

  a. "Collective" Self-Defense
     When a member of the United Nations is attacked, the other members have a right to engage in collective protection of that state by whatever means they deem necessary until the Security Council takes measures to maintain international peace and order. Measures taken in the exercise of this right must be reported to the Security Council.

b. Anticipatory Self-Defense
Since the right of self-defense is activated by the *threat* of force, self-defense may necessarily preempt the use of force by the offending state. However, anticipatory actions are generally limited to an appeal for aid to the Security Council. The development of nuclear arsenals has seemingly made more aggressive anticipatory measures simultaneously a greater necessity and danger.

5. Belligerency and Neutrality Under the Charter
Since the ratification of the U.N. Charter, the international community has seemingly made neutrality obsolete. However, in practice, neutral status continues to be a valuable political tool in modern day diplomacy. While declaring neutrality may in some way legitimize the conflict, a state may often feel that such a declaration is a political necessity.

II.   INTERVENTION IN CIVIL WAR

A. The Traditional Law

1. A Lack of Consensus
The absence of a consensus on the international stage has left actors with wide discretion as to when assistance may be given to legitimate governments engaged in civil war or when rebels may be given limited rights as "insurgents."

2. Supporting Governments or Recognizing Insurgents
Assisting insurgents, while at peace with the legitimate government, is generally seen as a violation of international law. This distinction is highly dubious since the exact point at which an insurgent force becomes a legitimate government is always open to debate.

B. Civil Strife and the United Nations Charter

The U.N. Charter says nothing about the contingencies of intervention in internal wars. There are many examples of military support for a recognized government before the rebellion has made much progress. But, the issue still remains whether intervention on either side of a civil war violates the Charter provision that members will not use force against the political independence or territorial integrity of another state.

1. Intervention by Force in Civil Wars
   States intervening in internal wars typically claim "counter-intervention" as their justification for stepping in to "protect the interests of the population." Receiving outside military support is the rule rather than the exception in modern internal conflicts.

2. Types of Conflicts (Falk)
   Civil strife may be analyzed according to three different models of conflict.

   a. Type I
      A conflict that involves the direct and massive use of military force by one political entity across a boundary of another, e.g., the Korean War.

   b. Type II
      A conflict that involves substantial military participation by one or more foreign nations in an internal struggle for control, e.g., the Spanish Civil War.

   c. Type III
      An internal struggle for control of a state's society, the outcome of which is virtually independent of external participation, e.g., the Russian Revolution.

3. Vietnam: A Case Study
   The judgment of international law regarding the Vietnam war largely depends on which model is used to characterize the war.

   a. Model A
      The war was a civil war within South Vietnam, with North Vietnam supporting one side and the United States assisting

the other. Here, neither side violated international law until the U.S. bombed North Vietnam making the civil war an international conflict.

b. Model B
The war was a civil war between North Vietnam and the Vietcong, on one hand, and South Vietnamese forces, on the other. Here, bombing North Vietnam would not necessarily violate the U.N. Charter, but the later bombing of Laos and Cambodia would be unjustified under the Charter.

c. Model C
The war was started when North Vietnam, using the Vietcong as its agent, attacked the Republic of South Vietnam. This view, officially adopted by the U.S. government, saw American action as part of an attempt at collective self-defense.

4. Is the Law of the Charter Still Viaole?
While the U.N. has largely failed as an international police force, the Charter may still be a legally viable document.

III. COLLECTIVE USE OF FORCE

The League of Nations, which was the first attempt at an international organization to deter war, failed due to the unwillingness or inability of the principle powers to deter Nazi-fascist aggression.

A. The United Nations

1. The Scheme of the Charter
The U.N.'s primary function is to maintain peace and security through an organized procedure authorizing the use of force against an aggressor. The executive authority was vested in the Security Council, led by the U.S., U.K., U.S.S.R., France and China. Japan and Germany were excluded as the recently defeated enemies of World War II. The advent of the cold war quickly undermined the ideal of the council acting in concert to avert military conflicts.

a. Collective Security
Until the 1990 Persian Gulf War, the only episode of collective security involving the U.N. was the Korean War of 1949-
53. With the Soviet delegate absent, the Security Council
issued a resolution ordering a cease fire and the immediate
withdrawal of North Korean troops from South Korea. The
measure failed to avert war.

b. U.N. Peacekeeping
U.N. sponsored troops have intervened in a peacekeeping
capacity in the Middle East, the Congo and Cyprus.

c. U.N. Sanctions
The U.N. has levied "collective sanctions" in Southern
Rhodesia and South Africa.

B. Regional Organizations and the Use of Force

Article 52 of the U.N. Charter provides that nothing in the Charter
shall preclude "the existence of regional arrangements or agencies
for dealing with such matters relating to the maintenance of
international peace and security." The Security Council encourages
parties to resolve local disputes through regional means.

1. The Inter-American System
The Organization of American States, consisting of twenty-five
North, South and Central American countries, was founded in
1948. It has addressed such serious international issues as the
Guatemalan invasions of 1954 and the Cuban Missile Crisis of
1962.

2. The Organization of African Unity (OAU)
Since its ratification by thirty-two African countries in 1963, the
Organization has addressed multiple border disputes and
internal wars within its sphere of influence.

3. Arab League
   This League of Arab States, founded in 1944, has been recognized as a "regional arrangement" under Article 52 of the U.N. Charter since the Anglo-French aggression in Egypt in 1956.

C. Collective Self-Defense Arrangement

Collective defense organizations have developed to present groupings of power made necessary by the corresponding power of the enemy and the inability of most existing states to defend themselves singly.

1. North Atlantic Treaty Organization (NATO)
   Born in 1949, NATO originally consisted of Belgium, Canada, Denmark, France, Iceland, Italy, Luxembourg, the Netherlands, Norway, Portugal, the United Kingdom, and the United States. Greece, Turkey and the Federal Republic of Germany joined later. The objectives of the treaty include: collective self-defense, peaceful settlement of disputes involving a member, and development of mutual relations. Parties to the treaty are not obligated to come to the aid of any member when an armed attack occurs. A member is only required to take action as it deems necessary to restore security.

2. Warsaw Pact
   Before the recent events in Eastern Europe, the Warsaw Pact consisted of Albania, Bulgaria, Czechoslovakia, the German Democratic Republic, Hungary, Poland, Romania and the U.S.S.R. In 1991, the member states of the Warsaw Pact agreed to disband.

3. Southeast Asia Treaty Organization (SEATO)
   Created in 1954, this Organization consists of the U.S., the U.K., Cambodia, France, Laos, Pakistan, the Philippines, Thailand, Vietnam, Australia, and New Zealand. This organization played a pivotal role in the militarization of South Vietnam during the Vietnam War. This collective self-defense organization is founded on the belief that an armed attack upon one member poses a threat to the security of the others.

4. Other Organizations
There are several other international organizations that were founded in the name of collective self-defense. Included in these organizations are the Central Treaty Organization (CENTO), originated with the Bagdad Pact of 1955, and the ANZUS Council made up of Australia, New Zealand and the United States.

IV.   THE LAW OF WAR AND THE CONTROL OF WEAPONS

A. The Law of War

The three areas addressed by the traditional rules of law are the definition of war, the conduct of war, and the relations between belligerent and neutral states. The law of wars is in an uncertain state in light of the U.N. provisions outlawing war in general.

1. The Conduct of War
In general, whatever force needed to overpower the enemy is allowed. Additional use of force or weapons that cause unnecessary suffering are often prohibited. The outlawing of war by the U.N. Charter has not invalidated laws regulating weapons.

2. Nuclear Weapons
In 1961, the General Assembly declared that the use of nuclear weapons violated the U.N. Charter. It should be noted that major world powers consider nuclear weapons to be a critical part of their national defense. For this reason the use of nuclear weapons is more likely to be dictated by the needs of military strategy rather than the rules of international law.

3. Treatment of POWs
After the maltreatment of prisoners in the two world wars, the Geneva Convention Relative to the Treatment of Prisoners of War established a comprehensive set of rules governing treatment of war prisoners. All prisoners are to be treated

equally and humanely by the detaining party. No prisoner is to be subjected to any form of torture or medical experimentation.

4. Enemy Nationals In Belligerent Territory
Customary law permits the confiscation of public and private enemy property. Often, war-ending treaties allow the victors to retain the seized property. The internment of enemy nationals is regulated, but not outlawed, by the Geneva Convention Relative to the Protection of Civilian Persons in Time of War.

5. Treatment of the Population of Occupied Territory
An occupying power has the right to maintain law and order by using the courts of the subservient government. The population of the occupied state may not be subjected to collective penalties, intimidation, terrorism, taking of hostages, and other acts of reprisal.

6. Enemy Ships
While the attack of merchant ships was outlawed between the two world wars, this regulation was largely ignored in World War II. The current status of the rules on the treatment of enemy ships is uncertain.

B. Arms Control and Disarmament

Disarmament has been viewed as a viable means of avoiding armed conflict since the end of World War I. On July 17, 1991, the United States and the Soviet Union agreed for the first time to reduce, as opposed to merely limiting, nuclear arsenals.

CASE CLIPS

The Caroline
(1906) HPSS
Facts: A group of armed Canadians attacked a ship full of insurgents who were docked on the American side of the border. Several of the

insurgents were killed. At trial, Canada claimed self-defense as a justification for the attack.

Issue: When may self-defense justify the invasion of another country?

Rule: Invasion of another country may be justified by self-defense if the threat is immediate, overwhelming, and leaves no alternatives or time for deliberation.

Judgement of the International Military Tribunal, Nuremberg (1946) HPSS, SOL

Facts: High ranking military and government officials of Nazi Germany were charged with planning and waging an "aggressive war." The indictment charged that the invasions of Austria and Czechoslovakia were part of preordained scheme.

Issue: Is it a crime to plan or wage a "war of aggression"?

Rule: It is a crime to plan or wage a "war of aggression" or a war in violation of international treaties.

Certain Expenses of the United Nations (ICJ 1962) HPSS, SOL

Facts: The General Assembly authorized peacekeeping forces in the Congo and sought an advisory opinion whether the expenditures relating to the United Nations operations in the Congo constituted "expenses of the Organization." It was argued that the expenditures were not expenses of the Organization since only the Security Council is authorized to deal with matters of international peace.

Issue: Is the General Assembly empowered to authorize actions that ought to be taken for the maintenance of international peace and security?

Rule: While it is the Security Council that, in practice, has the "primary" responsibility for the maintenance of international peace and security, the General Assembly is empowered to authorize measures for the maintenance of international peace. However, only the Security Council has the power to order coercive action.

Diggs v. Schultz, Security of Treasury (U.S. 1972) SOL

Facts: The President of the U.S. authorized the importation of certain materials into the U.S. from Southern Rhodesia. Ps sought to enjoin the importation, claiming that it violated the treaty obligations of the U.S. under the U.N. Charter.

Issue 1: In order for a plaintiff to have standing to sue, must there be a logical nexus between the status asserted and the claim sought to be adjudicated?

Rule 1: In order for a plaintiff to have standing to sue, there must be a logical nexus between the status asserted and the claim sought to be adjudicated.

Issue 2: May Congress nullify a treaty commitment of the U.S.?

Rule 2: It is settled constitutional doctrine that Congress may nullify, in whole or in part, a treaty commitment of the U.S.

Advisory Opinion On the Continued Presence of South Africa in Namibia (South West Africa) (ICJ 1971) HPSS, SOL

Facts: South Africa was given a mandate to administer Namibia. Finding that South Africa had failed to fulfill its obligations with respect to the administration; the Security Council sought an advisory opinion from the ICJ as to the legal consequences of South Africa's continued presence in Namibia.

Issue: If a state is under an obligation to withdraw its administration from a neighboring territory but fails to do so, what are the legal consequences for other states as a result of the continued presence?

Rule: If the U.N. has determined that a situation created by a particular state is illegal, states that are members of the U.N. are under an obligation to recognize the illegality of that state's actions and to refrain from any dealings with that state's government implying recognition of the legality of that state's actions. Moreover, it is incumbent upon states that are not members of the U.N. to give assistance to the actions taken by the U.N.

Chapter 10

BASES OF JURISDICTION

I. JURISDICTION UNDER INTERNATIONAL LAW

A. Jurisdiction Defined

In general, the term jurisdiction is used to explain the authority to affect legal interests. The three basic types of jurisdiction are legislative, judicial, and executive or enforcement.

B. General Rules of Jurisdiction

While international law has not developed a definitive set of rules for the jurisdiction of states and other international legal persons, there are some established guidelines.

1. Civil and Criminal Jurisdiction
   International law does not distinguish between jurisdictional requirements for civil and criminal matters.

2. Scope of Jurisdiction
   The International Court of Justice has said that an international legal person's jurisdictional range and restrictions are determined by the role that the person plays in the international community.

3. A Jurisdictional Presumption
   Traditionally, states have been presumed to have valid jurisdiction and the burden of proof has fallen on the party attempting to prove otherwise. In recent times, states have increasingly had to demonstrate jurisdictional validity for actions taken beyond their borders.

C. Criteria for Determining Jurisdiction

A state's jurisdiction depends on the interest that state may reasonably have in exercising the particular jurisdiction asserted and on the reconciliation of that interest with the interests of any other states.

1. Basic Principles

a. The Territorial Principle
A state has a primary interest in whatever happens in its territory.

b. The Nationality Principle
A state has a significant interest in exercising jurisdiction over persons or things possessing its nationality.

c. The Protective Principle
A state has an interest in protecting itself against persons or acts that threaten its existence or its proper functioning as an independent, sovereign nation.

d. The Universal Principle
Certain actions are so universally prohibited that all states have an interest in exercising jurisdiction to defeat them.

2. See specifically Restatement (Revised) §§402-403

II. THE TERRITORIAL PRINCIPLE

A. Scope

1. Persons and Things within the Territory
A state may exercise jurisdiction over all persons or things within its borders.

2. Persons and Things Not within the Territory
A state may exercise jurisdiction over persons or things not within its borders that have a direct and not overly tenuous

effect on matters within its borders.

III. THE NATIONALITY PRINCIPLE

A. Nationality over Natural Persons

Generally, a state may exercise jurisdiction over its citizens if public interest so requires, even if the citizen is residing in another state.

B. Nationality over Legal Persons

A state may generally exercise jurisdiction over corporations organized under its laws, but not over corporations that are merely owned or controlled by nationals of the state.

C. Nationality of the Victim

Although disputed, statutes giving a state extraterritorial jurisdiction based on a crime victim possessing its nationality are typically recognized.

D. Nationality of Vehicles and Objects

1. Maritime Vessels
   While vessels are generally considered to be the possession of the nation whose flag they fly, there must be a "genuine link" between the vessel and the state.

2. Aircraft and Space Vehicles
   An aircraft may be registered in only one state and it carries the nationality of that state. Likewise, objects launched into, or constructed in, outer space retain the nationality of the state from which they originated.

   a. Convention on International Civil Aviation (1944)
      All contracting states recognized that every state has complete and exclusive sovereignty over the airspace above

its territory. The convention establishes a legal basis for the regulation of flights of civil aircraft.

b. Convention on Offenses and Certain Other Acts Committed On Board Aircraft (1963)
The state of registration has jurisdiction over offenses and acts committed on board an aircraft.

c. Convention for the Suppression of Unlawful Seizure of Aircraft (Hijacking) (1970)
This Convention, followed by 121 states, was aimed at controlling attacks and sabotage against civil aircraft.

d. Treaty on Principles Governing the Activities of States In the Exploration and Use of Outer Space, Including the Moon and Other Celestial Bodies (1967)
This Treaty allows for the rescue and return of astronauts as well as the return of any objects launched into outer space.

3. Other Things
States have attempted, by and large unsuccessfully, to extend the argument used for jurisdiction over vessels and aircraft to other inanimate objects, such as artistic creations and cultural artifacts.

IV. PROTECTION OF STATE AND UNIVERSAL INTERESTS

A. The Protective Principle

A state may exercise jurisdiction to prohibit conduct outside of its territory by non-nationals that threatens the security of the state or other important state interests.

B. The Universality Principle

Some conduct is so universally condemned that a state may exercise jurisdiction in an effort to combat such acts. An example of jurisdiction exercised pursuant to this principle is the prosecution of pirates. Likening the Israeli capture of Nazi leader Adolf

Eichmann within its territory to piracy, Argentina failed in its attempt to use this principle.

V. AGREEMENT WITH THE TERRITORIAL STATE

A sovereign nation has jurisdiction to enforce a rule of law within the borders of another state if provided for by an international agreement with the other state.

A. NATO Nations and Their Forces

1. The NATO Status of Forces Agreement allows sending states to exercise criminal and disciplinary jurisdiction over their military personnel in a receiving state.

2. Authorities of the receiving state may exercise jurisdiction over members of a foreign military force and their dependents with respect to offenses committed within the territory of the receiving state and punishable by that state.

B. The U.N. Peacekeeping Force in Cyprus

Members of the Joint Force shall be subject to the jurisdiction of their respective national states in respect to criminal offenses committed while in Cyprus.

VI. CONFLICTS OF JURISDICTION

Conflicts in international jurisdiction often arise when two countries each claim jurisdiction using one of the above principles. For instance, Country A might utilize the nationality principle to gain jurisdiction over its nationals abroad, while Country B might claim jurisdiction over the same persons based on the territorial principle. See *Bank of Nova Scotia*.

VII. JURISDICTION TO ADJUDICATE

A state must have the consent of the "host state" to exercise judicial functions within the territory of another state. Alternatively, a state may typically exercise its judicial functions on matters unfolding in its own territory. Criminal prosecutions *in absentia* are a commonly allowed exception by which states may exercise jurisdiction over its nationals in other nations. See Restatement (Revised) §§ 421, 423.

VIII. JURISDICTION TO ENFORCE

If a state has proven legislative or judicial jurisdiction, it may also exercise the corollary executive jurisdiction in compelling compliance with its laws. Restatement (Revised) § 431.

IX. EXTRADITION

A. Definition

Extradition is the surrender of an individual accused or convicted of a crime by the state within whose territory he is found to the state under whose laws he is alleged to have committed, or been convicted of, the crime.

B. Problems

1. Difficult problems arise when the act committed by the fugitive is punishable in the requisitioning state but not in the asylum state.

2. Other problems arise when the crime was not committed in the territory of the state requesting extradition.

CASE CLIPS

United States v. Aluminum Co. of America
(U.S. 1945) HPSS

Facts: A Canadian corporation was formed to take over the properties outside of the United States belonging to Aluminum Co. of America. The United States brought suit claiming that Ds had violated the Sherman Anti-Trust Act by their participation in an alliance with several foreign producers.

Issue: Does a state have the authority to impose restrictions upon foreign persons outside of its territory if the activities of those persons have an effect within the state's territory?

Rule: A state may impose liability on foreign parties outside of its territory if the activities of the parties have a direct and not overly tenuous effect within the borders of the state.

Blackmer v. United States
(S.Ct. 1932) HPSS, SOL

Facts: Blackmer, a United States citizen living in Paris, was subpoenaed to appear in a District of Columbia court. Upon his refusal, he was charged with contempt.

Issue: May the United States require the return of one of its citizens for a domestic legal proceeding?

Rule: (Hughes, C.J.) If the public interest requires it, the United States has the authority to demand the return of its citizens living abroad and to levy penalties for the failure of such return.

Wilson v. Girard
(S.Ct. 1957) HPSS, SOL

Facts: Girard, while guarding a machine gun in his capacity as an officer in the U.S. Army in Japan, caused the death of a Japanese woman. He was indicted by Japanese authorities, but after receiving an injunction, he was not delivered to those authorities.

Issue 1: Does a state have exclusive jurisdiction to punish offenses committed within its borders?

Rule 1: A state has exclusive jurisdiction to punish offenses committed within its borders, unless it expressly or impliedly consents to surrender its jurisdiction.

Issue 2: May a state waive the limited jurisdiction conferred upon it by another?

Rule 2: There are no constitutional or statutory barriers that prohibit a state from waiving the limited jurisdiction conferred upon it by another.

United States v. The Bank of Nova Scotia
(U.S. 1982) HPSS

Facts: As part of a tax investigation, a United States grand jury asked D to produce records that were located in the Bahamas. D refused, claiming that compliance would violate Bahamian privacy laws.

Issue: May a party refuse to produce documents for a tax investigation using foreign privacy laws as a justification?

Rule: Since, in a world of international commercial transactions, it would be hazardous to allow parties to hide documents behind the veil of a foreign country's privacy laws, refusal to produce documents in tax investigations is not permitted.

J.H.G. v. Public Prosecutor
(Netherlands 1958) SOL

Facts: J.H.G. was banned from driving by a domestic law of the Netherlands. He was later charged with unauthorized driving in Germany.

Issue: Can a state prescribe rules of domestic law to govern actions beyond its territory?

Rule: A state's jurisdiction to legislate rules of domestic law is limited to its own territory.

Re Penati
(Italy 1946) SOL

Facts: Penati, a Swiss subject, was convicted of aiding the German occupation authorities in Italy. He appealed the conviction, claiming that since he was an alien he was not subject to the Italian rules of criminal law.

Issue: May an alien defendant in a criminal law case use the defense that the criminal law of their residing state doesn't apply to nationals of other states?

Rule: Aliens and nationals are equally subject to the criminal law of the state in which they reside.

Armengol v. Mutualité Socialé Agricole de L'Hérault
(France 1966) SOL

Facts: P, a national of Andorra, drove his sheep into France where they grazed and were looked after by his shepherds. A French court held that because his activities were performed on French territory he was liable to pay certain taxes.

Issue: Absent benefitting from a state's laws or protections, are aliens subject to the laws of a foreign state in which they temporarily reside?

Rule: Generally, a state has the authority to regulate, as it sees fit, the activities of aliens in its territory.

Gostelradio SSSR v. Whitney and Piper
(1979) SOL

Facts: Whitney and Piper, two American journalists, were sued for fabricating information about a Soviet radio broadcast. The Soviet Radio Corporation cited Soviet civil law in their action.

Issue: Can a foreigner be guilty of libel in a state in which the questioned information was not disseminated?

Rule: If libelous information is likely to reach a state, the defendant may be subject to that state's libel laws.

The "S.S. Lotus" (France v. Turkey)
(PCIJ 1927) HPSS, SOL

Facts: Following a collision between the French steamship *Lotus* and the Turkish steamship *Boz-Kourt*, in which eight Turkish nationals died, Turkey instituted a criminal proceeding against Lieutenant Demons, a French national.

Issue: Does a state have jurisdiction in its territory to prosecute foreign offenders for an act committed on the high seas but effecting its nationals?

Rule: A state has the right to prosecute foreign offenders for acts that effect its nationals even though they occurred beyond its borders, provided the jurisdiction does not conflict with a principle of international law.

Rivard v. United States
(U.S. 1967) SOL

Facts: Four Canadian nationals were indicted for conspiracy to smuggle heroin into the United States. They were extradited from Canada, tried, and convicted in a U.S. district court. Ds were, at all times prior to their extradition, outside of the U.S.

Issue: Does a domestic court have jurisdiction to try an alien for acts performed outside its nation's borders that aid the commission of a crime within that nation?

Rule: Applying the objective view of the territorial principle, that a nation's jurisdiction is extended over all acts that take effect within the nation, even though the violator is elsewhere, a domestic court has the power to try an alien for acts performed outside a nation's borders that aid the commission of a crime within that nation.

Residents of Okinawa
(Japan 1967) SOL

Facts: During the time the U.S. administered Okinawa, the accused, Japanese nationals, committed crimes in Okinawa and fled to mainland Japan where they were arrested and prosecuted for the crimes. The accused had their permanent domiciles in Okinawa and lived there since birth or infancy.

Issue: Does a state have jurisdiction over people who have its nationality, regardless of domicile?

Rule: The state reserves its personal sovereignty over a person who has its nationality, even if the person resides in another nation.

United States v. Pizzarusso
(U.S. 1968) SOL

Facts: D, a citizen of Canada, was indicted and convicted in the U.S. for knowingly making false statements under oath in a visa application to an American consular official in Canada, a violation of 18 U.S.C § 1546.

Issue: Does a state have jurisdiction to establish a rule attaching legal consequences to acts done outside its territory that threaten national security?

Rule: Under the protective principal, a state has jurisdiction to prescribe a rule of law attaching legal consequences to conduct outside its territory that threatens its security as a state or the operation of its governmental functions, provided the conduct is recognized as a crime under the law of states that have reasonably developed legal systems.

Harry Winston v. Tuduri
(Spain 1961) SOL

Facts: P, an American corporation, sued Tuduri, a Mexican citizen domiciled in Spain, to collect the sum due on a necklace bought from P in the U.S. or, alternatively, for return of the necklace. D challenged the jurisdiction of the Spanish courts to hear the case, claiming that only American or Mexican courts had jurisdiction.

Issue: When does a state have jurisdiction over an action between nationals of other countries?

Rule: A state has jurisdiction over all civil law questions that may be raised within its jurisdiction, irrespective of the parties' nationalities.

Arret Fornage
(France 1873) SOL

Facts: Raymond Fornage, a French citizen, appealed a French court's prosecution of a grand larceny committed in Switzerland, claiming that he could not be prosecuted in the French courts for a crime committed outside the country.

Issue: Do domestic courts have the power to try foreign nationals for crimes committed outside the country's territory?

Rule: Except when a foreign national has committed a crime against the security of the state, a state does not have the jurisdiction to try foreign nationals for crimes committed outside its territory.

The Schooner Exchange v. McFaddon
(S.Ct. 1812) HPSS, SOL

Facts: A French warship, the *Balaou,* was forced by bad weather to enter the port of Philadelphia where it was libeled by two American citizens who alleged that the ship was in reality the *Schooner Exchange,* a merchant vessel wrongfully seized and confiscated on the high seas by the French government.

Issue: What is the nature of a nation's jurisdiction within its territory?

Rule: (Marshall, C.J.) The jurisdiction of a nation within its territory is exclusive and absolute.

United States v. Lira
(U.S. 1975) SOL

Facts: D appealed his narcotics conviction, claiming that he was abducted from Chile and tortured by U.S Drug Enforcement Agents.

Issue: Does a country have jurisdiction over a criminal defendant if the person was forcibly abducted and brought into the country?

Rule: The general rule, known as the *Ker-Frisbie doctrine,* is that a court's power to bring a person to trial upon criminal charges is not impaired by the forcible abduction of the defendant into the jurisdiction.   However, the *Ker-Frisbie doctrine* is not applicable if the government itself abducts the defendant into the jurisdiction through the use of cruel and inhuman conduct.

Lawrence Jusko & Co., et Lawrence Jusko v.
Fortis Uhren Ag et Tribunal Superieur du Canton de Soleure
(Switzerland 1979) SOL

Facts: In a Swiss court, a creditor sought to enforce a judgment obtained in Canada against a Swiss national.

Issue: Is service of notice by mail from one state to another, a violation of that state's territorial sovereignty?

Rule: The service of any judicial document represents an act of judicial authority that requires consent of the state, thus, notice by mail from one state to another, without consent, is a violation of that state's territorial sovereignty.

Securities and Exchange Commission v. Briggs
(U.S. 1964) SOL

Facts: The SEC sought to enjoin Briggs, an American citizen, from violating the anti-fraud provisions of the Securities Act of 1933. Briggs, who was served by mail, was located, at the time, in Canada.

Issue: May a state serve notice on a citizen living in a foreign nation?

Rule: The serving of notice upon a citizen of one state, found in another, is not an invasion of the foreign state's sovereignty.

The State v. Schumann
(Ghana 1966) SOL

Facts: The West German government sought the extradition of Schumann, a doctor charged with conducting sterilization tests on mental patients and Jewish prisoners. He challenged the extradition, claiming that his crimes were of a political nature.

Issue: When is the "political offense" claim a valid defense against extradition?

Rule: Crimes of a political nature are generally exempt from extradition treaties. However, an offense is "of a political nature" only when there is either political disturbance or upheaval, or some physical struggle between two opposing political parties for governmental control and the crime in question was committed in furtherance of that disturbance or struggle.

Re Bressano
(Argentina 1965) SOL

Facts: Peru requested the extradition of Bressano on charges of bank robbery and assault committed in Peru. Argentina refused extradition on the ground that the offenses were political offenses.

Issue: Does the fact that a criminal offense is directed against an existing political order mean, without more, the offense is "political"?

Rule: Generally, a "political offense" must be an act taken against a tyrannical or despotic government. Furthermore, not all acts of guerrilla warfare against an existing state, despotic or otherwise, will qualify.

Quinn v. Robinson
(U.S. 1986) SOL

Facts: The United Kingdom sought extradition of Quinn, a citizen of Northern Ireland, from the United States to face murder and conspiracy charges.

Issue 1: Is the judiciary precluded from deciding the applicability of a political offense exception rule in an extradition treaty?

Rule 1: The judicial branch of the government has the jurisdiction to consider the applicability of an extradition treaty's political offense exception clause.

Issue 2: Can offenses committed in a nation other than that of the extraditee's citizenship be classified as "political offenses"?

Rule 2: Offenses committed in a nation other than that of the extraditee's citizenship do not come within the "political offense" exception.

Issue 3: What are the criteria for ascertaining whether an offense is political and, thus, not extraditable?

Rule 3: An offense is not extraditable based on the political offense exception if it meets the requirements of the incidence test. The incidence test has two components: (1) an uprising and (2) the charged offense must have been committed in furtherance of the uprising. Acts of international terrorism do not meet the incidence test and are thus not covered by the political offense exception. Crimes against humanity are also beyond the scope of the exception.

Tax Decision
(Federal German Republic 1971) SOL

Facts: The German tax administration sought to tax A for income received from a German movie company for work performed by A in Germany and Italy.

Issue: May a state tax income received by an individual from work performed abroad?

Rule: A state may tax income received by an individual for work performed abroad if the work is "utilized" (the economic effect of the work performed abroad is of direct benefit to the state imposing the tax) in that state.

Whitley v. Aitchison
(France 1958) SOL

Facts: Whitley (D), a major in the U.S. Air Force stationed in France, was driving his car at high speeds when the car crashed, killing Aitchison, a passenger in the car. Under the North Atlantic Treaty, France had the primary right of jurisdiction but waived this right upon the request of U.S. authorities. When U.S. authorities decided not to proceed against D, Aitchison's wife brought suit against D in the French courts.

Issue: Pursuant to the NATO Status of Forces Agreement, if the authorities of a state waive their primary right of jurisdiction, may the right be reinstated if other states decline to exercise jurisdiction?

Rule: Once a state waives its primary right of jurisdiction, the right may not be reinstated even if other states decline to exercise jurisdiction.

United States v. The Watchmakers of Switzerland Information Center, Inc.
(U.S 1965) SOL

Facts: The United States charged a group of Swiss and American watchmakers with violating the Sherman Anti-Trust Act by forming a monopoly in the watch-making industry. The watchmakers claimed that the Act had no authority over acts that took place primarily in Switzerland.

Issue: May the United States extend its anti-trust laws to actions taking place in other countries?

Rule: A United States court may only apply the Sherman Anti-Trust Act to acts taking place in foreign countries if the acts have a substantial effect upon the foreign and domestic commerce of the United States.

Timberlane Lumber Co. v. Bank of America, N.T. and S.A.
(U.S. 1976) SOL

Facts: P charged the Bank of America with blocking the acquisition of a lumber mill in Honduras. The Bank defended itself using the act of state doctrine. The district court found the doctrine applicable and P appealed.

Issue: May U.S. courts apply U.S. antitrust laws to cases involving activities occurring abroad?

Rule: U.S. courts may apply U.S. antitrust law to cases involving extraterritorial activity provided that the following three factors are met: (1) the restraint affects or was intended to affect the foreign commerce of the U.S., (2) the restraint is of such a magnitude so as to be deemed a violation of the Sherman Act and, (3) the extraterritorial jurisdiction of the U.S. should be asserted as a matter of international comity and fairness.

Timberlane Lumber Co. v. Bank of America, N.T. and S.A.
(U.S. 1984) SOL

Facts: P brought an antitrust suit against Bank of America in Honduras. The Bank sought to dismiss the action on jurisdictional grounds.

Issue: May the United States assert its extraterritorial jurisdiction when doing so would be inconsistent with principles of international comity and fairness?

Rule: The U.S. may assert its extraterritorial jurisdiction only if doing so would be consistent with principles of international comity and fairness. In order to determine whether the U.S. may exercise its extraterritorial jurisdiction, the following factors must be considered: (1) the degree to which the foreign law conflicts with U.S. law; (2) the nationality of the parties; (3) the ability to enforce a judgement; (4) the relative effect of the outcome on the United States and the foreign state; (5) the presence of an overt effort to effect American commerce; (6) the foreseeability of such an effect; and (7) the situs of the alleged illegal conduct.

American Banana Co. v. United Fruit Co.
(S.Ct. 1909) SOL

Facts: D, a New Jersey corporation, took extensive steps to establish a monopoly in the Panamanian banana trade. P, an Alabama corporation trying to set up a rival business in Panama, was thwarted by the use of Costa Rican troops and other acts that violated American antitrust laws.

Issue: Do the antitrust laws of the United States apply to American companies doing business in foreign countries?

Rule: (Holmes, J.) Generally, the character of an act as lawful or unlawful must be determined by the law of the country where the act is done.

Bersch v. Drexel Firestone, Inc.
(U.S. 1975) SOL

Facts: Thousands of international plaintiffs brought a class action against Drexel Firestone. Alleging fraudulent acts committed abroad, the class wanted the favorable security laws of the United States applied.

Issue: May the U.S. apply its federal securities laws to cases primarily involving foreign acts?

Rule: There is subject matter jurisdiction of fraudulent acts relating to securities that are committed abroad only when these acts result in injury to purchasers or sellers of those securities in whom the United States has an interest, but not where acts simply have an adverse affect on the American economy or American investors generally.

IIT v. Vencap, Ltd.
(U.S. 1975) SOL

Facts: Several securities violations were allegedly committed in the United States by a group of foreign investors. The repercussions of the acts were felt almost solely outside of the United States.

Issue: May the United States claim jurisdiction over actions of foreign nationals that take place within the United States?

Rule: The United States may apply its securities law to acts that take place in its territory, even if the impact of those acts is felt almost exclusively outside of the United States.

Securities and Exchange Commission v. Kasser
(U.S. 1977) SOL

Facts: The SEC attempted to invoke the jurisdiction of the United States federal courts over defendants who allegedly engaged in fraudulent conduct within the United States. The district court dismissed the complaint, claiming that it had no subject matter jurisdiction since the acts had little, if any, impact in the United States.

Issue: May United States courts exercise jurisdiction over allegedly fraudulent acts within its borders when the sole victim of the acts is a foreign corporation and when the purported fraud had little, if any, impact in the United States?

Rule: Conduct within the United States is alone sufficient to apply federal statutes in U.S. courts to a foreign corporation's acts having little or no impact in the U.S.

United States v. First National City Bank
(U.S. 1968) SOL

Facts: Citibank was served with a subpoena requiring the production of documents from their New York and Frankfurt branches. They refused to comply with the demand to produce documents from their Frankfurt branches, claiming that doing so would subject them to civil and criminal liability in Germany.

Issue: When may a party caught in a conflict between the laws of two sovereign states refuse to comply with a subpoena from one of the states?

Rule: If a party will be subjected to criminal or severe civil liability under the laws of its state of residence, it may refuse to comply with a subpoena from another, even if the requesting nation is the state of the party's nationality.

Laker Airways Ltd. v. Sabena, Belgian World Airlines
& KLM, Royal Dutch Airlines
(U.S. 1984) SOL

Facts: Laker Airways brought an action against several rival airlines, claiming fraudulent antitrust business practices. When several of the defendants obtained a British injunction blocking Laker's action, Laker sought an injunction from a U.S. district court barring the rest of the defendants from obtaining foreign injunctions.

Issue: Do United States district courts have the authority to enjoin a foreign litigant from receiving from a foreign court an injunction that would remove the action from the jurisdiction of the United States?

Rule: In order to prevent a party from fleeing American jurisdiction, U.S. district courts may enjoin a foreign defendant from obtaining an injunction from a foreign court.

Chapter 11

IMMUNITY FROM JURISDICTION

I. THE IMMUNITY OF FOREIGN STATES

Originally, jurisdictional immunity of sovereign states was absolute. But, as states have become increasingly involved in international commercial activity, limitations on state immunity have developed. Communist and third world states cling more tightly to the notion of absolute sovereign immunity.

A. Absolute Sovereign Immunity

This form of immunity is based on the fundamental idea that all states are equal and that no state may exercise authority over any other. See *The Schooner Exchange*.

B. Restrictive Sovereign Immunity

1. The "Commercial" Exception
   While the jurisdictional immunity of a sovereign state is still recognized for public acts, it is no longer recognized for private commercial acts. There is a strong trend among nations toward recognizing this commercial restriction to state immunity.

2. Other Restrictions
   In cases in which a right to property in the United States acquired by succession or gift is in question, foreign states may not claim sovereign immunity. The same exception applies to cases involving noncommercial torts.

C. Waiver of Immunity

1. Generally
   The Foreign Sovereign Immunities Act of 1976 recognizes three kinds of waivers: (1) waiver of immunity from jurisdiction, (2) waiver of immunity from attachment in aid of execution or from

execution, and (3) waiver of immunity from attachment prior to the entry of judgment.

2. The Effect of an Arbitration Agreement

Generally, if a specific site and method for arbitration of disputes has been agreed upon in advance, sovereign immunity is deemed to be waived.

3. Counterclaims

If a foreign state brings an action in a U.S. court or intervenes in an action, it waives its right of immunity for all potential counterclaims.

D. The Nature of the Restrictions On Immunity

As the exceptions to absolute sovereign immunity have increased in number, it has remained unclear whether these exceptions apply to judicial jurisdiction, legislative jurisdiction, or both. The most widely accepted view is that denial of immunity from judicial jurisdiction implies an absence of immunity from legislative jurisdiction.

E. The Role of the Executive Branch

The Foreign Sovereign Immunities Act of 1976 limits, and possibly eliminates, the role of the Executive Branch in the adjudication of claims of sovereign immunity. The Attorney General's Office contends that the Executive Branch may still participate in these proceedings by appearing as an *amicus curiae*.

F. Procedural Problems

1. Judicial Competence

There has been some question about the constitutionality of the subject matter competence of federal district courts to hear sovereign immunity cases.

2. *In Personam* Competence
Personal jurisdiction over a foreign state is said to exist in any case in which the district court has jurisdiction over sovereign immunity cases. This blanket provision has often been questioned on constitutional grounds.

3. *In Rem* Competence
A foreign state is seen as having waived immunity from attachment of its property in cases where jurisdiction has already been established and the attachment is to secure satisfaction of a judgment entered against the foreign state.

4. Service of Process
Special problems often arise in serving process on foreign states.

G. Immunity From Execution

As with judicial and legislative jurisdiction, a restricted version of sovereign immunity has recently been applied to execution. See also *First National City Bank*.

H. Subdivisions and Instrumentalities of a State Enjoying Immunity

In order for an agency of a foreign state to qualify for immunity, it must be a separate legal person, a subdivision of the state, and not a citizen of the United States or any third country.

II.　IMMUNITIES OF STATE REPRESENTATIVES

A. Diplomatic Representatives

1. Generally
Diplomatic agents of a foreign state have long been viewed as immune from the operation of municipal law. The primary reason for this is that states should not be hampered in their foreign relations by the arrest or subpoena of their diplomatic agents.

2. Vienna Convention on Diplomatic Relations
   This Convention, observed by 149 states, declares that a diplomatic agent has the right of immunity unless it is expressly waived. Furthermore, the right is implied in the case of a counterclaim to a claim brought by the agent.

3. Diplomatic Relations Act
   This Act addresses domestic complaints about various privileges enjoyed and abused by diplomats, including exemption from property taxes and illegal parking.

B. Consuls

Originally, consuls were solely concerned with commercial activities and had no right of immunity. Recently, however, consular and diplomatic activities have become inextricably intertwined, and consuls are sometimes granted the same immunities as diplomatic agents.

C. Special Missions

Generally, an official representative of a foreign state on a limited diplomatic mission enjoys immunity to the extent necessary in relation to her official duties. See Restatement (Revised) § 462

D. Representatives to International Organizations

Representatives of the United Nations enjoy a full range of immunities when acting in their official capacity. In practice, the United States has limited the immunity of some representatives to a twenty-five mile radius of the United Nations against the wishes of their native states.

III. IMMUNITIES OF INTERNATIONAL ORGANIZATIONS

Like states, international organizations need immunities to carry out their official functions without the interference of domestic courts. Unlike states, however, international organizations do not have a long history of recognized sovereign authority or immunity.

This sometimes results in a reluctance by some domestic authorities to recognize the immunity of international organizations and their agents.

CASE CLIPS

Dralle v. Republic of Czechoslovakia
(Australia 1950) HPSS, SOL

Facts: P's branch office in Bohemia (which became part of Czechoslovakia) was nationalized by the Czech government. P, a German firm, sued for an injunction to keep the newly nationalized firm from using the mother company's trademarks in Austria.

Issue: May a foreign state claim sovereign immunity in matters governed by private law?

Rule: The principle of exemption of foreign states from municipal jurisdiction does not apply in cases where a state's involvement in commercial activity is at issue.

First National City Bank v. Banco Para
el Comercio Exterior de Cuba
(S.Ct. 1983) HPSS

Facts: The Banco Para El Comercio Exterior De Cuba, tried to collect on a debt owed them by D, First National City Bank. D and its assets had been nationalized by the Cuban government. P was later dissolved and liquidated by Cuba as well.

Issue: Is a corporation that has been absorbed by a sovereign nation considered a separate legal entity?

Rule: (O'Connor, J.) If recognizing a dissolved corporation as a separate legal entity would result in unfairness to parties having dealings with the corporation, the recognition of separateness will not be granted.

Arcaya v. Paez
(U.S. 1956) HPSS

Facts: P, a Venezuelan citizen living in the United States, sued the consul general of Venezuela. After the suit was brought, D was appointed to a permanent post at the United Nations and claimed immunity due to his new position.

Issue: Is a defendant who obtains diplomatic status entitled to immunity if the court has already obtained jurisdiction over him?

Rule: Immunity can not be generated from a change in the defendant's status after valid jurisdiction has been obtained.

Lutcher S.A. Celulose e Papel v. Inter-American Development Bank
(U.S. 1967) HPSS

Facts: P claimed that D violated loan agreements with it by granting loans to P's competitors.   P further claimed that D waived its immunity in the instrument of its formation.

Issue: May an international organization that is entitled to immunity from suit waive that immunity?

Rule: International organizations have the right to waive their immunity.

Aldona S. v. United Kingdom
(Poland 1948) SOL

Facts: P worked as a typist for a weekly English publication published in Cracow by the British Foreign Office. When P was fired from her job without being paid the money she was owed, she filed a claim in the District Court of Cracow.

Issue: If a foreign state recognizes immunity from jurisdiction of another state, must the latter state recognize immunity from jurisdiction of the former state?

Rule: Since the question concerning immunity from jurisdiction of foreign states is based on the principle of reciprocity, if the courts of one state recognize immunity from jurisdiction of foreign states, the latter states are obligated to recognize immunity of jurisdiction of the former state.

Krajina v. The Tass Agency
(England 1949) SOL

Facts: Ps sued the Tass Agency of Moscow for libel. Tass submitted documentation for its claim that it was a department of the Soviet State with the rights of a legal entity and thus that the doctrine of sovereign immunity should apply.

Issue: Does the doctrine of sovereign immunity apply to departments of a sovereign state even if the particular department has the rights of a legal entity?

Rule: The doctrine of sovereign immunity applies to departments of sovereign states even when the particular department has the rights of a juridical or legal entity.

Berizzi Bros. Co. v. The Pesaro
(S.Ct. 1926) SOL

Facts: When The Pesaro, a merchant vessel operated by the Italian government, was threatened with a suit for libel, the Italian government invoked the doctrine of sovereign immunity.

Issue: Are the principles of sovereign immunity applicable to a government-owned merchant vessel in the same manner that they are applicable to public vessels of war?

Rule: The principles of sovereign immunity are equally applicable to all ships held and used by a government for a public purpose. A ship used by a government to advance the trade of its people is a public ship in the same sense that war ships are.

Isbrandtsen Tankers, Inc. v. President of India
(U.S. 1971) SOL

Facts: P, a shipowner, brought suit against D for damages resulting from a delay in a shipment of grain. The State Department suggested that the court dismiss P's suit, and the court complied.

Issue: Are courts obligated to comply with a State Department request to invoke sovereign immunity?

Rule: The courts must comply with a State Department request to invoke sovereign immunity.

United States (Director of the
U.S. Foreign Service) v. Perignon and Others
(France 1962) SOL

Facts: Ps sued the U.S. for money owed to it pursuant to a contract for the construction of buildings for American citizens. P claimed that the contracts did not involve a public service or public power. D pleaded the jurisdictional immunity of foreign states and also claimed that the court lacked jurisdiction because of provisions in the contract giving competence for the settlement of disputes of the parties to the contracting officer and then to the United States Secretary of State.

Issue: Does the principle of sovereign immunity apply to situations involving the fulfillment of private interests and the performance of a private act?

Rule: The principle of sovereign immunity applies only to cases involving either public service or public power and does not apply where private interests are at issue.

De Ritis v. United States
(Italy 1971) SOL

Facts: De Ritis, an assistant librarian for the U.S. Information Agency, filed suit against her employer, the U.S., in the courts of Italy. De Ritis claimed that the principles of sovereign immunity did not apply to relations of a purely private-law character and that, while the U.S. Information Agency performs a public function in a foreign state, in the capacity as assistant librarian, she was not involved in the public function of the Agency.

Issue: May an employee of a state agency invoke the jurisdiction of the courts of a foreign state?

Rule: An employee of a state agency may not invoke the jurisdiction of the courts of a foreign state, even if her role in the agency is in a smaller and more specific field than that involving diplomatic or military activities.

Neger v. Etat de Hesse
(France 1969) SOL

Facts: Neger filed suit against the government of the Land of Hesse, a part of the Federal German Republic, for money owed to him. The Government of Hesse pleaded sovereign immunity because it performed sovereign acts.

Issue: Does the doctrine of sovereign immunity extend to a member state of a federation that does not have the status of a completely independent state ?

Rule: The doctrine of sovereign immunity does not extend to a state that does not have an autonomous legal personality of its own.

Société Nationale des Transports Routiers v.
Compagnie Algérienne de Transit et d'Affrétement
(France 1979) SOL

Facts: Compagnie Algérienne de Transit et D'Affrétement (CATA) sued Société Nationale des Transports Routiers (SNTR) in the French courts when the Algerian government stripped CATA of its assets in Algeria and vested them in SNTR.

Issue: Is an entity acting on behalf of a foreign state entitled to jurisdictional immunity where the act giving rise to the proceedings was an act of public power or an act performed in the interests of a public service?

Rule: An entity acting as a representative of a foreign sovereign state is not entitled to jurisdictional immunity if the entity retains its own legal personality, even where the act giving rise to the proceedings was an act of public power or an act performed in the interests of public service.

Vencedora Oceanica Navigacion v. Compagnie
Nationale Algérienne de Navigation
(U.S. 1984) SOL

Facts: P, a Panamanian corporation, brought an action against Compagnie Nationale Algérienne de Navigation (CNAN), an instrumentality of the Algerian government, and the Republic of Algeria to recover for the loss of its vessel. P brought this claim under the Foreign Sovereign Immunities Act of 1976 (28 U.S.C. § 1605), alleging that the court's jurisdiction was based on CNAN's unrelated continuing business in the U.S. and thus that it came within the "commercial activity" exception created by the second clause of § 1605(a)(2).

Issue: Does a U.S. court have subject matter jurisdiction over a cause of action that is unrelated to the defendant's business in the U.S.?

Rule: In order for a U.S. court to exercise jurisdiction under the "commercial activity" exception created by the Foreign Sovereign Immunities Act, there must be a nexus between the cause of action and the defendant's business in the U.S.

**Société Européenne d'Etudes et d'Entreprises en Liquidité
Volontaire v. Socialist Federal Republic of Yugoslavia
(Netherlands 1973) SOL**

Facts: The Société Européenne d'Etudes et d'Entreprises sought to enforce an arbitral award made in its favor against Yugoslavia and brought suit in the Dutch courts to obtain an exequatur for the award.

Issue: May a foreign state ever be required to submit to the jurisdiction of another state?

Rule: The doctrine of sovereign immunity is not absolute; there are situations that require a foreign state to submit to the jurisdiction of another state.

**Kingdom of Morocco v. Stiching Revalidate
Centrum "De Trappenberg"
(Netherlands 1978) SOL**

Facts: The daughter of the caretaker of the Moroccan Consulate-General at Amsterdam was injured at the consulate and incurred extensive medical bills at the rehabilitation center where she was treated. The rehabilitation center asked the Court for a garnishee order on funds held by Morocco at a bank in the Netherlands to secure the debt.

Issue: Does the doctrine of sovereign immunity apply where a sovereign state is liable in tort for an actor's omission and the state is acting in a private capacity?

Rule: Where a sovereign state is acting in a private capacity the doctrine of sovereign immunity does not apply.

**National Iranian Oil Company Revenues From Oil Sales Case
(Federal Republic of Germany 1983) SOL**

Facts: On the application of various British and American companies, the Provincial Court of Frankfurt am Main made various orders for the attachment of assets of the National Iranian Oil Company.

Issue: Under international law, is a forum state precluded from attaching the assets of a foreign state held within the forum state where the attachment serves to provide security for a legal claim brought against the foreign state?

Rule: Assets of a foreign state serving sovereign purposes may not be attached; however, a forum state may attach the assets of a foreign state to provide security for a legal claim brought against the foreign state.

Broadbent v. Organization of American States
(U.S. 1980) SOL

Facts: Ps, seven former staff members of the General Secretariat of the Organization of American States, alleged that they were improperly discharged and brought an action for breach of contract.

Issue: May the courts exercise jurisdiction over the claims of employees of international organizations?

Rule: The relationship of an international organization with its internal administrative staff is noncommercial and, thus, the courts may not exercise jurisdiction over an action by an employee of an international organization against that organization.

The Iran-United States Claims Tribunal v. A.S.
(Netherlands 1985) SOL

Facts: P, a Dutch national, was fired from his job as an interpreter and translator for the Iran-U.S. Claims Tribunal. The Tribunal was a joint institution of the two states and had a legal personality derived from international law.

Issue: Is the dismissal of an employee from an international organization included within the category of *acta jure imperii* (acts of the state)?

Rule: The action of an international organization in firing one of its employees who performed tasks essential to the function of the organization is considered to be *acta jure imperii*.

Radwan v. Radwan
(England 1972) SOL

Facts: D, an Egyptian national domiciled in England, entered the Egyptian Consulate where he divorced his wife in accordance with Egyptian law.

Issue: Are the premises of an embassy or consulate part of the territory of the sending state?

Rule: The overwhelming opinion of legal scholars, courts of law abroad, and international conventions is that diplomatic premises are not part of the territory of the sending state.

Immeuble de la rue de Civry v. Issakides and Konstantis (France 1966) SOL

Facts: P brought a civil action against Konstantis and Issakides concerning apartments they occupied. Konstantis, who was a NATO official, claimed diplomatic immunity.

Issue: Is there a distinction between the diplomatic immunity granted for acts performed in the exercise of a diplomat's mission and those of a private character?

Rule: In accordance with the Vienna Convention, acts performed both in the exercise of a diplomat's mission and those of a private character are protected under diplomatic immunity.

Case Concerning United States Diplomatic and Consular Staff in Teheran II (United States v. Iran) (ICJ 1980) HPSS, SOL

Facts: The United States instituted proceedings against Iran for its role in the seizure of the American Embassy in Teheran and the taking of American diplomatic personnel as hostages.

Issue: Is the seizure of the premises of a diplomatic mission and the taking of diplomatic personnel as hostages a justified remedy for abuses by members of the sending nation?

Rule: Even in the event of an armed conflict or a breach in diplomatic relations, the receiving state must respect the inviolability of diplomatic personnel and missions.

Seizure of Arms in Baggage of Diplomat in Transit (1974) SOL

Facts: Dutch customs officials discovered ammunition in the bag of a diplomat *en route* to his assignment in South America. The Israeli government believing the arms were to be used in organizing an attack upon its embassy in Brazil, protested the Dutch decision not to press charges.

Issue: Does immunity extend to diplomats in transit?

Rule: Although immunity is extended to diplomats in transit, it is subject to strict limitations and should not be granted to acts outside of official functions or to cases of a flagrant offense.

Regina v. Governor of Pentonville Prison, Ex parte Teja
(United Kingdom 1971) SOL

Facts: D, an Indian national, had been chairman of the board of an Indian company. He later served as "economic adviser to Costa Rica in special mission," thus, claiming diplomatic status. As part of his mission, D traveled to various European countries, including the United Kingdom, where he was arrested and held for extradition to India to face charges of criminal breach of trust.

Issue: Does diplomatic immunity automatically commence once the individual is conferred with diplomatic status or must the receiving nation first accept the foreign representative's diplomatic status in that country?

Rule: No immunity can be conferred by reason of status. The receiving nation must accept the representative of the sending country and recognize his diplomatic status.

Dame Nzie v. Vessah
(France 1978) SOL

Facts: According to both French and Cameroon law, P filed for divorced in French court. Her husband was a diplomat of Cameroon.

Issue: Must a sending state expressly waive its diplomatic immunity before a receiving state's court may adjudicate a divorce proceeding against a diplomat?

Rule: A sending state must expressly waive the immunity of its diplomat before a receiving state may try a case against the diplomat.

J.A. Helinski v. B.B. 't Hart
(Netherlands 1976) SOL

Facts: P, a foreign diplomat, brought a civil suit against his landlord in the receiving state's court.

Issue: May a diplomat initiate civil proceedings in a receiving state's courts against a citizen of a receiving state without a sending state's express consent?

Rule: Express consent is not needed from a sending state before its diplomat may institute civil proceedings, unless a receiving state has an explicit provision requiring such consent.

Abdulaziz v. Metropolitan Dade County
(United States 1984) SOL

Facts: Abdulaziz, a member of the Saudi Arabian ruling family, resided in the United States. Police officers searched his apartment after P was accused of holding an Egyptian woman against her will. A scuffle ensued at the apartment, and P brought a § 1983 action against the county and the parties involved. Ds then filed a counter suit. At the time P brought the suit, he did not have diplomatic status, though papers were subsequently filed qualifying P for diplomatic status.

Issue: Absent diplomatic status, are *special envoys* to a foreign country protected by the Diplomatic Relations Act?

Rule: According to the Diplomatic Relations Act, *special envoys* are granted full immunity, absent diplomatic status.

Status of Husband-In-Fact of Woman Diplomat
(Switzerland 1977) SOL

Facts: This action involved a ruling on whether the *de facto* husband of a diplomat from Switzerland had diplomatic immunity.

Issue: Is a spouse-in-fact considered a member of a diplomat's family to be granted the immunity extended to family members?

Rule: The preferred evaluation of "members of family" refers to the common household, thus, a spouse-in-fact is classified as a member of the family.

Status of Private Servant of Counselor of Embassy
(Austria 1971) SOL

Facts: A servant of a Greek diplomat challenged the jurisdiction of an Austrian court to hear a paternity suit, claiming that his status as a private servant of a diplomat entitled him to diplomatic immunity.

Issue: May diplomatic immunity be extended to the private servants of diplomats?

Rule: The private servants of diplomats do not enjoy diplomatic immunity.

Re Rissmann
(Italy 1970) SOL

Facts: The Italian government brought charges against Rissmann, Consul General for Germany in Genoa, for his role in helping a minor, with dual Italian-German citizenship, obtain a passport and leave Italy.

Issue: Is a consular official immune from prosecution for acts occurring within the scope of his duties?

Rule: Consular officials are exempt from prosecution for acts performed within the scope of their duties.

L. v. The Crown
(New Zealand 1977) SOL

Facts: L, a Vice-Counsel of a Pacific island country, was accused of sexually assaulting an applicant for a passport. L challenged the jurisdiction of the court to try the case, claiming diplomatic immunity.

Issue: Does the immunity granted to consular officials extend to criminal acts committed within the performance of official duties?

Rule: The immunity extended to a consular official is not a personal immunity, it is, rather, an immunity for the benefit of the sending state, limited to acts that properly occur in the course of the performance of consular duties, thus, excluding immunity for criminal acts.

People v. Leo
(United States 1978) SOL

Facts: D was a Tanzanian national employed by the United Nations as an Economic Affairs Officer. While working, D received a call from his wife advising him that a woman refused to leave their apartment despite requests that she do so. Upon his arrival, a scuffle broke out with the woman. D was arrested and charged with assault and resisting arrest. D challenged the court's jurisdiction, asserting diplomatic immunity.

Issue: What is the scope of the immunity granted employees of the United Nations?

Rule: The immunity granted to an employee of the United Nations is limited to acts committed in the course of accomplishing his functions.

United States ex rel. Casanova v. Fitzpatrick
(United States 1963) SOL

Facts: Casanova, a Cuban national, attaché, and Resident Member of the Staff of the Permanent Mission of Cuba to the United Nations, was arrested and charged with conspiracy to commit sabotage and violating the Foreign Agents Registration Act.

Issue 1: Does Article 105 of the United Nations Charter confer diplomatic immunity to representatives and staff members of United Nations Missions?

Rule 1: Article 105 of the United Nations Charter does not confer diplomatic immunity to representatives and staff members of U.N. missions.

Issue 2: Is the status of attaché and Resident Member of a United Nations mission an automatic entitlement to diplomatic immunity?

Rule 2: The United Nations Headquarters Agreement specifies that diplomatic immunity is accorded only after the U.N. Secretary-General, the Government of the United States, and the Government of the member state, concerned agree to confer the immunity.

Anonymous v. Anonymous
(United States 1964) SOL

Facts: P brought a paternity suit against D, an Ambassador to the U.S., and requested that the court issue an arrest warrant to prevent him from fleeing.

Issue: Does an Ambassador to the United Nations have the same immunity as a foreign diplomat accredited to the United States?

Rule: According to the United Nations Headquarters Agreement, an Ambassador to the United Nations has the same immunity as a foreign diplomat accredited to the United States.

Chapter 12

HUMAN RIGHTS

I. INTRODUCTION

Originally, international law was only concerned with the relations between sovereign states. The treatment of nationals by their government was solely the concern of domestic law. Events such as the death of slavery in the West, the U.S. response to nineteenth century Russian pogroms, and the world's horrible realization of the Holocaust are evidence of the international community's slow embrace of the nebulous idea that is now called "Human Rights."

II. UNIVERSAL HUMAN RIGHTS LAW

A. The Substantive Law of Human Rights

1. Charter of the United Nations

a. Article 55
This article is the heart of the Charter's stance on human rights. Generally, it states the U.N.'s objective to promote higher standards of living and universal respect for human rights without distinction as to race, sex, language, or religion.

b. Article 56
Members of the U.N. pledge to take the actions necessary to achieve the purposes of Article 55.

c. Problems
The weak and general nature of the language in the Charter has often led to unsuccessful attempts to invoke its provisions in U.S. courts. Yet, some suggest that many of the Charter's provisions have reached customary status in the international community.

2. The International Bill of Rights

    a. Universal Declaration of Human Rights
       Drafted by the General Assembly in 1948, this document sets out fundamental claims about human equality and the right of all people not to be discriminated against due to race, color, sex, language, religion, political or other opinion, national or social origin, property, birth or other status.

       i. Not a Treaty
          This declaration was passed by a vote of the General Assembly as a "common standard of achievement." As such, the declaration is not considered legally binding.

       ii. Authoritative Interpretation
          Despite its nonbinding nature, the declaration has come to represent the authoritative interpretation of human rights and is often viewed as customary international law.

    b. The Principle Covenants
       The Universal Declaration was divided into two principle covenants: the Covenant on Civil and Political Rights and the Covenant on Economic, Social, and Cultural Rights. This bifurcation allowed political-civil matters to be placed beneath the rubric of "rights," while socio-economic matters simply remained aspirations or plans.

3. Customary International Law of Human Rights
   A state violates customary international law if it practices, encourages, or condones genocide, slavery, murder, torture, prolonged arbitrary detention, or systematic racial discrimination. (Restatement (Revised) § 702).

    a. Invocation
       The Nuremberg Charter's charging of Nazi leaders with "crimes against humanity" marked one of the first times that the customary law of human rights was invoked in court.

b. Scope of the Restatement List
The Restatement list includes only those human rights whose status as customary law is most generally accepted. Rights not on the list that have gained widespread acceptance include the right against systematic religious or sexual discrimination and basic due process rights, such as appeal, impartial tribunal, counsel, and protection against self-incrimination oneself.

c. Departure from State Autonomy
The fundamental notion that states are subject to some minimum level of human rights obligations is contrary to the general unwillingness of international law to restrain state sovereignty.

d. Derogations From Rights in Emergencies
The Covenant on Civil and Political Rights provides that a state, if its very existence is threatened, may derogate from its obligations under the Covenant to the strict extent necessary in the particular situation. However, an "emergency" will not justify discrimination solely on the basis of race, color, sex, language, religion, or social origin. Derogations from guarantees to the right to life and against torture, slavery, and servitude are also prohibited.

B. Implementation and Enforcement of Human Rights

In general, enforcement of human rights law is more problematic than enforcement of other areas of international law. Where international law is generally observed, it is because violations directly affect state interests; conversely, human rights violations generally injure the inhabitants of the violating state.

1. International Agreements

a. Convention on the Prevention and Punishment of Genocide
Contracting parties may call upon departments of the U.N. to take whatever actions deemed appropriate for the

prevention of acts of genocide. However, no dispute under the Genocide Convention has ever reached the ICJ.

b. International Covenant on Civil and Political Rights

   i. Reports
Parties to the covenant submit reports on the measures they have taken to implement the rights recognized by the covenant. Included in the reports should be any observations or comments relating to the implementation of the relevant rights.

   ii. Human Rights Committee
This eighteen-member committee is the principal committee responsible for implementing the covenant's goals.

c. Optional Protocol to the International Covenant on Civil and Political Rights
By voluntary acceptance of this protocol, member states can accept the competence of the Human Rights Committee to receive and consider communications from individuals claiming to be victims of a human rights violation. States that are not members to the Protocol do not have their human rights matters submitted to the Committee.

d. International Covenant on Economic, Social and Cultural Rights

   i. Reports
As with the Covenant on Civil and Political Rights, members submit reports on the measures that they have adopted in achieving the observance of the rights enumerated in the Covenant.

   ii. Use of the Committee on Human Rights
The Economic and Social Council, formed as the administrative agency of the Covenant, also submits recommendations to the Committee on Human Rights.

e. Domestic Jurisdiction
Like the breach of any other international agreement, the breach of human rights agreements offers remedies to the wronged state. Human rights agreements are no less enforceable simply because they benefit third parties (the inhabitants of the countries party to the agreement) rather than the states themselves.

2. Individual Remedies Under International Agreements

a. Perspective One
A simple view of human rights agreements sees only arrangements between states. The only rights and duties are thus between the state-parties to the agreement.

b. Perspective Two
A second view of international human rights agreements would admit that individuals hold rights, but that these rights are only enforceable by interstate remedies. Here, an individual might have the ability to submit petitions to the appropriate arbitral bodies, but would be unable to receive personal reparations.

c. Perspective Three
A third perspective sees human rights agreements as giving individuals claims for any violations within their own society.

3. Enforcement of Customary Law of Human Rights

a. Remedies
Violations of customary human rights law generally entail remedies for the state and the individual that is victimized by the violation. Any state, regardless of its relation to the violation, may make a claim against the violating state.

b. Nationality of the Victim
The remedies available to all states for violations of customary laws of human rights are not dependent upon the

nationality of the victim. Although, it is most common for states to intervene on behalf of their own nationals or individuals with whom they have some connection.

c. Use of Force
The right of a state to intervene in another state, without its consent, with military force to prevent or put a stop to human rights abuses has not been agreed upon by a consensus of states.

d. Sanctions
A state may use trade, aid, or other national policy sanctions to criticize and dissociate itself from other nations that have violated the customary law of human rights.

e. Apartheid
The institution of apartheid as it exists in the Republic of South Africa has been the subject of special investigation by the Economic and Social Council. The Council found that apartheid, by its fundamental tenets, amounted to systemic discrimination and consequently violated customary law on human rights.

4. National Enforcement of International Human Rights Obligations
International law supplements the weak areas of various national laws on human rights protection, but it does not replace national institutions of administration and enforcement. Even though human rights are seen as universal, they are still, in their most fundamental form, claims of individuals against the state in which he lives.

a. Covenant on Civil and Political Rights
It is the obligation of each signatory state to ensure, to the extent possible, that no person within its territory suffers from a violation of the rights enumerated within the Covenant. Also, in the case of a violation, the state must provide the victim an effective remedy and procedural due process.

b. The Position of the United States
The U.S. is not a party to the Covenants or most other human rights conventions. However, aliens may, in some situations, obtain a remedy in U.S. courts for human rights violations by foreign officials. See *Filartiga v. Pena-Irala* and *Tel-Oren v. Libyan Arab Republic*.

III. REGIONAL HUMAN RIGHTS LAW

A. The European Human Rights System

The European Convention for the Protection of Human Rights and Fundamental Freedoms went into effect in 1953 establishing a major, comprehensive human rights program for Europe.

1. The Rights and Freedoms Protected

a. List of Rights
The substantive provisions of the European Convention include the right to life, freedom from torture, freedom from slavery, liberty and security of person, the right to a fair trial, respect for privacy and family life, freedom of thought and religion, freedom of expression and association, the right to marry, and freedom from invidious discrimination.

b. Comparison with the International Covenant
The European Convention contains no reference to a right of peoples to self-determination or "economic self-determination"; rights of persons belonging to ethnic, religious or linguistic minorities; the right to recognition everywhere as a person before the law; and the right to equality before the law and the equal protection of the law. All of these provisions are included in the International Covenant.

2. The System of Implementation and Enforcement

   a. The Basic Framework
     The elaborate administrative system of the European Convention consists of a department of inquiry and conciliation, the Commission, a political decision-making department, the Committee of Ministers of the Council of Europe, and a judicial department, the European Court of Human Rights.

   b. The European Court of Human Rights
     The court hears interstate complaints that are referred to it by the Committee of Ministers. Individuals have no independent standing, although they may appear before the court to aid in the presentation of a case.

   c. Committee of Ministers
     The Convention confers a judicial role upon the committee, a political group consisting of one representative for each member state of the Council of Europe. The committee takes a case if the Human Rights Commission fails to resolve a dispute and the matter is not referred to the European Court.

   d. The European Commission of Human Rights
     The commission is comprised of twenty-one members, with no more than one member per state. The commission is the group to which all claims introduced by a state party or an individual must first be submitted.

3. The European Social Charter

   a. In General
     Parties to the Charter resolve "to make every effort in common to improve the standard of living and to promote the social well-being of both their urban and rural populations by means of appropriate institutions and actions."

b. Requirements
Each state must select a specified number of social rights
with which they agree to comply.

c. Enforcement
Reports to the Committee of Ministers must be made at
two-year intervals by each state party to the Charter.

B. The Inter-American Human Rights System

The Western Hemisphere has taken a keen interest in human
rights law ever since the shocking events surrounding the end of
the Second World War. The Charter of the Organization of
American States says that, "[States] shall respect the rights of the
individual and the principles of universal morality." These have
been seen as legally binding words.

1. The Rights and Freedoms Protected
The American Declaration and the American Convention
closely parallel the Universal Declaration and the International
Covenant on Civil and Political Rights. However, unlike the
latter two documents, the American Declaration recognizes the
right of reply to anyone injured by inaccurate or offensive
statements as well as the right of asylum.

2. Implementation of Human Rights in the Inter-American System
The Inter-American Commission of Human Rights is the
primary administrative agency of the American Human Rights
System. The Commission has read its mandate very broadly, but
has met with mixed success in actually implementing its ambitious goals of human rights recognition.

C. The African Human Rights System

In 1979, the Organization of African Unity drafted an African
Charter on Human and Peoples' Rights. It is now popularly called
the Banjul Charter.

1. The List of Rights and Freedoms Protected
   The Charter protects the right to equal protection of the law;
   the right to life; freedom from slavery, torture, and cruel,
   inhuman or degrading punishment and treatment; the right to
   liberty and freedom from arbitrary arrest or detention; the
   presumption of innocence in a criminal trial and the right to
   counsel; freedom of conscience, profession, religion, expression,
   association, assembly, and movement; the right to leave and
   return to one's own country; the right to seek and obtain asylum
   when persecuted; the right to participate freely in government;
   the right to property; the right to work under equitable and
   satisfactory condition; the right to enjoy the best attainable state
   of physical and mental health; the right to an education;
   freedom from discrimination; and against prohibition of mass
   expulsion of aliens.

2. The System of Implementation and Enforcement
   The African Commission of Human and Peoples' Rights was
   established by the Charter to promote and ensure protection of
   human rights in Africa.

CASE CLIPS

Lawless Case
(1961) HPSS

Facts: Ireland detained a member of the IRA, without charge or trial,
at a time when increased terrorism had led to a state of national
emergency.

Issue: When does a state of emergency warrant incarceration of an
individual without charge or trial?

Rule: In the event that a public emergency is an exceptional
situation of crisis, effects the whole population, and constitutes a
serious threat to the organized life of the community of the state, a
state may detain individuals without trial if the response is strictly
limited to that which is required by the situation at the time.

Roberts (United States) v. United Mexican States
(1926) SOL

Facts: Roberts was arrested in Mexico and held without a trial for a period exceeding the constitutional limit.

Issue 1: Do an arresting country's constitutional standards regarding the minimum time a prisoner may be held without a trial apply when the prisoner is an alien?

Rule 1 : An alien prisoner must be tried for crimes according to the same standards that are applicable to that state's citizens.

Issue 2: What are the standards of treatment established by international law regarding prison conditions?

Rule 2: Prison conditions are required to meet the ordinary standards of treatment recognized by civilization.

Cantero Herrera v. Canevaro & Co.
(Peru 1927) SOL

Facts: After P lost an appeal in Peruvian courts, the Cuban envoy wrote a letter requesting that the Peruvian government overturn the decision.

Issue: May a state justify diplomatic intervention on behalf of its citizens challenging a judgment in foreign civil proceedings?

Rule: Except in instances of extreme denial of justice, the general rule is that a nation should refrain from diplomatic intervention that challenges the legitimacy of a foreign state's judgment.

Chattin (United States) v. United Mexican States
(1927) HPSS, SOL

Facts: The Mexican government arrested Chattin for embezzlement. P charged that the government violated his right to a fair trial and subjected him to cruel and inhumane treatment.

Issue: Is a state responsible to aliens for holding proceedings and establishing prison conditions that sink below minimum international standards?

Rule: A state is liable for failing to maintain minimum international standards of a fair trial and prison conditions.

Dissent: A state should not have to account for minor variations of international judicial standards.

Neer and Neer (United States) v. United Mexican States
(1926) SOL

Facts: After the murder of Neer in Mexico, his wife and daughter brought a suit charging the Mexican government with lack of diligence in the investigation and prosecution of the murderers.

Issue: Under what circumstances would an international tribunal charge a state with delinquent criminal proceedings?

Rule: Outrageous conduct, bad faith, willful neglect of a state's duties, or insufficiency of governmental action to the extent that it does not meet recognized international standards are circumstances that justify an international tribunal in charging a state with delinquent criminal proceedings.

Advisory Opinion on the Continued Presence of
South Africa in Namibia (South West Africa)
(ICJ 1971) HPSS, SOL

Facts: After World War I, South Africa occupied Namibia pursuant to the Covenant of the League of Nations. Subsequently, the United Nations declared South Africa's presence in Namibia illegal and called upon the member states to act accordingly.

Issue: Does the denial of human rights and the suppression of freedom to particular segments of society violate the purposes and principles of the U.N. charter?

Rule: Distinctions, exclusions, restrictions, and limitations exclusively based on race, color, descent, or national or ethnic origin violate the purposes and principles of the U.N. charter.

South West Africa Cases
(Ethiopia v. South Africa; Liberia v. South Africa)
(ICJ 1986) SOL

Facts: Ethiopia and Liberia brought this action seeking either to compel South Africa's compliance with the League of Nations Mandate for South West Africa or initiate the dissolution of the Mandate.

Issue: Are humanitarian considerations sufficient to create a legal right in an unaffected member state of the United Nations thereby permitting them to bring a cause of action against a state allegedly acting inhumanly?

Rule: A state has jurisdiction to bring a cause of action against another state only if it has a genuine interest or is a party to an obligation the defendant state breached.

Dissent: The Genocide Convention recognizes the right of states without a specific interest to turn to the ICJ for interpretation, application, or fulfillment of a treaty having a humanitarian interest.

Advisory Opinion on the Western Sahara
(ICJ 1975) HPSS, SOL

Facts: The United Nations General Assembly requested an advisory opinion on claims by Morocco and Mauritania to the former Spanish colony of Western Sahara.

Issue: When the U.N. requests an advisory opinion regarding a territorial dispute from the ICJ, must the ICJ obtain consent from the effected state?

Rule: The ICJ does not need to obtain consent from the affected state to give an advisory opinion regarding a territorial dispute.

Sendic v. Uruguay
(1981) SOL

Facts: The Uruguay government arrested Raul Antonaccio. He was subjected to torturous prison conditions and denied contact with family, counsel, and U.N. human rights observers.

Issue: Does a state have the right to subject a political prisoner torturous prison conditions or to hold him incommunicado?

Rule: Political prisoners may not be subjected to torturous prison conditions, nor may they be held incommunicado.

Salgar de Montejo v. Colombia
(1982) SOL

Facts: The Colombian government convicted Salgar de Montejo for illegally selling a gun. The government denied de Montejo the right to appeal, justifying its action by declaring a state of siege.

Issue: Is the denial of the right to appeal a human rights violation?

Rule: A state is, at all times, obligated to grant an individual the right to appeal a conviction and failure to do so is a human rights violation.

Filartiga v. Pena-Irala
(U.S. 1980) SOL

Facts: P brought an action in tort against D for wrongfully causing the death of his son Joelito Filartiga, who D kidnapped and tortured.

Issue 1: Does international law prohibit "official torture"?

Rule 1: International consensus recognizes basic human rights and obligations including the right to be free from "official torture."

Issue 2: May U.S. courts adjudicate tort actions brought by foreign individuals against foreigners?

Rule 2: U.S. courts may adjudicate tort actions brought by foreigners against foreigners. Under 28 U.S.C.§ 1350, U.S. courts have jurisdiction on all actions where an alien brings a tort action and alleges a violation of international law.

Tel-Oren v. Libyan Arab Republic
(U.S. 1984) SOL

Facts: Ps, survivors and representatives of persons murdered in a terrorist attack in Israel, brought suit in a federal district court against the Palestinian Liberation Organization. Ps asserted jurisdiction under 28 U.S.C. § 1350, which confers jurisdiction over actions by an alien alleging a tort committed in violation of the law of nations or a treaty of the U.S.

Issue: Do U.S. courts have jurisdiction over civil actions between foreign nationals occurring in a foreign state?

Rule: Rule not provided.

Concurrence: (Edwards, J.) Although 28 U.S.C. § 1350 gives aliens the right to sue in federal court for violations of international law occurring on foreign territory, this right arises only where the violation is perpetrated by a party that, unlike here, is recognized by the community of nations or a state official acting under color of state law.

Concurrence: (Bork, J.) There must be an explicit grant of a private right of action in order for a plaintiff to plead principles of international law in a federal court.

Concurrence: (Robb, J.) This case presents a nonjusticiable political question.

Case of Ireland v. The United Kingdom
(1978) SOL

Facts: In response to increasing Irish Republican Army violence, the United Kingdom instituted extrajudicial detention procedures. Additionally, the authorities instituted "disorientation" or "sensory deprivation" techniques that consisted of wall-standing, hooding, subjection to noise, and deprivation of sleep, food, and drink. These techniques were later renounced.

Issue 1: Should the European Court decline to decide the legality of a practice when the practice has been renounced?

Rule 1: Because one of the European Court's functions is to safeguard and develop rules that contribute to the observance by states of obligations undertaken as contracting parties, the Court should decide the legality of a practice even though a practice has been renounced.

Issue 2: What factors determine whether an interrogation technique will be classified as torture or cruel and inhuman treatment?

Rule 2: In determining whether an interrogation technique is classified as torture, a court will look to the intensity of the suffering inflicted. The court will classify the technique as torturous if the severity of the technique was such that it deliberately caused very serious and cruel suffering.

Issue 3: Does the European Court have the power to direct a state to institute criminal or disciplinary proceedings against members of its security forces who have violated human rights?

Rule 3: The European Court does not have the power to direct a state to institute criminal or disciplinary proceedings against violators of human rights.

Dudgeon Case
(1981) SOL

Facts: Dudgeon asserted that laws enacted in the United Kingdom against consensual homosexual conduct between adults violated the Convention for the Protection of Human Rights and Fundamental Freedoms.

Issue: Do laws infringing upon an individual's right to privacy violate the Convention for the Protection of Human Rights and Fundamental Freedoms?

Rule: According to Article 8 of the Convention, a state may not interfere with an individual's right to privacy. Consequently, there is a duty to respect freedom of choice regarding one's private sex life.

Advisory Opinion On Compulsory Membership In
An Association
(1985) SOL

Facts: Costa Rica sought an advisory opinion from the Inter-American Court on Human Rights on the validity of a law prescribing compulsory membership in a journalist association.

Issue: May a state seek an advisory opinion on an issue that is related to an issue that is being adjudicated in another forum?

Rule: A state may seek an advisory opinion on a issue that is related to an issue that is being adjudicated in another forum.

Chapter 13

RESPONSIBILITY FOR INJURY TO ALIENS

I. CONFLICTING VIEWS ON BASIC PRINCIPLES

A. Basic Principles

1. Subjection to Local Law
   A national of one state who enters into the territory of another state becomes subject to the local laws of that state.

2. When State Responsibility Arises for Injury to an Alien
   A state is responsible for the injury of an alien when:

   a. Acts
      The state injures the alien through its actions; or

   b. Omissions
      An alien is injured within the state's territory by non-state action and the state fails to provide effective local remedies for the alien's loss.

   c. International Minimum Standard of Justice
      Unless the legal system falls below international standards, the minimum standard of justice is met where an alien and national benefit equally from the state's laws.

B. The International Minimum Standard of Justice and the Principle of Equality

1. Hull Doctrine
   The United States contends that there is a ground for complaint regarding treatment of aliens by a nation if that nation's domestic legal system falls below an international standard. In

this context, it asserts that the international standard for compensation to aliens in the case of nationalization of their property requires adequate, effective, and prompt compensation.

2. Calvo Doctrine — Equality of Treatment
Mexico contends that international law does not require minimum standards of justice, but rather that an alien who voluntarily subjects himself to the law of a nation be treated on a basis legally equal to nationals. Therefore, in the context of compensation for the nationalization of property, international law allows the state to determine, by its internal law, the time and manner in which compensation is to be made, as long as aliens are not discriminated against on the basis of their alienage.

3. Conflict between First and Third World
The distinction between the Calvo and Hull Doctrines illustrates the conflict between first and third world nations. The third world nations assert that they are in a disadvantaged position due to exploitation by the first world and its multinational corporations. Further, they contend that they should not be expected to sacrifice their much needed economic development to reach standards that only the first world can afford.

C. Protection of Nationals Abroad
There has been considerable controversy between the first and third worlds over the protection of nationals abroad. While the Permanent Court of International Justice claimed that diplomatic protection was a fundamental principle of international law, several U.N. resolutions have disagreed.

1. First World
Customary law requires states to adhere to an international minimum standard of justice in their treatment of aliens, or face international responsibility for their actions. This is supported by the development of human rights and humanitarian law.

2. Third World
   In the third world, there is no international minimum standard of justice, but customary international law requires that state sovereignty may not be infringed.

   a. No Principle of State Espousal of Claims
      There is no international principle that requires a state to espouse the claim of one of its nationals abroad. If done, it is merely custom and is rapidly being undermined by the development of the right of the individual to make claims on his own behalf.

   b. Principles of State Sovereignty

      i. Sovereign Equality
         The sovereign equality of states entitles a state to be free from any interference by other states regarding matters within its territory.

      ii. Alien Equality
          Aliens are entitled to no greater rights than nationals. Aliens that voluntarily avail themselves of the benefits of a forum must accept its limitations.

      iii. National Courts
           National courts have exclusive jurisdiction over all matters within their territory.

3. Socialist States
   Socialist states have adopted the position of the third world that there is no international minimum standard of compensation and that this falls entirely within domestic jurisdiction. They have also taken the position that equality of treatment between national and alien corporations is not compatible with the socialist system.

D. Treatment of Alien Property

The third world maintains that the present international economic order, in which third world countries account for 70 percent of the world's population and only 30 percent of the world's wealth, is due to the colonialist domination of the first world and may only be redressed by allowing nations complete sovereignty over all property and resources within their territory.

II.   CONDITIONS AND PROCEDURAL ASPECTS OF ASSERTION OF A CLAIM

A. General Considerations

1. Who Can Bring International Claims

   a. Traditional Law
   An individual cannot bring a claim against a state in an international tribunal, only states may bring such claims. However, the injured person generally has the right to request that the state of her origin intercede on her behalf to present a claim for any injury she has suffered due to acts or omissions (such as failure to redress an injury caused by a private person) of the foreign state that are violative of international law. The theory is that, although the individual is harmed, the injury is to the state of which that individual is a national.

   b. Human Rights Standards
   As human rights law develops, states are beginning to invoke international human rights standards as a basis for state claims for injury. It is also becoming a basis for claims brought by the individual on his own behalf.

2. No Duty of State to Espouse Claim
   International law does not impose a duty on a state to espouse the claim of its injured national.

3. State Control
   If a state does choose to espouse a claim, it has complete and exclusive control over the claim.

4. Measure of Compensation
   The measure of compensation is based on the injury to the individual, rather that the injury to the state.

B. Duty to Exhaust Local Remedies

The individual has a duty to exhaust local remedies before his state of origin can espouse the claim and before he can resort to international law.

1. Requirements
   Before remedies may be considered exhausted, all contentions of fact and law must have been raised at the municipal level.

2. Claims that are Bound to Fail

   a. Procedural Grounds
      If an appeal is bound to fail under domestic law on procedural grounds, the right to appeal is not an effective remedy and need not be exhausted.

   b. Well-Settled Point of Law
      If an alien loses on a point of law in the national court of first instance and the appellate courts regard the point as well settled, the alien must still appeal unless the highest court in the country had also made a pronouncement on that issue effectively precluding successful appeal.

3. Involuntary Contacts Exception
   The local remedies rule is inapplicable where the injured aliens have established no voluntary contacts with the injuring state (e.g., a state accidently sinks a cruise ship with a misfired missile).

4. Dominant State Claim
The local remedies rule is also inapplicable where the state of the alien's nationality is bringing a separate and dominant claim on its own behalf arising out of the same facts.

5. Waiver
A state may waive the requirement of exhaustion of its local remedies and allow an alien to go directly to an international court.

C. Waiver By Individual Claimant

If an injured alien waives or settles a claim under domestic law, this is a defense on behalf of the respondent state to a subsequent claim under international law.

1. Calvo Clause
Many third-world states have Calvo Clauses in their law that state that every foreigner who establishes voluntary contact with the state waives all international claims and agrees to submit herself to national tribunals. There is a controversy over whether this merely restates the exhaustion of domestic remedies rule or goes beyond.

2. United States and First World Position — No Waiver
Many first-world states, as well as the International Court of Justice, maintain that the right of protection by a state of its nationals is an immutable right of the individual.

a. Logic
First-world states claim that this is a right of the state to grant as a result of citizenship and that denial of this right to an individual is an infringement on the rights of the state.

b. Flaw in Logic
However, individuals can waive or settle claims as a result of submission to domestic remedies and, thereby, deny their state of origin the right to bring the claim since the state's claim is derivative of the individual's claim.

D. Nationality of Claimant

1. Corporations
   The traditional rule is that a corporation's nationality is of the country where it has been incorporated and where it has its registered office. However, there is no absolute test of corporate nationality that has been generally accepted. There must be minimum contacts between the state and the corporation, such as: incorporation under domestic law, corporate offices on domestic territory, or a majority of stockholders of domestic nationality. However, none of these alone are dispositive.

2. Corporate Claims
   When an unlawful act has been committed against a company representing foreign capital, the state of the company alone has the right to bring a claim.

3. Shareholder's Rights
   Generally, the only time a country may sue on behalf of its nationals who are shareholders in a foreign corporation is when the foreign country in which the corporation was incorporated caused the corporation's injury.

4. Employees of International Organizations
   International law recognizes parallel rights of protection in the case of an individual serving an international organization.

E. Attribution of Conduct to a State

When any person concerned with the discharge of government functions at any level improperly discharges his functions and this results in a failure of the nation to abide by its obligations under international law, the state is responsible for these actions.

1. Actions in Excess of State Authority
   Any subdivision of the state, even if it has exceeded its authority or violated specific instructions, may create international responsibility for the state.

2. Non-State Entities
The state is responsible for the actions of those entities that are not subdivisions of the state but have been empowered to exercise functions of the kind normally exercised by government officials. It is also responsible for private persons employed by the state, such as mercenaries.

F. Circumstances under Which Otherwise Unlawful Conduct Does Not Give Rise to International Responsibility

1. Circumstances
Circumstances such as necessity and *force majeure* (natural disasters) may make conduct, which would otherwise result in international responsibility, permissible. Also, acts that are necessary to protect currency or foreign exchange are usually permissible even if they violate international responsibility.

2. Permissibility Requirements
According to the Restatement (Second), in order for acts that would normally violate international responsibility to be permissible, they must be:

a. Reasonably Necessary
Reasonably necessary to achieve an objective;

b. Consistent with Standards
Consistent with international standards; and

c. Nondiscriminatory
Not unreasonably discriminatory against the nationals of a foreign state.

III.   SUBSTANTIVE BASES OF RESPONSIBILITY

A. General

1. Human Rights
International customary law creates state responsibility for violations of human rights caused by an official act or omission.

    a. Civil and Political Rights Based on Citizenship
Customary law does not create state responsibility for the guarantee of rights that are based on a person's citizenship, such as the right to vote and hold office.

    b. Civil and Political Rights of All Humans
Customary law does create state responsibility for the guarantee of rights that are based on the dignity of the human being, such as the right to life and freedom from persecution.

2. Denials of Justice
Customary law also creates state responsibility for violations of due process protections and the failure to provide legal remedies.

3. Property and Economic Interests
There is no agreement between the third and first worlds on whether property or economic interests that are infringed due to acts or omissions of the state create international liability for the state. Customary law does not grant these rights, but it does forbid unreasonable discrimination between aliens and nationals.

B. Failure to Protect Aliens or Apprehend Defendants

1. Due Diligence — Prevention
International law requires states to provide adequate police protection to prevent injuries to aliens.

    a. Special Protection — Prior Constructive Notice
A state must have prior constructive notice that there is a need for special protection. A number of similar crimes or terrorist acts in the past constitutes prima facie notice, as does a high level of lawlessness in an area.

 b. Measures

 The required measures taken to prevent injuries to, or crimes against, aliens must be reasonable under the circumstances. This takes into account a lack of resources on the part of any state to prevent all crimes.

2. Due Diligence — Apprehension

 International law requires states to take prompt and efficient action to apprehend a private individual who has caused injury to an alien. It does not require a state to succeed in its attempt to redress the injury.

3. Prosecution

 As long as due process is observed, the state is under a duty to prosecute, but not to convict.

4. Punishment

 The punishment must not be disproportionate to the crime committed.

5. Extradition

 International law does not impose a duty of extradition in the absence of a treaty.

6. Terrorists

 a. Support or Complicity

 A state is internationally responsible if it supports or complies with terrorists.

 b. Encouraging

 A state is only internationally responsible for encouraging terrorists if a causal link can be established between the encouragement and a terrorist act.

c. Prevention

    i. Identity of Assailant
The state is not responsible for inability to prevent an injury if the identity of the assailant cannot be ascertained.

    ii. Suddenness of Act
If an act is sudden and unexpected, the state will be presumed to not have had constructive notice.

d. Punishment or Extradition
A state is not always internationally responsible for the punishment or extradition of terrorists in the absence of a treaty. While a state will be responsible for exercising due diligence regarding the apprehension and punishment of terrorists who both committed acts and are based in its territory, it is not necessarily responsible for terrorists who committed acts abroad and fled into its territory.

C. Denial of Procedural Justice

Although states are internationally liable for its denial, procedural justice is not clearly defined under international law. Denial of procedural justice is generally deemed to include denial of: (1) an interpreter; (2) information about the charges against a defendant; (3) the opportunity to confront the witnesses against a defendant; and (4) access to counsel or the representatives of one's government. Furthermore, any treatment of an alien that violates international law, departs from generally accepted standards of substantive law, or fails to afford an adequate remedy constitutes a denial of procedural due process.

D. Injury to Economic Interests of Aliens

1. Non-Commercial Risk
Examples of non-commercial risk are nationalization of assets without proper compensation, imposition of foreign exchange

restrictions that prevent remittance of profits abroad, and import restrictions that prevent the acquiring of necessary equipment or raw materials.

a. Creeping Expropriation

Creeping expropriation is the use of subtle measures that hinder the operations of a foreign corporation until it eventually can no longer operate. Examples of this are delays in the granting of necessary permits or taxes that constitute *de facto* discrimination against aliens.

b. Intangible Property

Non-commercial risks pose a particular problem in relation to intangible patent or intellectual property rights that the foreign company may have lost due to nationalization.

c. Letter of Credit

Transactions or loans that are not conducted with an irrevocable letter of credit are in danger of default of payment due to lack of foreign currency, payment in inconvertible currency, or refusal to pay.

2. Protection Against Non-Commercial Risk

a. Special Assurances – National Protection

Most developing countries grant special assurances to foreign investors against these non-commercial risks. The grave need for foreign capital has prompted this contradiction of the Calvo Doctrine, in the form of broad based incentive programs to encourage foreign investment. These assurances are usually given on an *ad hoc* basis in concession or guarantee agreements or through instruments of foreign investment approval. In addition to such assurances, incentive programs often contain favorable tax and tariff plans. Examples of special assurances are guarantees of the ability to repatriate profits and capital; the availability of foreign currency to repay loans or pay royalties; and the ability to bring in key materials and personnel from abroad.

b. Protection By International Law
Most protection is in the form of bilateral treaties as the dispute between the third and first worlds over the legality of nationalization of foreign assets indicates. Customary law offers little protection.

3. Expropriation of Alien's Property

a. What Constitutes a Taking
As previously stated, there is a dispute over the legality of takings (See § I,B above). Some takings are always violations of international law, such as takings in violation of a treaty.

i. Constructive Taking (Creeping Expropriation)
A constructive taking is interference with property rights that amounts to less than an outright expropriation, but denies the alien of effective ability to benefit or use his property. The Restatement Revised § 712 regards this as a constructive taking, even if it is only for a short period of time.

ii. Overseas Private Investment Corporation (OPIC)
The OPIC program, which is sponsored by the United States government to encourage foreign investment by providing insurance against non-commercial risk to all American investors willing to invest abroad, defines a taking as any foreign action condoned by the government that has the effect of depriving the foreign investor of exercising effective control over a substantial amount of his property for a period of a year or more.

iii. Not A Constructive Taking
Any exercise of state power that is reasonable and in pursuance of its power to regulate public order, health, safety, currency, fiscal matters, taxes, interest rates, or foreign exchange is not a constructive taking no matter how it alters rights of aliens. Generally, the word of a

head of state that an action was necessary to protect state fiscal matters is beyond dispute.

b. For a Public Purpose

International law requires that takings must be for a public purpose. This requirement was included in General Assembly Resolution 1803 on Permanent Sovereignty of Natural Resources and has probably reached the status of customary law. However, there is no clearly defined international standard as to what constitutes a public purpose. It should be noted that nationalizations that are not for economically sound reasons occur frequently, apparently to alter the balance of power between less-developed countries and multinational corporations.

c. Nondiscriminatory

International law requires that takings must not discriminate against a particular class of aliens. Discrimination must not be unreasonable or arbitrary. Discrimination may be deemed legitimate if it is necessary to accomplish a specific and legitimate public purpose that could not otherwise be accomplished.

   i. Political Purpose

   If the purpose is political, such as the retaliation against the homeland of certain aliens, or is based on prejudice against a social group, the taking is not legitimate.

   ii. Economic Purpose

   If the discrimination is due to economic reasons, it is probably legitimate.

d. Compensation

International law requires that some compensation must be paid in the event of a taking of an alien's property. As previously stated, there is a dispute as to the amount of compensation required under international law. (See § I,B above).

i.   Just Compensation
The Revised Restatement § 712 requires that the amount of compensation must be an amount equivalent to the fair market value of the property at the time of the taking and must be paid at the time of the taking or in a reasonable time, with interest. It is unclear to what extent just compensation should reflect lost profits and other intangibles, such as technical expertise.

ii.   Exceptions to the Just Compensation Rule
Takings resulting from damage during war are valid without the requirement for just compensation if they are incidental to the act of war. Takings on the ground of land reform programs may be deferred, although the total amount of payment may not thereby be reduced.

iii.   Invalid Just Compensation Exceptions
According to the Revised Restatement § 188, exceptions are not valid when: the alien company was specifically encouraged or authorized by the state to locate within the state; the company taken is not dismantled, but run by the state; or takings did not apply equally to nationals. Takings of neutral vessels or of alien property during war must be compensated if the taking is intended to promote the war effort, even if justified by necessity.

iv.   Appropriate Compensation
Appropriate compensation under the circumstances is an alternative to just compensation and is more widely accepted. This does not require full compensation in all cases, but rather an inquiry into all of the circumstances of an expropriation. It includes the principle of unjust enrichment of an alien corporation that may have unfairly reaped benefits at the expense of its host nation while it was in operation.

4. Breach by a State of an Agreement with an Alien
   While a state is responsible for injuries caused to aliens, aliens do not have the same rights under contracts that foreign states do under treaty law.

   a. *Pacta Sunt Servada*
      By the doctrine of *pacta sunt servada*, international law generally requires states to honor their agreements with aliens. However, there are exceptions.

   b. Contractual Breaches as Violations
      Contractual breaches are violations of international law only if they are arbitrary. They are arbitrary if the following criteria are met:

      i. Departure From Governing Law
         The breach clearly departs from the law of the state or the law governing the contract;

      ii. Departure From Contract Law
          The breach is an unreasonable departure from the principles of contract law; and

      iii. Violation
           The breach amounts to a violation of a treaty.

   c. Non-Violating Contractual Breaches
      Breach of contract is not a violation of international law if it results from an inability to perform due to a dispute about the nature of the performance required by the contract or is motivated by commercial considerations and the state is willing to pay damages.

   d. Individual Rights and Capacity
      Individuals have rights under international law, although they cannot invoke these rights because their capacity as a subject of international law is limited. The international capacity of the individual depends on the recognition granted to him by

the state in its legal relations with him (See § III,D,4,f,(3), below).

e. Determining Breach
To determine whether there has been a contractual breach, it is necessary to look to the contracting parties' choice of law.

    i. Choice of Law
International law guarantees the parties to any contract made under international law the right to choose the law that will govern the contract. They may choose the law of the state of one of the parties, principles common to the nations of each of the parties, international law, or a combination thereof.

    ii. No Choice of Law
International law looks to the law of the state to which the contract has the closest connections if the parties do not designate a choice of law.

    iii. Choice of International Tribunal
The choice of an international tribunal in reference to the resolution of disputes indicates a rejection of the presumption in favor of the municipal law of one of the contracting states and may indicate rights on the part of the individual to international remedies, rather than the intervention of his state of origin on his behalf.

    iv. General Principles of Law
Reference to general principles of law always signifies the internationalization of a contract.

f. Stabilization Clauses
Stabilization clauses stabilize the positions of the contracting parties *vis-à-vis* each other. They do not impair state sovereignty, but represent an agreement on the part of the state not to legislate in a manner that would impair the

operation of the other parties to the contract. A nationalization in breach of such a clause is a breach of good faith under international law and may result in a remedy of restitution or specific performance.

g. Contracts that Can Be Amended Unilaterally
Administrative contracts can be amended unilaterally by a state. The following are characteristics of an administrative contract:

    i.   Management Objective
    The object of the contract is the management of a public service.

    ii.   Administrative Capacity
    The administrative authority in control of that particular service entered into contract in its administrative capacity.

    iii.   Unusual Rights Granted
    The contract specifically confers rights, such as the right to unilateral amendment, that are not usually found in a civil contract.

h. Economic Development Contracts
Economic development contracts are contracts that are: (1) long term; (2) concerned with close relationships between the host state and the investor; and (3) require permanent installations and technical assistance rather than isolated performance. These contracts may be internationalized even without any indication of the intention to do so on their face.

IV. REPARATION

A violation of international law creates an obligation on the part of the violator to make reparation. The purpose of reparation is to put the injured party in the position he would have been in had the illegal act not been committed. Reparation may consist of restitution, money damages, indemnity, or satisfaction.

A. No Individual Right

When an alien is injured, the state of which that alien is a national has the right to bring a claim for reparation on his behalf. The individual does not have an independent right to bring a claim on his own behalf.

B. Scale of Damages

The measure of damages caused to a state by the harming of one of its citizens is always different from the amount of damages suffered by the individual himself.

C. Reparation Payable

Reparation is always paid to the state, and it is within the discretion of the state to compensate its injured citizen.

D. Money Damages

Money damages are usually awarded because restitution and specific performance are often not possible.

E. Where Compensation Can Make an Illegal Act Lawful

If an expropriation is of such a type that reparations render the act lawful, the ICJ will calculate reparation as equal to the value of the property taken at the time, plus interest.

F. Lost Profits

Lost profits will be awarded under certain circumstances provided they are not too speculative.

1. Tortious Violation
Where compensation cannot make an illegal act lawful, reparation will be equal to the value of the property at the time it was

taken, plus compensation for lost profits if the lost profits are reasonably certain.

2. Contract Breach

Lost profits may also be awarded in breach of contract.

G. Personal Injury

In cases of personal injury, victims are awarded damages that are equal to the individual loss suffered, including medical expenses, loss of earnings, and pain and suffering.

H. Lack of Diligence in Apprehending

If a state is internationally liable for not prosecuting a national who has injured an alien, the measure of damages is the loss suffered to the individual alien, not the gravity of the state's delinquency.

V. BILATERAL TREATIES

In order to avoid the uncertainties of protection of international law for nationals who invest abroad, many states have concluded bilateral treaties to secure assurances against non-commercial risks.

A. Friendship, Commerce and Navigation Treaties (FCN Treaties)

Treaties of friendship, commerce, and/or navigation usually secure most favored nation status for nationals (both individuals and corporations). They may also ensure that, in the case of the imposition of exchange restrictions, the nationals abroad will be able to remove their profits in convertible currency or that payments will be made in convertible currency not withstanding the restrictions. They may also contain assurances against measures that would impair the interests of nationals within the territory.

B. Investment Treaties

These treaties are like FCN treaties; however, they contain more detailed and specialized provisions.

VI. UNITED STATES LAW ON FOREIGN INVESTMENT

A. The Act of State Doctrine (see also, Chapter 3, § II,C,6) (P. 63)

The United States considers commercial transactions as excepted from the act of state doctrine.

B. The Second Hickenlooper Amendment (see also Chapter 3, § II,C,8)

This is an exception to the act of state doctrine. It is limited to actions asserting title to specific property within the United States.

C. First Hickenlooper Amendment

1. Power to Suspend Aid
   This amendment gives the president power to suspend aid to any country that meets the following criteria:

   a. Nationalized Property
      The state has nationalized the property of an American national or a company that is at least fifty percent owned by American nationals.

   b. Imposed Restrictions
      The state may also have imposed restrictions that have the effect of nationalizing the property of an American national or a company that is at least fifty percent owned by American nationals.

   c. Repudiated a Contract
      The state repudiated a contract with an American national or a company that is at least fifty percent owned by American nationals.

2. Exception
The U.S. may not suspend aid if the offending country has taken steps within six months to "discharge its obligations under international law" (as the United States defines them). These steps include:

a. Submission to arbitration; or

b. Provision of prompt compensation in convertible currency for the full value of property taken or damages incurred. (The Hull Formula)

NOTE: The First Hickenlooper Amendment was only invoked once, against Ceylon (Sri Lanka) in 1963.

CASE CLIPS

Claim of Finnish Shipowners
(Finland v. Great Britain)
(1934) HPSS

Facts: Finnish ship owners sued in British courts for compensation for requisitioned ships. They lost and did not appeal. Subsequently, Finland sought to espouse their claims in an international court on the basis that they did not need to appeal to exhaust domestic remedies since their dispute was based on a question of fact, not of law.

Issue: Does a domestic legal remedy that is bound to fail come under the ineffective remedy exception to the exhaustion rule?

Rule: If an appeal is bound to fail under domestic law on procedural grounds, the right to appeal is not an effective remedy, and need not be exhausted. However, all contentions of fact and law must have been brought before the domestic court before domestic remedies may be considered exhausted.

The Ambatielos Claim
(Greece v. the United Kingdom)
(U.N. 1956) HPSS, SOL

Facts: A Greek national decided not to call a witness in British court, because he did not expect to win the case and was afraid that he would thereby be precluded from calling the witness in an international tribunal.

Issue: Does the failure to call an available witness preclude the exhaustion of local remedies.

Rule: Failure to call an essential witness in a national court is a breach of the exhaustion of local remedies rule, and therefore the case cannot be brought before an international tribunal.

Case Concerning The Barcelona Traction, Light and Power Co.
(Belgium v. Spain), Second Phase
(ICJ 1970) HPSS, SOL

Facts: Barcelona Traction was incorporated under the laws of Canada. The majority of its shareholders were Belgian nationals. The company suffered injury in Spain. The Canadian government did not have enough interest in the claim to pursue it on behalf of the company, so the Belgian government wished to espouse the claim.

Issue: Does a nation have the right to bring a claim if its nationals have suffered infringement of their rights as shareholders in a foreign company?

Rule: A nation does not have a right to bring a claim on behalf of its nationals who are shareholders in a foreign corporation, unless the country that caused injury to the corporation is the country of origin of the corporation.

William T. Way Claim
(United States v. Mexico)
(1928) HPSS

Facts: An American was killed by law enforcement authorities under the direction of a local Mexican sheriff who issued a warrant that was void on its face. The Mexican government took no action to punish the authorities.

Issue: Does misconduct of minor government officials give rise to the international responsibility of a state?

Rule: When any person concerned with the discharge of government functions at any level improperly discharges his functions and this results in a failure of the nation to live up to its obligations under international law, the state is responsible for the actions.

Laura M.B. Janes Claim
(United States v. Mexico)
(1926) HPSS

Facts: An American who worked at a mine in Mexico was shot by a former employee. The Mexican authorities delayed their investigation and did not exert a reasonable effort to apprehend the killer.

Issue: Is a state internationally responsible for injury to an alien caused by a private individual?

Rule: If law enforcement authorities of a state fail to take prompt and efficient action to apprehend a private individual who has caused injury to an alien, the state is internationally responsible.

B.E. Chattin Claim
(United States v. Mexico)
(1927) HPSS, SOL

Facts: An American was arrested solely on the basis of an accusation by a convict. He was denied an interpreter, information about the charges against him, and an opportunity to confront the witnesses against him.

Issue: Does a state incur international liability for not conforming with internationally recognized standards of procedural justice?

Rule: If the conduct on the part of a national judiciary amounts to a wilful neglect of duty, bad faith, or insufficient government action that is recognizable as unjust by a reasonable man, the state is internationally responsible for denial of procedural justice.

Texaco Overseas Petroleum v. Libyan Arab Republic
(1977) HPSS

Facts: Libya became angry with the American government and nationalized all of Texaco's property in retaliation. This violated a deed of concession that granted Texaco the right to do business in Libya.

Issue: May a state nationalize property of an alien in order to retaliate against the government of that alien?

Rule: International law, by the principle of good faith, prohibits nationalization of property for the purpose of political retaliation against a contracting party's government.

Chapter 14

INTERNATIONAL ECONOMIC LAW AND ORGANIZATIONS

I.   INTRODUCTION

International economic law principally deals with agreements concerning the restriction or regulation of the actions states may take that affect the interest of other states or their nationals. These restrictions and regulations include imposition of taxes, exchange controls, tariffs, import quotas, export subsidies, environmental controls, and safety regulations.

II.   INTERNATIONAL TRADE

A. The General Agreement on Tariffs and Trade (GATT)

1. Generally

a. The Objectives
Formed immediately following World War II, GATT was the first global commercial agreement in history. It was largely an effort to eliminate protectionist measures that had crippled the world economy in between the two world wars.

b. The Status
GATT was originally intended to be one part of the structure of an International Trade Organization. However that organization never materialized; as a result, GATT, originally designed as a temporary agreement, is the principal international method for regulating trade.

2. Outline of GATT
The bulk of GATT is detailed tariff schedules that fill many volumes of text. But the primary elements of GATT is contained in about eighty pages called the "General Articles." These articles contain the general rules pertaining to tariffs and other obligations of the cosignatory states.

3. Tariffs

Through the mandatory most-favored-nation status and the agreement on tariff schedules found in GATT, tariff reduction negotiations have met with widespread international success.

4. Quantitative Restrictions

Quantitative restrictions on imports (quotas) are generally prohibited under GATT. Exceptions include agricultural or fisheries products, prevention of deceptive practices, and protection of public morals, national treasures or human or animal health. Even these restrictions must be administered in a manner not discriminatory to any single nation.

5. Indirect Barriers to Imports

GATT also prohibits indirect trade restraints, such as internal taxes, that affect local sales, purchases, transportation, distribution, or use of imported goods.

6. Subsidies and Countervailing Duties

Under GATT, only developing nations may put a subsidy on exports, driving the export price lower than the domestic price.

7. Dumping and Anti-Dumping Duties

Exporting products at below the "normal value" is combatted by GATT's Anti-Dumping Code, which allows an importing state to place a duty on any imports to bring them up to their "normal value."

8. Protection of Domestic Producers by Emergency Action

If a state realizes that an imported product is seriously threatening its domestic producers, it may utilize GATT's escape clause and suspend its obligation or withdraw a concession in respect to a product.

9. Customs Unions and Free Trade Areas

Customs unions and free trade areas may be formed under GATT as long as tariffs and restrictions on third parties are not increased as a result of the agreement.

10. Developing States
GATT allows states with a low standard of living or in the early phases of development to impose tariffs or quotas, grant subsidies, and take other actions to protect their domestic industries.

11. Commodity Agreements
There are three kinds of commodity agreements.

a. One
Importers and exporters are obligated to buy or sell guaranteed amounts of a commodity at a price with stipulated maximum and minimum boundaries.

b. Two
This kind of agreement establishes an international buffer stock monitored by an administrative body that buys or sells the commodity in an effort to stabilize the commodity's price.

c. Three
This kind of agreement allocates export quotas and forces participating importers to limit their imports from non-participants in an effort to assure fair export allocation between competing exporters of a commodity that is in surplus.

12. Export Controls
GATT prohibits a member state from imposing export controls in order to achieve economic advantage for its goods. All other controls are generally permitted.

B. The U.N. Conference on Trade and Development (UNCTAD)

UNCTAD is a permanent department of the United Nations that strives to reduce the trade gap between developed and developing states. UNCTAD is especially concerned with the improvement of trade conditions for the developing countries' wide variety of basic commodities exported to developed nations.

III. INTERNATIONAL MONETARY LAW

A. The Bretton Woods Institutions

In 1944, at a meeting in Bretton Woods, New Hampshire, the United States and Great Britain spearheaded a conference that gave birth to the International Monetary Fund (IMF) and the World Bank. These institutions coordinated the post-war effort to eliminate wartime restrictions on, and discriminatory policies toward, trade, while at the same time encouraging post-war growth in trade.

B. The IMF

1. Introduction
   The principle function of the IMF was to make funds available to nations with temporary balance of payment problems. Nearly all nations except the Soviet Union and its former satellites belong to the IMF. A fundamental change occurred in 1973 when the United States abandoned the gold standard. The international monetary system became a system of floating exchange rates, rather than a system where specific exchange rates with other currencies or gold were maintained.

2. The Principle Features of the IMF
   The funds that make up the IMF come from its member states on a quota system reflecting the relative position of the state in the world economy. One-quarter of a country's contribution must be made in the form of specified, convertible currencies. The remaining three-quarters may come in the state's own currency. The IMF may supplement these funds by borrowing from the "Group of Ten" (United States, Netherlands, United Kingdom, Japan, Italy, Canada, Belgium, France, Deutsche Bundesbank, and Sveriges Riksbank).

3. Structural Framework

   a. Organization
   Twenty-two executive directors supervise the daily operation of the IMF. Six directors are appointed by the six nations with the largest quotas (U.S., U.K., France, Germany, Japan, and China). The remaining directors are elected at two-year intervals by the remaining members of the IMF.

   b. Voting
   The IMF has an unequal voting scheme determined by the size of the nation's quota. In 1985, the United States had the most votes (179,433 or 19% of the total) and the Maldives had the fewest (270).

4. Moving from Fixed to Floating Exchange Rates
   Originally, gold was the main reserve asset of the system, but gold convertibility soon became inadequate. When the United States abandoned the gold standard, the IMF Articles had to be amended to allow member currencies to "float," unbacked by gold.

5. Revision of the System
   In 1971, the Group of Ten amended the IMF to abolish the central role of gold. At the same time, they developed the "high" majority, whereby 85 percent of the IMF vote is needed to approve major decisions, such as exchange rate provisions.

6. Use of IMF Resources by Member States
   A member state may withdraw up to one-quarter of its quota from the IMF without any strings attached. Further borrowing comes only through the promise of repurchase by the borrowing state.

7. Obligations of Member States

   a. Exchange Arrangements
   Generally, states are obligated to use exchange arrangements that promote economic growth and provide price stability.

No exchange arrangements that discriminate against the currency of another state are permitted.

b. Consultation and Cooperation
Each member state must relay to the IMF all of its relevant exchange rate policies every eighteen months.

c. Exchange Restrictions
Member states may use controls that are needed to regulate international movement of capital, but they may not restrict payment of current transactions without the approval of IMF.

d. Sanctions
The IMF allows for a variety of sanctions, including punitive rates of interest, ineligibility for new resources, and publishing of a members financial status.

IV. INTERNATIONAL DEVELOPMENT

A. Introduction

The fundamental goal of international economic development is to encourage the flow of technology and capital to developing countries in an effort to benefit their populations through economic growth.

B. The World Bank and Accompanying Developmental Organizations

1. World Bank and the International Finance Corporation (IFC)
Made up of the International Bank for Reconstruction and Development (IBRD), and the International Development Association (IDA), the World Bank's objective is assisting the economic growth of developing nations.   IFC coordinates private investment in developing countries.

a. Functions

The IBRD, IDA, and IFC have three closely related functions: (1) to lend funds, (2) to provide advice, and (3) to stimulate the investment of other states.

b. Financial Strength

The IBRD only gives loans to low risk borrowers for projects that promise to have a positive economic influence in the borrowing country.

2. Growth in World Bank Assistance

The Bank is the world's leading provider of development assistance. Bank assistance generally covers a third to a half of a project's funding, with the bulk of the remaining capital coming from the country's own investors

a. Lending Criteria

The Bank only lends money based on economic criteria. Consequently, support for a project's military or political objectives is not a valid reason to request funding.

b. The Graduation Process

Most of the poor countries that have borrowed money from IBRD and IDA have attained sufficient economic stability so that they no longer need to borrow. Some former borrowers, such as Colombia, Japan and the Republic of Korea, have turned their economies around to the extent that they now contribute to the World Bank's institutions.

c. IFC's Complementary Role

IFC supplements the funding of the World Bank with its own funding and by organizing and encouraging capital investments in developmental programs.

C. The Overseas Private Investment Corporation (OPIC) and Eximbank Investment Guaranties

1. OPIC
OPIC oversees the insurance and guaranty of American private investment in less developed countries. There are three major risks insured against: (1) inconvertibility of foreign currency into dollars, (2) expropriation of investment by the host government, and (3) war, revolution, civil strife, and insurrection.

   a. Inconvertibility Coverage
   OPIC assures the investor that any rights or guarantees with respect to convertibility and repatriation of earnings and capital that the investor enjoys at the time of the original investment will continue for the life of the contract.

   b. Expropriation Coverage
   If the host government nationalizes or takes other less dramatic action against investor property, OPIC insures compensation in dollars.

   c. War, Revolution, Insurrection and Civil Strife Coverage
   OPIC's basic coverage compensates any damage caused by the hostile acts of any national or international forces.

2. Export Credit Insurance Programs
These programs offer insurance, available through the Export-Import Bank of Washington, D.C. (Eximbank), for exports to developing countries that are likely to be of high risk.

D. Multilateral Efforts to Produce Investment Codes

Efforts to codify the law of state responsibility have largely failed due to the dramatically different positions of developed and developing countries.

E. U.N. Commission and Centre on Transnational Corporations

The Centre is principally focused on furthering the understanding of transnational corporations and their political, legal, economic and social effects on home and host countries.

F. Settlement of Investment Disputes

The International Center for Settlement of Investment Disputes has the jurisdiction to handle any legal dispute arising directly out of an investment between a member state and the national of another member state, that the parties to the dispute consent in writing to submit to the Center.

G. Multilateral Investment Insurance

The Multilateral Investment Guarantee Agency (MIGA) is the latest proposal to form an international agency to insure investments in the less developed countries.

H. United Nations Industrial Development Organization (UNIDO)

UNIDO was created in 1966 with the goal of promoting and accelerating industrial development in the developing countries and strengthening cooperation in, and coordination of, all U.N. activities in this area.

CASE CLIPS

United States v. Texas Instruments, Inc.
(U.S. 1980) SOL

Facts: Texas Instruments won a verdict at the Court of Customs Claims on the classification of imported integrated circuit devices used in digital watches. The Government appealed, arguing that the legislative history of the Tariff Schedules of the United States suggests a different classification.

Issue: Does the Court of Customs Claims have the authority to interpret the meaning of national tariff schedules in the case of importation disputes?

Rule: It is the responsibility of the Court of Customs Claims (now the United States Court of International Trade) to interpret the meaning of the Tariff Schedules of the United States.

Canadian Meat Council v. United States
(U.S. 1986) SOL

Facts: The members of the Canadian Meat Council challenged a final affirmative subsidy determination by the Department of Commerce. They claim that the duty order on imports of live swine does not apply to their importation of fresh, chilled, or frozen pork.

Issue: Can a party challenge a final affirmative subsidy determination by the Department of Commerce?

Rule: A party is permitted to challenge a final affirmative subsidy determination where a final negative injury determination is the subject of a pending appeal.

BP Exploration Co. v. Libya
(1973) SOL

Facts: The Libyan government nationalized the state's oil industry, thus breaching a contract with P. P brought suit for specific performance against the government.

Issue: What remedies are available to a party that is the victim of a breach of contract due to government nationalization of an industry?

Rule: Following the government nationalization of an industry, the only remedy available to nonbreaching parties is a suit for damages.

Saudi Arabia v. Arabian American Oil Co. (ARAMCO)
(1963) SOL

Facts: In 1954, Saudi Arabia entered into a contract with the Onassis Tanker Co. granting the company priority in shipping oil from areas in Saudi Arabia. ARAMCO challenged the validity of the agreement on the ground that it conflicted with a prior contract between themselves and the Saudi state dating back to 1933.

Issue: Can a state violate a prior contract for oil rights with a foreign party by creating a conflicting agreement with a third party, also a foreigner?

Rule: If the law of the grantor state and world-wide business practice suggest that a prior agreement has vested a property right in oil concessions, that agreement can not be breached by the grantor state.

Owners of the Tattler v. Great Britain
(1920) SOL

Facts: In 1905, the Tattler, a fishing vessel of United States nationality, was detained by Canadian authorities on charges of having violated an 1818 treaty on fishing territory. The owners of the Tattler waived all rights of protest on this charge. The United States Government later brought a claim protesting the detention.

Issue: Can a protest be brought on behalf of a party that has previously waived all rights pursuant to an earlier charge.

Rule: The waiver of rights by a private party precludes any future claims made within the scope of the waived rights.

Société Nationale Industrielle Aérospatialle v.
U.S. District Court for Southern District of Iowa
(S.Ct. 1987) SOL

Facts: The petitioners, two French airplane manufacturers, built and sold the "Rallye" airplane. In 1980, a Rallye crashed in Iowa injuring the pilot and a passenger. During the ensuing action, discovery was carried out by both sides pursuant to the Federal Rules of Civil Procedure. However, when the plaintiffs sought the production of documents and interrogatories, the petitioners filed for a protective order, arguing that the Hague Convention on the Taking of Evidence Abroad in Civil and Commercial Matters controls evidentiary procedures for retrieving evidence from foreign countries who are signatories to the convention. The district court and the court of appeals found that the Federal Rules of Civil Procedure are the sole source of evidentiary procedure in the United States.

Issue: Must a federal district court consult the procedures set forth in the Hague Convention when litigants seek answers to interrogatories, the production of documents, or admissions from foreign nationals of signatories to the Convention?

Rule: (Stevens, J.) The application of the procedures in the Hague Convention are only permissive, thus allowing a federal district court to order the discovery of evidence in foreign countries pursuant to the Federal Rules of Civil Procedure only.

Dissent: (Blackmun, J.) Viewing the Hauge Convention as optional ignores the importance of the Convention in accommodating divergent procedural interests. Instead, there should be a presumption that courts should resort first to the Convention procedures.

The Santa Fe Case
(Switzerland 1983) SOL

Facts: The SEC discovered the possibility of illegal stock trading between an American and Kuwaiti corporation in Switzerland. The U.S. Department of Justice asked Switzerland to compel the disclosure of relevant information held by Swiss banks.

Issue: Is a state required to mandate the disclosure of confidential securities information to facilitate another nation's investigation?

Rule: A nation does not have to mandate the disclosure of confidential securities information for a securities regulation investigation conducted by another country.

The Second Santa Fe Case
(Switzerland 1984) SOL

Facts: The SEC discovered the possibility of illegal stock trading between an American and Kuwaiti corporation in Switzerland. The U.S. Department of Justice asked Switzerland to compel some Swiss banks to disclose confidential securities information. When the Swiss Supreme Court failed to mandate the disclosure, the U.S. renewed the request, alleging acts that violated Swiss law as well.

Issue: Can a state obtain assistance from another state when conducting a securities investigation and alleging acts that are illegal under the assisting state's law?

Rule: Investigative authorities of one nation can rely on the judicial assistance of another nation when alleging the violation of laws within the assisting state.

Chapter 15

THE LAW OF THE SEA

I.   INTRODUCTION

A. Development

For hundreds of years, the sea was considered a part of the international community belonging to everyone. This principle was known as *mare liberum* (the sea free).   As the coastal states challenged the theory of universal possession, exceptions began to develop. Eventually, the principle of *mare liberum* was refined, and zones of "national jurisdiction" for the coastal states, the territorial sea, the continental shelf, and exclusive economic zones were recognized.

B. Modern Nautical Law

The law of the sea was mainly customary until the United Nations Conference on the Law of the Sea in 1958. This Conference, not signed by the United States, has, in large part, become the guideline for modern nautical law. A modified convention was ratified, but still without the support of the United States, in 1982.

II.   VESSELS

A. The Nationality of Vessels

1. The Right of Navigation
   All states have the right to sail vessels flying their national flag on the high seas.

2. Nationality of Ships
   States establish the rules for nationality of their own vessels. Unless conclusively proven otherwise, vessels are assumed to belong to the nation whose flag they fly.

3. Status of Ships
Ships are to have the sole nationality of the country's flag that they are flying. Ships flying more than one flag are seen as without conclusive nationality.

B. Jurisdiction Over Vessels

1. Requisition and Control of National Vessels
Sometimes vessels will fly "flags of convenience" (i.e., different from that of their national ownership). However, it is the nation that is responsible for the ship's conformity with international law that may control the movement and activities of the ship.

2. Jurisdiction Over Acts Committed on National Vessels
Restatement (Revised) §502 says that it is the obligation of the flag state to exercise effective authority and control over the ship.

III.   DEROGATIONS FROM "COMMONAGE"

The notion of "territorial waters" developed with the idea that coastal states had a special interest in the waters adjacent to their shores. Today, coastal states have exclusive economic rights and sovereignty over the continental shelves beneath their territorial waters as well as a contiguous zone that may extend up to twenty-four nautical miles from the state's low-water coast.

A. The Territorial Sea

1. Definition and Delimitation
The traditional three-mile belt, which was established based on the distance of a cannon shot, has been extended to twelve nautical miles. The baseline for measuring the breadth of the territorial sea is the low-water line along the coast.

a. Bays
Special disputes have arisen involving bays. Unless a bay is seen as an "historic" part of a nation, it's mouth must be no more than twenty-four miles across for a state to claim territorial sovereignty over all of its waters.

b. Mid-Ocean Island Archipelagoes
Nations, such as the Philippines and Indonesia, have said that their archipelagoes have been viewed historically as single entities. The U.N. Convention on the Law of the Sea says that as long as the archipelagic state has a water-to-land ratio not greater than nine-to-one, the outer points of the islands may be joined by contiguous territorial baselines.

2. Passage Through the Territorial Sea

a. Innocent Passage
The vessels of all states enjoy the right of innocent passage through the territorial sea. Passage is innocent as long as it doesn't disturb the peace, good order, or security of the coastal state.

b. International Straits
The 1982 Convention gave vessels the right of passage through international straits between one part of the high seas or an exclusive economic zone and another part of the high seas or an exclusive economic zone. See also *Corfu Channel Case*.

c. International Canals
The privilege of free passage through the three major interoceanic canals of the world, Suez, Panama, and Kiel, has been created by treaty.

d. Archipelagic Sea-Lane Passage
All states enjoy the right of passage through or above all routes designated by the archipelagic state for international navigation or overflight.

3. Jurisdiction over Acts on Foreign Vessels in Territorial Seas

   a. Jurisdiction of the Coastal State
   A coastal state should only exercise jurisdiction over a foreign vessel passing through territorial waters if there has been a crime that has disturbed the peace of the state or if such measures are necessary for the suppression of illicit traffic in drugs. See *The David* and *Wildenhus' Case* for the uncertainty of the law concerning vessels in a foreign port.

   b. Jurisdiction of the Flag State
   When there is no breach of the peace in the coastal state, acts committed aboard a vessel are considered to be within the jurisdiction of the country whose flag the ship is flying. See *U.S. v. Flores*.

4. The Contiguous Zone
   The contiguous zone is an area just outside of a nation's territorial sea, not more than twenty-four nautical miles from the baselines by which the breadth of the territorial sea is measured. Within a contiguous zone a state has the authority to prevent and punish infringement of its customs, fiscal, immigration or sanitary laws.

   a. Customs Zones
   Before the Convention of 1982, states often enforced anti-smuggling laws well beyond the twenty-four mile boundary of contiguous zones. The status of international law on anti-smuggling jurisdiction today is unclear.

   b. Hot Pursuit
   The hot pursuit of a foreign ship may be undertaken when the authorities of the coastal state have good reason to believe that the ship has violated the laws of that state. Only military or other clearly marked ships and aircraft may engage in hot pursuit.

c. Security Zones
While not recognized in international law, states have historically claimed a right to protect themselves against foreign aggression by taking action in waters beyond their territorial limit.

d. Anti-Pollution Zones
Canada has declared an anti-pollution zone of 100 nautical miles around its Arctic coast. There is no such right formally recognized in international law.

B. Economic Resources Beyond the Territorial Sea

1. The Continental Shelf

a. Definition
Article 76 of the 1982 U.N. Convention states, "The continental shelf of a coastal State comprises the sea-bed and subsoil of the submarine areas that extend beyond its territorial sea throughout the natural prolongation of its land territory to the outer edge of the continental margin, or to a distance of 200 nautical miles from the baselines from which the breadth of the territorial sea is measured where the outer edge of the continental margin does not extend up to that distance."

b. Delimitation Between States
Article 83 of the 1982 Convention allows for the settlement of continental shelf boundary disputes by the International Court of Justice. See *The North Sea Continental Shelf Cases*.

2. The Exclusive Economic Zone
Countries have long claimed and observed sovereignty over all resources found within territorial waters. The first codification of these economic rights was in the 1958 Geneva Conference.

a. Fishery Conservation and Management Act of 1976
The United States granted itself exclusive fishery management authority over a zone contiguous to its territorial sea
called the fishery conservation zone.

b. The Exclusive Economic Zone in the 1982 Convention
The Convention defined an exclusive economic zone as "an
area beyond and adjacent to the territorial sea, subject to the
specific legal regime established in this Part, under which the
rights and jurisdictions of the coastal State and the rights and
freedoms of other States are governed by the relevant
provisions of this Convention." The breadth of the exclusive
economic zone is not to extend beyond 200 nautical miles
from the coastal state's low-water coastline.

IV.   THE REGIME OF THE HIGH SEAS

The high seas are defined by the 1982 Convention as "all parts of
the sea that are not included in the exclusive economic zone, in the
internal waters of a State, or in the archipelagic waters of an
archipelagic State."

A. The Principle of Freedom

The high seas are open to all states for navigation, overflight, the
laying of submarine cables and pipelines, the construction of
artificial islands, fishing, and scientific research.

B. Limitations on Freedom

In general, a state can not excavate an area on which another
nation has already staked a claim. When conflicting uses of high
sea territory arise they are most commonly dealt with through
international negotiation and agreement.

1. Uses Impinging on Coastal State Interests
Offshore "pirate" broadcasting was outlawed in 1967. Now,
broadcasting from international waters must receive proper

licensing from the coastal states at whom the broadcasts are aimed.

2. Prohibited Activities

a. Slave Transport
No state may allow its flag to be flown on a vessel engaged in the transport of slaves,

b. Piracy
Every state has the right, and under some conditions the duty, to seize vessels engaged in piracy.

c. Right of Visit
According to the U.N. Convention on the Sea (1982), in the event a warship encounters a foreign ship on the high seas the crew is permitted to board the ship only if there is reasonable ground for suspecting the ship is engaged in piracy, slave trade, or unauthorized broadcasting; or the ship is without nationality, flying a foreign flag or refuses to show its flag is in reality the same nationality as the warship.

C. Military Uses of the High Seas

There has been recent, widespread support for the idea that international seas and seabeds, like outer space, should be completely demilitarized by U.N. resolution. Nations, such as the United States, that use the sea as a critical part of their national defense are not likely to support a demilitarization of international waters.

D. Exploitation of Resources beyond National Jurisdiction

1. Mineral Resources of the Seabed
An ever growing issue in international law involves who is entitled to exploit resources found beneath the high seas. One basic view urges that the seas' treasures are there for the taking and that the most technologically advanced states should be given incentives to retrieve the seas' resources as quickly and as

efficiently as possible. The opposing view contends that now is the time to lay down "preventive laws" restricting the exploitation of the resources beneath the high seas.

2. Living Resources
Fishing on the high seas must be conducted with "reasonable regard" for the interests of other states.

V.   MARINE ENVIRONMENT

The problem of pollution by sea vessels has been specially addressed by the International Maritime Organization.

VI.   MARINE RESEARCH

Marine scientific research on the high seas remains unrestricted, but subject to the control of the coastal state in territorial waters.

VII.   SETTLEMENT OF SEA DISPUTES

The U.N. has also established a Law of the Sea Tribunal, including a Seabed Disputes Chamber, with jurisdiction over international disputes involving issues of the law of the sea.   The ICJ also occasionally hears sea disputes.

CASE CLIPS

Corfu Channel Case
(United Kingdom v. Albania)
(ICJ 1949) HPSS, SOL

Facts: A channel that was part of Albanian waterways was mined by Albania. The mines damaged British vessels and killed Britons.
Issue: Does a nation have an obligation to warn other nations of dangers within its territorial waters?
Rule: A nation must warn other nations of dangers in territorial waters that are used for international navigation.

The David
(United States v. Panama)
(1933) HPSS

Facts: The steamer *Yorba Linda*, owned by an American corporation, collided with the steamer *David*, owned by a Panamanian corporation. The United States claimed that the collision took place in American territorial waters.

Issue: Does a foreign vessel have immunity from jurisdiction during innocent passage through another country's territorial waters.

Rule: The fact that a vessel is sailing through another nation's territorial waters on an innocent passage does not give that vessel jurisdictional immunity.

Wildenhus' Case
(S.Ct. 1887) HPSS, SOL

Facts: While on board a Belgian vessel docked in Jersey City, Wildenhus (D) killed a fellow Belgian. Belgium claimed to have exclusive jurisdiction over the events on its vessel

Issue: Who has jurisdiction over a vessel moored to a foreign dock?

Rule: (Waite, C.J.) In general, when a vessel docks, it subjects its self and its crew to the jurisdiction of the host country, especially if the disorder involves a breach of the peace.

United States v. Flores
(S.Ct. 1933) HPSS

Facts: Flores killed a fellow American citizen while on board an American vessel docked in the Belgian Congo. The district court dismissed the case under *Wildenhus* saying that it didn't have jurisdiction.

Issue: Do United States' courts have jurisdiction over crimes committed on American vessels in foreign territorial waters?

Rule: (Stone, J.) The United States only has judicial and legislative jurisdiction over crimes committed on American vessels in foreign waters if the host nation has waived jurisdiction or has failed to assert its own jurisdiction.

Church v. Hubbart
(S.Ct. 1803) HPSS

Facts: P owned a vessel that was seized by Portuguese authorities four or five leagues off of the Brazilian coast due to the fact it was engaged in illegal trade. P tried to collect on two insurance policies that he had purchased from D. Each policy excluded losses from illegal trade.

Issue: Does a nation have jurisdiction in areas contiguous to its territorial waters?

Rule: (Marshall, C.J.) A state may exercise its jurisdiction in contiguous zones to prevent or punish infringement of its customs, fiscal, immigration, or sanitary laws.

North Sea Continental Shelf Cases
(ICJ 1969) HPSS

Facts: The Netherlands and Denmark claimed that the boundaries between their continental shelves and West German territories should be determined by the principle of equidistance in Article 6 of the Geneva Convention of 1958. Germany was not a party to the Convention.

Issue: What is the proper method for delimiting the continental shelf between states?

Rule: The only legally recognized method of demarcating continental shelf boundaries is by an agreement between the states involved.

Public Ministry v. Mogens Glistrup
(Denmark 1967) SOL

Facts: A vessel belonging to a Danish corporation, registered in Denmark, and flying the Danish flag, was leased without provision of officers or crew by the Danish company to an American company, which used it in Nigerian waters. The crew assigned by the American company to the vessel did not meet the requirements of the Danish government.

Issue: Is the nationality of a ship dependant upon a genuine link between the state and vessels flying its flag?

Rule: Article 5 of the Geneva Convention on the High Seas makes the nationality of vessels dependant upon the existence of a genuine link between the state and vessels flying its flag. This test is applicable even if a nation has not ratified the Convention. A genuine link implies that the state effectively exercises its jurisdiction and its control.

The People v. Robert J. Thomas
(Ireland 1954) SOL

Facts: Thomas, who was not an Irish citizen, was convicted in Ireland of the manslaughter of Humphries, which occurred on board the Irish ship *Munster*.

Issue: Does a nation's jurisdiction extend to a foreigner on board a ship flying that nation's flag outside that nation's territory?

Rule: A country has the right to control the conduct of those on board a ship flying that nation's flag outside that nation's territory, irrespective of citizenship.

Re Bianchi
(Argentina 1957) SOL

Facts: Bianchi, a member of the crew of an Argentine ship, was charged with committing theft on board the ship while it was anchored in a Brazilian harbor. Argentina asserted its jurisdiction to try the case after no action was instituted by the Brazilian authorities.

Issue: Does a flag state have jurisdiction over offenses committed on board the ship while in foreign territorial waters if the local authorities do not institute any action?

Rule: Offenses committed on board a vessel in foreign territorial waters can be prosecuted by the flag state if the local authorities waive jurisdiction.

Note: Brazil's failure to prosecute constituted a jurisdictional waiver.

Hoff, Administratrix
(United States v. United Mexican States)
(U.N. 1929) SOL

Facts: An American schooner entered a port in Mexico after a severe rainstorm damaged the boat. The Mexican government seized the schooner and its cargo. Subsequently, the Mexican government assessed triple damages against the cargo seized, and both the schooner and cargo were sold to satisfy the judgment.

Issue: Is a merchant vessel that enters the territorial waters of a foreign nation subject to the foreign nation's laws without exception?

Rule: Generally, a merchant vessel entering the territorial waters of a foreign nation is subject to the foreign nation's laws. However, there are two exceptions granted: (1) vessels in distress and innocent passage

Public Prosecutor v. Kairismaa
(Sweden 1960) SOL

Facts: Kairismaa, a Finnish citizen, was brought to trial in Sweden for fraudulently obtaining a loan from a fellow Finnish passenger. The alleged fraud occurred on board a Finnish ship in Swedish territorial waters.

Issue: Is a crime committed by an alien on board a foreign ship against another alien punishable by a nation in whose territorial waters the ship has entered?

Rule: A court has the jurisdiction to try a case against an alien who committed a crime against another alien while on board a foreign ship that is in the territorial waters of the adjudicating nation.

Re Martinez
(Italy 1959) SOL

Facts: Martinez and others, who were foreign nationals, were convicted in Italy of smuggling. The alleged criminal act occurred when their ship was in a declared *zone of vigilance* (contiguous zone) nine miles off the coast of Italy.

Issue: Does a state have a right to declare the extent of its territorial waters and contiguous zones and, if so, to what extent will that state's law apply?

Rule: Since there is no existing customary international law on how far from the coast sovereignty and jurisdiction is extended, the area of territorial waters and its contiguous zone is determined by the domestic law of each nation. However, sovereignty over a contiguous zone permits only police and preventive measures.

Re Pulos and Others
(Italy 1976) SOL

Facts: A Greek boat anchored outside of Italian territorial waters was used as a motherboat to smuggle cigarettes into Italy. The Italian authorities pursued the boat on the high seas, seized it, and arrested everyone on board.

Issue: Can a state seize a foreign vessel on the high seas?

Rule: Article 23 of the Geneva Convention on the High Seas permits a state to seize a foreign vessel on the high seas if the foreign craft violated or threatened to violate law within the territorial waters of the arresting state.

United States v. Florida
(S.Ct. 1976) SOL

Facts: Florida and the United States were in dispute over resource rights in waters abutting the state.

Issue: Who owns the natural resources found in a state's coastal waters?

Rule: (By Decree) State ownership over resource rights in its coastal waters extends up to three miles from its coast, the remaining area belongs to the United States government.

Odeco (Ocean Drilling and Exploration Co.) v.
Torao Oda, Superintendent of Shiba Revenue Office
(Japan 1982) SOL

Facts: Odeco challenged the right of the Japanese government to assess taxes on the income earned from boring activities beyond the reach of Japan's territorial waters but on its continental shelf.

Issue: May a nation have sovereignty over regions beyond its territorial waters?

Rule: Although customary law has evolved to the point where a nation has sovereignty over the seabed on its continental shelf, no such sovereignty exists for the water and airspace over extraterritorial regions.

Chapter 16

INTERNATIONAL WATERWAYS AND
OTHER COMMON AREAS

I.   INTRODUCTION

There are several geographic areas, accessible by man, that have not been brought under the sovereignty of any state.   These include Arctic and Antarctic regions, international waterways, the high seas, the moon, and outer space.

II.   INTERNATIONAL WATERWAYS

A. Concept and Scope

The two fundamental types of international waterways are contiguous rivers, which serve as the boundary between two states, and successive rivers, which run through more than one state. Often such waterways are the subject of treaties that outline the conditions for shared use.

B. Use and Diversion

1. Definition of International Drainage Basin
An international drainage basin is a geographical area extending over two or more states determined by the watershed limits of the system of waters, including surface and underground waters, flowing into a common terminus.

2. Uses
Initially, the law of international waterways dealt primarily with problems concerning navigation. Modern uses of waterways and scarcity of water has caused the law governing international

waterways to deal with such issues as irrigation, power, flood control, industry, and waste disposal as well as navigation.

3. Physical Linkages
Due to reductions in water supply, physical linkages of a river basin, including tributaries, are recognized as part of the "system."

4. General Rules
In general, a basin state is a state whose territory includes a portion of an international drainage basin. Each basin state is entitled, within its territory, to a reasonable and equitable share in the beneficial uses of the waters of an international drainage basin. See *Lake Lanoux Case*.

C. Navigation

A state controlling both banks of a river can, absent the exceptions of a treaty, regulate and block shipping through their link of the river. However, treaties of necessity or convenience generally avert river blockades.

III.   THE POLAR REGIONS

A. The "Sector Theory"

Nations such as Great Britain, Canada, New Zealand, France, Russia, and Norway have claimed that polar regions are divided based on the projection northwards or southwards of the areas bordering the respective maritime territories. This variation on the theory of geographical continuity has not gained legal acceptance.

B. The Antarctic

Various nations, including the United States, the United Kingdom, and Australia, have claimed sovereignty over, or established an occupying presence in, Antarctica. To date, no state has sovereignty over the region. In 1959, states with interests in Antarctica signed the Antarctic treaty and agreed that the area would be used only for peaceful and purely scientific activity.

IV.   THE MOON, CELESTIAL BODIES AND OUTER SPACE

In 1967, a treaty involving nations with developed space programs was signed. It declared that, "outer space, including the moon and other celestial bodies, shall be free for exploration and use by all states without discrimination of any kind, on a basis of equality and in accordance with international law, and there shall be free access to all areas of celestial bodies." The treaty further provided that: "outer space, including the moon and other celestial bodies, is not subject to national appropriation by claim of sovereignty, by means of use or occupation, or by any other means."

A. The Geostationary Orbit

In 1976, eight states with territory on the equator claimed sovereign rights over that segment of the "geostationary" orbit above their territories. The orbit is used by hundreds of satellites and is the most valuable and most utilized segment of outer space. The United States has rejected the claims of the equatorial states in favor of a policy of "first come, first serve." For obvious reasons, states with lesser developed space programs have protested the American policy.

B. The Moon Treaty

This treaty, which was adopted by the General Assembly in 1979, has failed to gain the acceptance of nations with developed space programs. These nations object to the clause stating that "the moon and its natural resources are the common heritage of mankind," which in effect relinquishes the monopolistic control of those nations with developed space programs.

C. Military Uses of Outer Space

The 1967 Treaty on Principles forbids those states that are parties to the treaty from placing objects carrying nuclear weapons or other weapons of mass destruction in other space. The use of outer space for "defensive" weapons presents new questions concerning space as a purely peaceful domain.

D. Remote Sensing From Outer Space

In 1985, the U.N addressed the issue of gathering military intelligence through geostationary satellites. Generally, the sensed state has a right to all data gathered, and the sensing state has an obligation to disclose any information regarding possible harms to the world environment.

E. Broadcasting From Outer Space

The U.N. General Assembly voted 108 to 13 that a state could not broadcast radio or television frequencies into another state without the prior consent of the receiving nation. The United States and Western European countries opposed this resolution, citing the right to a free flow of information.

CASE CLIPS

Lake Lanoux Case
(1957) HPSS

Facts: In 1866, France and Spain signed an agreement not to interfere with the natural flow of water into the River Carol, an outlet of Lake Lanoux. Spain claimed that a French plan to use the lake for hydroelectric power would violate this treaty.

Issue: Do parties to a treaty have a right to negotiate in the event that a dispute arises out of the treaty between them?

Rule: Parties to a treaty must strive to resolve, through negotiations, any dispute that might violate their treaty.

Chapter 17

THE ENVIRONMENT

I. THE EMERGING INTERNATIONAL LAW OF THE ENVIRONMENT

The role of international law in the increasingly visible issues of the environment is unconcern. However, it is likely that international law will help determine the regulation of environmental issues involving common areas, such as the high seas, Antarctic areas, and outer space. The Restatement (Revised) § 601 holds that a state is responsible to all other states for any violations of internationally accepted rules and standards for the prevention, reduction, and control of injury to the environment of another state.

II. TRANSBORDER POLLUTION

A. Generally

A Convention on Long-Range Transboundary Air Pollution, signed in 1979, has set guidelines for limiting and, to the extent possible, reducing or eliminating long-range transboundary air pollution. See also *The Trail Smelter Case.*

B. Chernobyl

The 1986 explosion at this Soviet atomic power plant evoked fears throughout the international community about a state withholding information concerning incidents within their own borders that are likely to have an effect on the worldwide environment.

C. Institut De Droit International, Resolution On Pollution

This resolution, adopted in 1979, defines "pollution" as any physical, chemical, or biological alteration in the composition or quality of waters that results directly or indirectly from human action. Generally, the resolution lays the groundwork for co-operation and information transfer in environmental matters.

III. MARINE POLLUTION

The U.N. Convention on the Law of the Sea sets out provisions prohibiting polluting the marine environment. Coastal states are left with the responsibility of monitoring and enforcing their territorial waters. The Restatement (Revised) § 603 requires states to maintain vessels flying their flag in accordance with international regulations on marine pollution.

IV. WEATHER MODIFICATION AND CLIMATE CHANGE

The law relating to weather modification is developing, as is the technology in this area. In 1977, the U.N. banned the military use of environmental modification techniques having wide-spread, long-lasting, or severe effects. Recently, "human induced" climatic changes have also been the focus of much debate, but international law is yet to directly address these potential threats.

Chapter 18

ORGANIZATIONS FOR TECHNICAL, SOCIAL, AND CULTURAL COOPERATION

I. INTRODUCTION

All of the international organizations for technical, social, and cultural cooperation maintain close working relationships with the United Nations, although each of these organizations maintains its own administrative structure.

II. EDUCATION AND CULTURE

A. United Nations Educational, Scientific and Cultural Organization (UNESCO)

UNESCO was founded in 1946, with the goal of promoting team-work among nations in the fields of education, science and culture. UNESCO's international unity was damaged in the mid-1980s when the United States and the United Kingdom both withdrew from the organization, claiming a bias against the West.

B. World Intellectual Property Organization (WIPO)

WIPO administers almost twenty globally scattered unions with the goal of promoting the protection of intellectual property through-out the world. Generally, WIPO requires that member states grant foreign nationals the same advantages as residents regarding the protection of trademarks, inventions, designs, and copyrights.

C. World Tourism Organization (WTO)

WTO attempts to promote tourism with the goal of prompting economic expansion, cross-cultural learning, and peace.

III.   AVIATION

A. International Civil Aviation Organization (ICAO)
The dramatic increase in the use of the airplane during World War II brought about the need to regulate its use. ICAO enforces the basic principle of the Convention on International Civil Aviation that every state has complete sovereignty over the airspace above its territory.

B. Bilateral Agreements

Most of the individualized decisions on commercial air rights and obligations are determined through bilateral agreements.

IV.   COMMUNICATIONS

A. International Telecommunication Union (ITU)

ITU is the administrative body created by, and charged with, enforcing the International Telecommunication Convention. The ITU was founded with the goal of maintaining and extending international cooperation for the improvement and rational use of telecommunications. Specifically, ITU oversees the allocation of the radio-frequency spectrum, combats harmful signal interference, and promotes progress and safety in the field.

B. International Telecommunications Satellite Organization (INTELSAT)

INTELSAT is open to any state that belongs to the International Telecommunication Union. The primary goal of INTELSAT is to provide "fixed or mobile telecommunications services which can be provided by satellite and which are available for use by the public." In a unique arrangement, the United States' representative to INTELSAT is Comsat, a private corporation.

C. Universal Postal Union (UPU)

The UPU was founded in 1874, with the goal of organizing and improving the international cooperation in global postal operations.

V.   SHIPPING

A. International Maritime Organization (IMO)

IMO generally endeavors to aid cooperation in the regulation and shipping practices of international trade. In addition, the IMO seeks to promote the highest standards of maritime safety and to facilitate the use of shipping for international commerce.

B. International Maritime Satellite System (INMARSAT)

INMARSAT was developed under IMO with the goal of providing a space segment in a satellite system for international maritime communications.

VI.   LABOR

A. International Labour Organization (ILO)

1. History
The ILO is one of the oldest specialized agencies; its constitution created in the Treaty of Versailles of 1919. For its first twenty-five years, ILO was primarily involved with labor conditions, such as working hours, female labor, industrial injury, and unemployment compensation programs. During World War II, ILO changed its focus to the social, spiritual, and economic welfare of people. Specifically, ILO embraces the ideas that labor is not a commodity and that all people have a right to pursue their own goals with freedom, dignity, and equal opportunity.

2. Organization

   a. The Structure
   Each member state has four representatives: two from government, one from labor, and one representing employers. Difficulty in selecting delegates has arisen in nations where there is no formal organization of workers or employers.

   b. The Legislation
   Between 1919 and 1976, 147 Conventions and 155 Recommendations have been adopted covering a range of topics, including basic human rights, labor administration, industrial relations, working conditions, social security, and the employment of women and children.

3. Problems in a Changing World
   During the Cold War, noncommunist states often challenged the method of selection used by communist states for their labor representatives in the ILO. In the 1970s, the United States briefly withdrew from the ILO to protest the activities of nondemocratic governments in the organization.

VII. AGRICULTURE

A. Food and Agriculture Organization (FAO)

The FAO provides an international framework for national development of farming, forestry and fisheries. It's general focus is on raising nutritional levels, improving the efficiency of the production and distribution of food, and advancing the condition of the world's rural population. The FAO, along with other international organizations, assists developing countries in formulating national food security policies and advises them on how to increase foreign exchange and employment.

B. International Fund For Agricultural Development (IFAD)

IFAD was organized to mobilize capital for increasing food production and improving the nutritional intake of the world's poorest populations.

VIII. WEATHER

The World Meteorological Organization (WMO) was founded to standardize meteorological observations and to coordinate international weather statistics.

IX. HEALTH

The World Health Organization (WHO) was founded with the lofty objective of attaining the highest possible level of health for all people. Specifically, WHO has the authority to adopt regulations relating to sanitary and quarantine requirements, medical nomenclature, international diagnostic standards, and the safety of biological and pharmaceutical products in international commerce.

X. ATOMIC ENERGY

The International Atomic Energy Agency (IAEA) is an autonomous body organized to promote the safe use of atomic energy. The primary practical function of IAEA is the on-site inspection of potential atomic energy problems.

CASE CLIPS

Powers Case
(USSR 1960) SOL
Facts: D, a CIA agent, intruded into Soviet air space on an espionage mission, with the knowledge of the U.S. government, and collected

information of strategic importance that constituted a state and military secret of the Soviet State.

Issue: May a state punish an individual who collects information constituting a state or military secret by invading that state's air space?

Rule: Since international law establishes the exclusive sovereignty of every state over the air space above its territory, a state may punish an individual who invades its air space on an espionage mission.

Silberwacht v. Attorney General
(Israel 1953) SOL

Facts: An employee of an Israeli airport challenged his conviction for smuggling, claiming that he could not be convicted since once the goods entered Israel's airspace they had already been smuggled.

Issue: Does a state's territorial sovereignty include authority over its airspace?

Rule: The law governing territorial sovereignty of a state includes authority not only over the surface of the land but also over the skies.

Chumney v. Nixon
(U.S. 1980) SOL

Facts: Chumney claimed that while on a charter flight from Rio de Janeiro to Memphis, Tennessee, Nixon physically assaulted him. At the time of the alleged assault, the aircraft was flying over the Brazilian jungle. Chumney claimed that 49 U.S.C. § 1472(k)(1), pertaining to the special aircraft jurisdiction of the U.S., was applicable to the facts of this case.

Issue: Do the U.S. courts have jurisdiction over civil actions arising out of assaults committed on aircrafts in another country's airspace over another country's airspace, whose final destination is the U.S.?

Rule: As Congress has given the federal courts jurisdiction to impose criminal penalties against those who commit felonious assaults on aircraft over another country's airspace, the U.S. courts may, consistently with this congressional legislative scheme, exercise jurisdiction over civil actions as well.

Trail Smelter Case (United States v. Canada)
(1941) SOL

Facts: Consolidated Mining and Smelting Company of Canada operated a smelting plant in Canada that emitted sulphur dioxide fumes into the air and caused damage in the U.S.

Issue: May a state bring a suit for damages caused by air pollution emanating from a plant operated on the territory of another state?

Rule: Under the principles of international law, no state has the right to use or permit the use of its territory in such a manner as to cause injury by fumes in, or to the territory of, another or the properties or persons therein; thus, a suit lies if pollution emanating from one state damages another state.

Nuclear Tests Case (Interim Protection Order)
(Australia v. France)
(ICJ 1973) SOL

Facts: Australia instituted proceedings against France based on a dispute concerning the atmospheric testing of nuclear weapons by the French government in the Pacific Ocean that caused wide-spread radioactive fallout on Australian territory. Australia sought an injunction against further testing pending a final decision.

Issue: Where damage from the testing of nuclear weapons may prove to be irreparable, may a court order a state to cease such testing pending a final decision in the case?

Rule: Where damage from the testing of nuclear weapons may prove to be irreparable, a court may order a state to cease the testing pending a final decision in the case.

Chapter 19

REGIONAL ECONOMIC COMMUNITIES

I. THE EUROPEAN COMMUNITIES

A. European Economic Community (EEC)

1. Developments Leading to Its Creation

a. Introduction
Following World War II, many people in Europe were attracted to the idea of political and economic unity, as achieved in the United States, for Europe. This kind of integration in Europe was seen by its supporters as a way to achieve economic prosperity and maintain post-war peace.

b. Benelux
Before World War II had ended, Belgium, the Netherlands, and Luxembourg agreed to drop all customs duties and economically unify the three states.

c. A Failed Attempt: France and Italy
With an admiring eye upon the recently developed Benelux customs union, France and Italy negotiated a similar alliance. The agreement, however, was never ratified.

d. Organization for Economic Cooperation and Development (OECD)
The Organization for Economic Cooperation and Development was created in conjunction with the Marshall Plan in an attempt to coordinate the economic union of the Atlantic Community, including the United States and Canada. The OECD attempts to solve the economic problems of the Atlantic Community and to provide aid to underdeveloped countries.

e. Council of Europe
Following the creation of the EEC, European leaders decided to organize this council to coordinate and discuss mutual political and economic issues.

f. European Coal and Steel Community (ECSC)
Joined by France, Germany, Italy, and the three Benelux countries, the ECSC was formed in 1952 to achieve economic coordination and integration of the member states' steel and coal industries.

g. The Failure of the European Defense Community
Realizing the value of economic integration, this attempt at political integration was signed in 1952, but the treaty dissolved two years later when France, concerned about German rearmament, withdrew.

h. The Treaties of Rome
Following the dissolution of the European Defense Community, the six parties to the ECSC decided to adhere to economic integration. These agreements laid the groundwork for the EEC to take effect on January 1, 1958.

i. Growing Numbers
In 1973, the United Kingdom, Ireland, and Denmark joined the EEC, leading to a much broader and more diverse European coalition. In 1986, Greece, Portugal, and Spain joined the EEC.

j. Treaty Revision
In 1986 a supplement to the EEC Treaty was signed, adding such subjects as research, technological development and the environment.

2. The Structure, Goals, and Administration of the Treaty

   a. The General Structure of the Treaty
     The Treaty is divided into six major parts: Principles, Bases of the Community, Policy of the Community, The Association of Overseas Countries and Territories, Institutions of the Community, and General and Final Provisions.

   b. The Objectives of the EEC
     The goals of the EEC extend far beyond the elimination of inter-European tariffs. The broader goals of the Community are to establish a closer union among the European peoples and a complete economic integration of Europe.

   c. The Means for Attaining the Objectives
     Article 3 of the Treaty lays out the specific steps that are to be taken toward integrating the European economy.

   d. Discrimination
     Article 7 of the Treaty prohibits any discrimination on the basis of nationality.

   e. The Time-Tables
     The elaborate economic transformation mandated in the Treaty could not be implemented overnight. The Treaty allows for a twelve-year transitional period consisting of three stages.

   f. The Institutions of the EEC
     The four principal institutions of the EEC are the Assembly, the Council, the Commission, and the Court of Justice

     i. The European Parliament
       Also referred to as the Assembly, this body is made up of 518 members elected by direct universal suffrage. The body has no actual legislative power and is purely advisory in nature.

ii. The Council
Each member country sends one representative to this body, which has both legislative and executive powers.

iii. The Commission
The Commission is the principal executive department of the EEC. It has seventeen members, appointed by the twelve member countries by "common agreement."

iv. The Court of Justice
The Court of Justice is composed of thirteen members serving six-year terms. Half of the judges are appointed every three years.

g. Means of Implementation of Treaty Provisions
There are five ways in which the Council and the Commission can exercise their implementation powers.

i. Regulations
Regulations are legislative measures that are directly binding on all member states.

ii. Directives
Directives are binding orders addressed to member states requiring them to accomplish a stated purpose, while leaving them free to select the form in, and the means by, which that purpose is to be achieved.

iii. Decisions
Decisions are orders binding only upon the states to whom they are addressed.

iv. Recommendations or Opinions
Recommendations or opinions are nonbinding findings on various subjects by EEC bodies.

h. Financial Affairs
The Commission combines the proposed budgets of the various EEC institutions. The Council consults the institutions whose proposed budget it wishes to amend and then drafts the Community budget. Each member must make a contribution to the budget according to an established formula.

i. Admission to, and Agreements with, the Community

   i. Admission to Membership
Any European state may address an application for membership to the EEC. The recent changes in Eastern Europe may dramatically change the composition of the EEC.

   ii. Agreements of Association
The EEC may negotiate association agreements with the government of any independent sovereign state. These agreements have been reached with Cyprus, Algeria, Turkey, Malta, and Morocco.

   iii. Tariff and Commercial Agreements
The Community may also participate in negotiations with countries involved in the General Agreement on Tariffs and Trade (GATT).

3. Implementation of the Common Market

a. Rules Dealing with Specific Aspects of Economic Life

   i. Free Movement of Goods
In order to achieve a free movement of goods within the Community, the Treaty eliminated internal customs duties and equivalent levies. Internal and external tariffs are also restricted and regulated within the Community.

ii. Common Agricultural Policy
Due to the uncertainty surrounding agricultural production, the Community leaves open the option of free competition in agricultural matters. However, since its inception, the Community has opted for a regulated economy more often than not.

iii. Free Movement of Persons, Services, and Capital
These provisions eliminate the restrictions on the free movement of persons, services, and capital. The only restrictions that are permitted are those designed to protect the public order, safety, or health.

iv. Transportation
While ground transportation is still the subject of national regulation, the EEC Treaty provides that all states should make their transportation systems compatible with other systems within the community. Road transportation has been easier to integrate than rail transportation. The Community has implemented a system of licenses and a standard rate system for Community wide road transportation.

b. General Policies

i. Antitrust Policy
One of the most fundamental tenets governing the EEC Common Market is free competition in place of extensive official regulation. For this reason, the Commission is selective about declaring agreements invalid based on monopolistic practices.

ii. Tax Policy
The Treaty provides for the modification of national tax policies that obstruct the Community's goals. Specifically, the EEC required that member states replace their systems of turnover taxes with a system of taxation on added value.

iii. Harmonization of Laws
In addition to the specific areas outlined above, the EEC
has reserved the authority to harmonize the laws of its
member states in any area that has a direct influence on
the functioning of the common market.

iv. Policy in Regard to Business Cycles
The Council has the power to adopt, by unanimous vote,
whatever measures may be appropriate to lessen the ill
effects of business cycles and to implement these measures by directives adopted by majority vote.

v. Balance of Payments Policy
The basic goal of the Treaty, in regard to the balance of
payments of the member states, is to achieve equilibrium
in the balance of payments in regard to both member and
nonmember states.

vi. Common Commercial Policy
The Treaty prescribes the development of a common
policy in regard to trade with nonmember states and
charges the Commission with the duty of submitting
proposals for appropriate action, to the Council, on tariff
negotiations with nonmember states concerning the
common customs tariff.

vii. Social Policy
Provisions under the rubric of "social policy" deal with
issues including labor legislation, social security, trade
union regulation, workers' compensation, nondiscriminatory employment practices and paid vacation. The
Council has also negotiated an agreement with the
International Labor Organization providing for a joint
effort in the improvement of living and working conditions of workers.

B. European Coal and Steel Community (ECSC)

Developed under the "Schuman Plan" of 1950, the ECSC establishes a common market assuring the adequate supplies of coal and steel at the lowest economic prices to the member nations of France, West Germany, Italy, the Netherlands, Belgium, and Luxembourg.

C. European Atomic Energy Community (EURATOM)

EURATOM was formed to develop research, disseminate information, enforce uniform safety standards, facilitate investment, ensure regular and fair distribution of supplies of nuclear material, guarantee that nuclear materials are not used for nondesignated uses, exercise certain property rights in respect of such materials, create a common market for the free movement of capital for investment and personnel for nuclear industries, and promote the peaceful uses of atomic energy.

D. European Free Trade Association (EFTA)

EFTA is composed of the nations not in the original EEC and known as the "outer seven." They are Austria, Denmark, Norway, Portugal, Sweden, Switzerland, and the United Kingdom. EFTA is similar in purpose to the EEC, but lacks the elaborate supranational powers of the Community.

E. Council For Mutual Economic Assistance (CMEA)

CMEA, also known as COMECON, was the East European counterpart to the EEC. Created under the watchful eye of the Soviet Union, its members were the USSR, Bulgaria, Czechoslovakia, Hungary, Poland, Romania, Albania and the German Democratic Republic. Mongolia and Cuba became the group's two non-European members and North Korea and Vietnam joined as observers. The underlying principles of the organization are: respect for state sovereignty, independence and national interests, equality, mutual advantage, and comradely assistance. Unlike the

EEC, the CMEA is unable to make commitments on behalf of its member states and thus the governments of CMEA countries must participate in all negotiations and agreements.

II. LATIN AMERICAN REGIONAL ORGANIZATIONS

A. Latin American Free Trade Association (LAFTA)

Formed with the goal of establishing free-trade in Latin America, LAFTA is composed of Argentina, Brazil, Chile, Mexico, Paraguay, Peru, Uruguay, Colombia, Ecuador, Venezuela, Bolivia.

B. Latin American Integration Association (LAIA)

LAIA has replaced LAFTA as the instrument for achieving the establishment of a Latin American common market.

C. Central American Common Market (CACM)

Modelled after the EEC Common Market, CACM has found success in integrating Latin American economies, while lowering tariffs and other trade restrictions in the area.

D. Andean Common Market (ANCOM)

Joined by Bolivia, Colombia, Chile, Ecuador, and Peru, ANCOM's objectives include promotion of development of member states, acceleration of economic growth rates, and assurance of local benefits from a common market.

III. AFRICAN REGIONAL ORGANIZATIONS

A. Central African Economic and Customs Union (UDEAC)

1. History
This union is the latest in a series of attempts to join the economic interests of the French speaking nations in Central Africa.

2. Objectives

The objectives of UDEAC include extending the national markets of member states through the removal of barriers to interregional trade, the adoption of a procedure of equitable distribution of industrialization projects, and the coordination of development programs for the various production sectors.

3. Membership

Membership in UDEAC is open to any interested African state. The original members are Cameroon, Central African Republic, Congo, Gabon, and Chad. These five nations cover as much territory as the whole of Western Europe, but average only nine people per square mile. Poor transportation and communication between the states has proved a major obstacle to economic integration.

B. Economic Community of West African States (ECOWAS)

The development of economic unity in West Africa has been slow. ECOWAS, formed in 1975 with the signing of fifteen nations, has made little progress.

C. Southern African Development Coordination Conference (SADCC)

SADCC was formed in 1980 by nine countries opposed to the system of apartheid in South Africa and its economic domination of the region. Unlike many other African economic coalitions, SADCC has achieved many of its goals. It has made major improvements in transportation and communications between the member states and is currently trying to improve the supply and distribution of food in the region.

IV. THE MID-EAST: ARAB ECONOMIC UNION

Consisting of Kuwait, Egypt, Iraq, Syria, and Jordan, the Arab Economic Council has made little progress due to heated internal disagreements between the member states.

CASE CLIPS

Italian Finance Administration v. Simmenthal S.p.A.
(1978) HPSS

Facts: The Pretore of Susa called on the Court of Justice for a ruling on the applicability of European Economic Community law when it is in conflict with national law.

Issue: When there is a direct conflict of law between the members of the EEC, does the law of the EEC or the relevant national law take precedence?

Rule: In cases of conflicting law, EEC law takes precedence over the law of a single sovereign nations.

Opinion of the Court Given Pursuant
to Article 228 of the EEC Treaty
(1975) HPSS

Facts: The EEC brought a case before the Court of Justice to determine what authority they had to conclude economic treaties pursuant to Article 228 of the EEC Treaty of 1975.

Issue: What power does the EEC have in relation to the conclusion of economic treaties within the community?

Rule: The EEC has the exclusive power to participate in conventions and treaties that relate to commercial policy regarding their member states.

Defrenne v. Sabena
(1976) HPSS

Facts: Defrenne, an airline attendant, brought suit in Belgian courts charging her employer with gender based discrimination. She claimed Article 119 of the European Economic Community Treaty as the basis of her claim.

Issue: Do EEC provisions on sexual discrimination have authoritative effect in the national courts of member states?

Rule: The national courts of EEC member states are obligated to enforce the EEC provision that men and women must be paid equal wages for the same work.

BLOND'S™ LAW GUIDES

Precisely What You Need to Know

Civil Procedure
Cound
Field
Rosenberg
Louisell

Contracts
Farnsworth
Dawson
Kessler
Fuller
Murphy

Criminal Procedure
Kamisar
Saltzburg
Weinreb/Crim.Process
Weinreb/Crim.Justice
Miller

Evidence
McCormick
Green
Weinstein
Kaplan
Cleary

Property
Dukeminier
Browder
Casner
Cribbet

Torts
Prosser
Epstein
Keeton
Franklin

Constitutional Law
Barrett
Brest
Ducat
Gunther
Lockhart
Rotunda
Stone

Criminal Law
Kadish
LaFave
Kaplan
Weinreb
Dix
Johnson
Inbau

Corporate Tax
Lind
Kahn
Wolfman
Surrey

Corporations
Cary
Choper
Hamilton
Henn
Jennings
Solomon
Vagts

Family Law
Areen
Foote
Krause
Wadlington

Administrative Law
Bonfield
Breyer
Gellhorn
Cass
Schwartz
Mashaw

International Law
Sweeney
Henkin

Income Tax
Klein
Andrews
Surrey
Kragen
Freeland
Graetz

ORDER FORM

Sulzburger & Graham Publishing
P.O. Box 20058
Park West Station
New York NY 10025

(800)366-7086
Orders shipped
within 24 hours

BLOND'S LAW GUIDES @ $13.95 per copy.
Name of book

_____ $_____

_____   _____

_____   _____

_____   _____

_____   _____

_____   _____

_____   _____

_____BLOND'S MULTISTATE @ $26.95 per copy   _____

_____BLOND'S T-SHIRT @ $9.95   _____

_____WHAT YOU AREN'T... @ $14.95 per copy   _____

Shipping and handling @ 2.25   _____
Total $_____

☐ Check or money order (payable to Sulzburger & Graham)
☐ MasterCard   ☐ Visa   ☐ American Express   ☐ DiscoverCard
Charge Card No. _____
Exp. Date _____   Signature _____

Name _____
Address _____
City/State/Zip _____
Phone # _____
Law School _____
Graduation Date _____

All orders are shipped UPS same or next business day. Delivery time will vary, based on distance from New York City.
Washington/Boston corridor can expect delivery 2 working days after shipment. West Coast should allow 6 working days. UPS
overnight, Federal Express, and 2d day air available at extra cost.